Gordon McLendon

Gordon McLendon from Ebbets Field. *Photo courtesy of The McLendon Companies.*

Gordon McLendon

THE MAVERICK OF RADIO

Ronald Garay

CONTRIBUTIONS TO THE STUDY OF
MASS MEDIA AND
COMMUNICATIONS,
NUMBER 32

Greenwood Press

NEW YORK
WESTPORT, CONNECTICUT
LONDON

Library of Congress Cataloging-in-Publication Data

Garay, Ronald.
Gordon McLendon : the maverick of radio / Ronald Garay.
p. cm.—(Contributions to the study of mass media and communications, ISSN 0732-4456 ; no. 32)
Includes bibliographical references and index.
ISBN 0-313-26676-X (alk. paper)
1. McLendon, Gordon. 2. Radio broadcasting—United States—Biography. 3. Executives—United States—Biography. 4. Motion picture producers and directors—United States—Biography.
I. Title. II. Series.
PN1991.4.M38G37 1992
791.44′028′092—dc20 91-35968
[B]

British Library Cataloguing in Publication Data is available.

Library of Congress Catalog Card Number: 91-35968
ISBN: 0-313-26676-X
ISSN: 0732-4456

First published in 1992

Greenwood Press, 88 Post Road West, Westport, CT 06881
An imprint of Greenwood Publishing Group, Inc.

Printed in the United States of America

The paper used in this book complies with the Permanent Paper Standard issued by the National Information Standards Organization (Z39.48-1984).

10 9 8 7 6 5 4 3 2 1

Copyright Acknowledgments

The author and publisher are grateful to the following for allowing the use of materials:

The March 1969 Gordon McLendon interview by Dr. Clifton Ganus, reprinted by permission of Harding University.

Bart McLendon for permission to quote from archival items contained in the McLendon papers housed at Texas Tech University's Southwest Collection.

This book is dedicated to my wife,
Mary Sue,
a proud Texan

Contents

Preface

Preface

My first encounter with the Gordon McLendon legend came while a novice disc jockey at radio station KPET in Lamesa, Texas. The station aired a modified Top 40 format, which quite likely had been inspired by the innovative format that Gordon had co-invented and popularized. Several years later, while a student at Texas Christian University in Fort Worth, I experienced the McLendon Top 40 sound at close range by listening to Gordon's KLIF in Dallas.

At one point during those college years, I actually met Gordon McLendon. The occasion was a National Association of Broadcasters meeting, and the encounter was a brief one—a handshake and, as well as I can remember, a "Hello. Nice to meet you."

Some twenty years were to pass before my attention turned to a serious scholarly investigation of just what it was that made Gordon McLendon so important to U.S. radio history. The catalyst for that investigation came during a conversation I had with Dennis Harp, a professor in the Texas Tech University Department of Mass Communications, during a broadcasting seminar in New York. Dennis casually mentioned that Gordon had donated many of his private and professional papers to Texas Tech's Southwest Collection and that this massive assortment of documents had been dented only slightly by anyone with scholarly intent.

The idea to conduct a thorough examination of the McLendon papers immediately took hold. Little did I know that my intended quick glance at this archival treasure trove would turn into a project of nearly five years and result in this book.

Acknowledgments

A project of this size and duration obviously requires the help and support of many persons. To all who have played a part in bringing this book to its completion I extend a collective thank you. There are some people, however, who are deserving of special thanks.

Dennis Harp not only ignited my interest in writing about Gordon McLendon, but kept the fire stoked in many, many ways. Dennis provided me with audio and video tapes of McLendon interviews; he offered his own recollections about his many years of friendship with Gordon McLendon; he provided me with entree to the research facilities at Texas Tech University; and he even provided lodging during several of my research trips to Lubbock, Texas. In other words, there is much of Dennis Harp in this book. I treasure his friendship, and I shall be forever grateful for his tremendous help and unselfish generosity.

My mind often has wandered back to that one chance encounter I had with Gordon McLendon. Had I only known that some day I would be writing a book about him, I would have made every effort to stretch that encounter into hours, if not days. Unfortunately, Gordon's life ended just as my research on his life began. Because of that loss, I came to rely on the observations and recollections of Gordon's relatives, friends and close business associates. During my conversations with these persons, I was struck by the admiration and love that practically all of them had for Gordon. Those conversations were a genuine delight for me. I met fascinating people, gained invaluable insights into my subject and generally had a marvelous time in the process.

Among those persons whose memories form the nucleus of this book, a special debt of gratitude is owed Don Keyes, Edd Routt, Ken Dowe, Les

Vaughn, Glenn Callison, Bart McLendon, Billie Odom, Dorothy Manning, Bill Meeks, Tom Merriman, Marcus Cohn, Chuck Blore, Joseph Sitrick, Gary Owens, Lindsey Nelson, Dave McKinsey, George Sandlin and Bob Porter. All of these persons generously gave of their time, whether in home, office or by phone, to accommodate my interview schedule. My thanks to each and every one of them.

My gratitude extends as well to the many archival and library personnel who assisted in my research. At the head of that list must be David Murrah and his helpful staff at Texas Tech's Southwest Collection. I always looked forward to the many days spent at the Southwest Collection because of the friendly atmosphere that David and his very competent staff created.

Big thank yous also go the staffs of the Barker Texas History Center at the University of Texas at Austin, the Texas/Dallas Collection of the Dallas Public Library, the Houston Public Library's Metropolitan Research Center, and the libraries at Texas Tech University, the University of Texas at Austin, the University of Houston, Southern Methodist University, the University of Texas at Arlington, the University of North Texas, Louisiana State University, Southern Methodist University School of Law and Louisiana State University School of Law.

I am also deeply indebted to the following persons for their help and support: Allen and Laurie Sanders, who graciously allowed me to interrupt their busy lives and provided me with lodging during my many Dallas research trips; Al and Dorothy Bankston, who became the "keepers of the text" for a paranoid writer; Ed Glick, who, as a Gordon McLendon scholar himself, provided information for my own study; David MacFarland, whose definitive study of Top 40 radio helped fill in many of the blank spots in my own rendition of the McLendon Top 40 years; the Harding University Library, for providing me recordings of a lengthy 1969 interview conducted by Harding University President Clifton Ganus, Jr. with Gordon McLendon; Joseph Berman, for sharing with me his love and knowledge of electronic media history; and my wife Mary Sue, who, with infinite patience and humor, allowed the writing of this book to intrude time and time again into her ordered life.

A final word of appreciation goes to the Louisiana State University Council on Research for its financial support in helping defray a portion of the expense incurred while conducting research for this book.

Introduction

Gordon McLendon's birth was, coincidentally, nearly simultaneous with the birth of the U.S. broadcasting industry. The two would mature together and in time each would have a profound influence upon the other.

Together with his father and business partner B. R. McLendon, Gordon would head a vast business and entertainment enterprise. He would become famous and wealthy and develop an enormous capacity for hard work and achievement. Yet Gordon never would lose the common touch, nor would he allow life's serious side to interfere with his capacity to see its humorous side. The playful twinkle in Gordon's eye and his wide grin would be as much a part of his personality as would be his no-nonsense work ethic.

Gordon's exploits would be adventuresome, controversial, sometimes failures but most often wildly successful. Very few things that Gordon McLendon would do or attempt to do ever would be considered ordinary. His greatest joy would come from charting new territory, in doing what others had not done, and in challenging what most thought to be impossible.

Gordon was a person of keen intellect and nearly limitless creative talent, whom many would call a genius. And certainly, his contributions to the U.S. radio industry were to make Gordon a legend among his fellow broadcasters.

This book is a biography of Gordon McLendon's public and professional life. It documents his career principally in the radio industry, but it also touches lightly upon Gordon's long career in the motion picture industry and his shorter career in Texas politics. Only as a means to illustrate how personal life intermingled with professional has there been any effort to peer beyond the "Old Scotchman" persona most often heard, seen and appreciated by the public.

Early chapters of this book have been arranged as nearly as possible in chronological order. However, Gordon's multiple roles as broadcast executive, motion picture producer, politician and investment expert during the 1960s and 1970s made chronological order in later chapters impossible. For this reason, those chapters have been organized topically rather than chronologically.

1 *Childhood, Education and Military Career*

Gordon McLendon would be born a Texan. On that, his father already had decided. No matter that Barton Robert (B. R. for short) McLendon and his expectant wife Jeannette happened to live in the tiny southeastern Oklahoma town of Idabel, ten or so miles north of the Texas border. B. R. had made up his mind, and there would no dissuading him. His son would be born in Texas.

Why B. R. was so insistent that his first-born be a native Texan is uncertain. B. R. himself had been born and raised in Mississippi, and in 1917 had settled in Idabel ("Movie Theater Owner," 1982). Other than Idabel's close proximity to northeast Texas, there was nothing in particular connecting B. R. with the Lone Star State.

B. R. and Jeannette Eyster had met and married during B. R.'s first year in Idabel ("McClendon [sic] Services Set," 1985). At that time, B. R. operated an insurance agency and studied law part-time under the tutelage of his father, Jefferson Davis McLendon ("Media Pioneer Dies," 1982). The senior McLendon had practiced criminal law in Mississippi before moving to Idabel, where he served as McCurtain County judge and guardian to some 6,000 Choctaw Indians ("McLendon Rites Set," 1954).

B. R. was about to launch his own law career in 1921 when the birth of his and Jeannette's first child came due. The second of their two children, Frances Marie, was born the following year (" 'Mr. Mac,' " 1969).

As delivery time approached, B. R. hurriedly transported his wife by car nearly seventy miles from Idabel across the Red River to Paris, Texas. There, on June 8, 1921, Gordon Barton McLendon was born (McLendon, 1969a).

The circumstances of birth were unusual, certainly, but they were quite fitting for someone whose life was destined to assume extraordinary dimensions. Actually, Gordon was to misunderstand for most of his life the reason why his father chose Paris, Texas for his birth. Gordon assumed that because Idabel had no hospital, his parents decided to journey to Paris where there was one. But regardless of how logical or how sound from a health perspective, this was not at all the real reason. Not until 1968 did Gordon learn the true story behind his Texas birth. As Gordon told it, after he had recounted to a friend what he understood to be the circumstances of his birth, B. R., who was standing nearby, corrected him. At that moment Gordon discovered that his father's trip to Paris was made primarily so that he could be born a Texan (McLendon, 1969a).

LIFE IN IDABEL, OKLAHOMA

Texan though he was, Gordon was carried back north after two days in the Paris hospital, and for the next fourteen years spent his life in Idabel (McLendon, 1969a). From all accounts Gordon had a happy and fulfilling childhood, despite the economic woes being experienced in Depression-era Oklahoma. Gordon remembered those days not because of any hardships that he himself suffered but because of those suffered by his father, who had to struggle to keep his law practice afloat (McLendon, 1969a). To a sensitive boy like Gordon, the experience of living through a Depression did not have to affect him directly in order to leave a lasting impression.

Regardless of the economic conditions, Gordon recalled years later that Idabel had provided him an especially good place to grow and learn. Gordon credited the Idabel public schools as being particularly instrumental in nurturing an intellectual curiosity that would become a lifelong fascination with learning (McLendon, 1969a).

Education aside, there were other things about small-town Idabel that attracted young Gordon's attention. For one thing, Idabel was located very near the Choctaw Indian Reservation that Jefferson Davis McLendon administered. Gordon's friendship with the Choctaw Indians was strong enough that he learned their language—not a simple task by any means, and one that gives some indication of Gordon's linguistic skills. Eventually, he would speak six languages (Tolbert, 1952, pp. 57–59).

Gordon developed a close bond with his father during his youth. That relationship later grew into a partnership that would last for nearly four decades. Much of the success that Gordon would experience came not only because of the verbal urging and support of his father, but because B. R. was able and willing to finance his son's many ventures. The foundation for that McLendon father/son partnership occurred in peculiar fashion when in 1932 (Gordon was eleven at the time) B. R. purchased a movie theater from a struggling law client (" 'Mr. Mac,' " 1969). B. R.'s first order of business was to change the name of the small Idabel theater from the Brent to the State Theater ("Movie Theater Owner," 1982). Then, borrowing money from the bank, B. R. began heavily promoting the movies that played at his new theater (Meeks, 1990).

What could have turned out to be a white elephant for the successful attorney instead became quite an investment. Later, the State Theater in Idabel became the cornerstone of the Tri-State Theatre Circuit that B. R. would command (" 'Mr. Mac,' " 1969).

As important a role as B. R. would play throughout Gordon's life, that role was overshadowed to some degree by the influence of Gordon's paternal grandparents. The couple lived nearby in Oklahoma, and so it was fortunate for Gordon that when his mother became ill he was able to move in briefly with the elder McLendons (McLendon, 1969a).

Gordon's grandfather, Jefferson Davis McLendon (called "Jeff" by his friends) was especially solicitous of his grandson's every need. Jeff placed Gordon on a pedestal, and Gordon in turn revered his grandfather (Manning, 1990). Gordon later would describe Jeff McLendon's influence on him as "enormous" (McLendon, 1969a).

Jeff McLendon "was a brilliant criminal lawyer," Gordon remarked proudly. His oratorical skills were such that he often could bring jury members to tears. And of the nearly five hundred cases tried by Jeff McLendon, Gordon said that his grandfather never lost a single defendant to capital punishment (McLendon, 1969a).

One might have expected Gordon to be inspired enough by the courtroom exploits of his grandfather to look toward the legal profession himself. But there were other forms of inspiration imparted by Jeff McLendon that did fashion Gordon's future. Granddad McLendon, said Gordon, "was an avid reader, a great wordsman, and simply a master of himself and of his audience on his feet." He also had a knack for writing, added Gordon. Jeff McLendon often wrote stories especially for his grandson that not only were fun to read, but also contained what Gordon later realized were grains of wisdom meant to inspire and teach (McLendon, 1969a).

Jeff McLendon's love of writing and speaking would profoundly affect Gordon's future. No less effective, though, would be the elder McLendon's politics. Jeff McLendon, of course, had been a politician of sorts at one time, having served what Gordon recalled was either one or two terms as a county judge. Gordon cited his grandfather as the source both for his own interest in politics and for his own particular political philosophy. As long as he could remember, Gordon said in 1969, he had been a conservative. And by no one else but Granddad McLendon could the seeds for such political conservatism have been planted (McLendon, 1969a).

Jeff McLendon's active role in Gordon's young life—teaching him political and intellectual values—led to a momentous event for Gordon. The event occurred when Gordon was fourteen years old and involved a contest sponsored by *Young American* magazine, a popular periodical among teens and pre-teens of the day. As Gordon remembered, Jeff McLendon picked up a copy of the magazine one day just to find out what his grandson was reading. He spied an announcement for an essay contest sponsored by the magazine in which a boy and girl whose winning essay on "What I Would Do If I Were President" would receive an expense-paid trip along with their chaperones to Washington, D.C.

Gordon said that he had paid little attention to the contest. His vision of the world and the events that shaped it was confined almost exclusively to the immediate environs of Idabel, Oklahoma. The rest of the world seemed remote. Moreover, what could Gordon McLendon do or say that would have the least bit of interest to anyone outside of Idabel (McLendon, 1969a)? Gordon admitted to having no great ambition at age fourteen and no thoughts of amounting to very much. The extent of his travels at that point had been only short trips with parents or grandparents to Texarkana, Texas.

Nonetheless, after sufficient badgering from his grandfather, Gordon did enter the contest. And to his amazement, he won it. Gordon had been reluctant to compete with children from across the country, whom he considered were better educated. Winning the essay contest filled him with tremendous pride and confidence (McLendon, 1969a).

Gordon had just cause to be proud. Thousands of essays had been submitted in the contest, and final essay judging had been done by none other than Arthur Brisbane, Walter Lippman and Henry R. Luce. U. S. Congressman Wilburn Cartwright, who represented southeastern Oklahoma, included a copy of Gordon's essay in the *Congressional Record*. The essay might appear somewhat radical by today's standards, but in an America still beset by the Depression its words represented ideals that conservatives might have applauded. And it is highly likely that most anyone reading the essay would have been amazed to find that the essay's author was but fourteen years of age.

In part, Gordon had written that if he were President he would "encourage Congress to conclude its labors and return home"; avoid membership in the World Court and League of Nations; withdraw support from legislative proposals that "encroach upon State rights"; advocate dropping taxes on incomes of less than five thousand dollars but "increase taxes on incomes and inheritances in the higher brackets"; increase military readiness; and build and maintain a "navy comparable to the navies of the other great powers" (*Congressional Record*, 1935).

Gordon accepted his essay contest award by traveling with his grandfather to Washington and there meeting with Speaker of the House Joseph W. Byrns, First Lady Eleanor Roosevelt and a number of senators and congressmen. When he returned from his two-week train trip to Washington, he found himself to be "quite a celebrity." The entire experience had been an inspiration, said Gordon some years later, because it had expanded his horizons and shown him "all of the things that could be" (McLendon, 1969a).

Gordon would go on to receive countless awards and honors during his lifetime, but none would mean as much or carry the same impact as his first award for winning the essay contest (McLendon, 1969a). The fact that the award was bestowed while the admiring eyes of Jefferson Davis McLendon looked on must have made the whole occasion that much more satisfying to Gordon.

LIFE IN ATLANTA, TEXAS

Not long after Gordon's eventful trip, the McLendon family moved to Atlanta, Texas, some twenty-six miles south of Texarkana in the piney woods of East Texas (McLendon, 1969a). The move to Atlanta would allow B. R. to be closer to his parents, who had moved there from Idabel in 1930 ("McLendon Rites," 1954), as well as allow him to be closer to the Atlanta movie theater he had bought recently (Patoski, 1980, p. 103).

Gordon would excel in Atlanta. If his Washington trip had shown him all the things that could be, here in Atlanta is where he would begin the exciting journey of realizing just what he actually could accomplish. And there would be no hesitation in getting on with matters. Jeff McLendon had made certain that Gordon forever would be setting his sights on hard-to-reach goals and then steadfastly moving toward achieving those goals with a minimum of wasted time (McLendon, 1969b, p. 3).

Gordon began pushing for success in whatever way he could attain it. Even at the age of fourteen he seemed a driven person. His singular ambition for success, his constant effort to develop and improve himself, kept him very busy and left little time for friends. In fact Gordon said that he did not have his first date until age sixteen because he was so busy doing other things (McLendon, 1969a).

Gordon's non-school-related activities were fairly typical for a boy of his age. It was in scholastic activities, though, that Gordon excelled. Debate, for instance, was one of his specialties. Gordon later admitted that both he and his debate partner were not very good at first, but they improved so much by their sophomore year that they won the Texas state debating championship (McLendon, 1969a).

That he was able to improve his debating skills so quickly and so effectively indicates something about Gordon's growing fascination with language. The *Young American* essay had been a testament to the power of words and how one might use words to inform and persuade. Now that Gordon understood that he had a knack for speaking as well as writing, he would endeavor to practice both skills in whatever ways he could.

Gordon's interest in writing led quite naturally to an extracurricular stint with his high school newspaper. He had always been an avid newspaper reader, confining his interest mostly to the sports section. But after his Washington trip, Gordon expanded his reading to include the front page as well (McLendon, 1969a).

Gordon's newspaper activities were extensive, to say the least. To begin with, he was the editor of the Atlanta High School student newspaper (Patoski, 1980, p. 103). He also, at the age of fourteen, had arranged to become a stringer for several nearby newspapers and one news service. As such, he would submit stories to the newspapers about matters happening in or around Atlanta, Texas. If the stories were printed, Gordon was paid a fee by subscriber newspapers that generally amounted to about $100 per month. The money—a hefty sum for a high school student in those days—was put to good use: within two years, Gordon had launched his own weekly newspaper. The paper, which was hand-set on a hand press, was called the *Atlanta News* (McLendon, 1969a).

It became apparent to Gordon early on in his neophyte newspaper career that an occupation centered on words would require a vocabulary more extensive than the average teenager's. There were always words popping up in news stories that were unfamiliar to Gordon, and it alarmed him. Gordon decided to remedy the situation. He fashioned a project for himself in which he would use flash cards with new words on them to increase his vocabulary. For the next two or three years Gordon religiously worked at learning five new words every day (McLendon, 1969a).

Gordon's meticulous attention to linguistic details was only fitting for someone whose career would rely on words. And although his writing skills would be of extreme professional importance, it was Gordon's speaking skills that would make him famous. More important in the beginning of his professional career, though, would be his ability to combine radio speaking skills with a vast knowledge of and love for sports.

Long before high school Gordon had busied himself learning about sports—mostly baseball and football. He shortly would become somewhat of an authority on present and past sports events (McLendon, 1969a).

But Gordon was an active boy whose interest in sports was not confined just to intellectual matters. He was also a participant, playing on his high school golf and tennis teams and later on his college tennis team. Gordon loved baseball, but since Atlanta High School had no organized baseball team, his baseball playing was limited to intramural games that pitted one grade against another.

Participating in sports did not appeal nearly so much to Gordon as did the idea of covering sports events on the radio. There was no doubt in Gordon's mind that his future was bound in that direction. Ambition finally had grabbed hold of him in high school, and as Gordon told an interviewer in 1981, "I wanted to be a sports broadcaster in the worst possible way" (McLendon, 1981b). Being on radio, Gordon imagined, would be every bit as glamorous, romantic and exciting as being a movie star or even President of the United States (Patoski, 1980, p. 103).

Gordon dated the beginning of his love for radio from the Saturday afternoons of his childhood, when he would climb into an armchair to listen to

"Ted Husing's great football broadcasts" on the family's "old Majestic radio" (McLendon, 1957b, p. 7). And while Gordon listed a trio of sports announcers—Ted Husing, Bill Stern and Graham McNamee—as among his idols (McLendon, 1981b), Ted Husing was, by far, the stand-out favorite. "I always thought that he was the best sports broadcaster . . . that ever lived," Gordon said of Husing (McLendon, 1978). Here was Gordon's idea of what a sports broadcaster should be.

The "radio bug" that afflicted Gordon developed into the serious pursuit and lifelong practice of doing whatever was necessary to develop and perfect his radio performance. He turned first to the development of his diction, his speaking style. As a model whose style he wanted to emulate, Gordon naturally chose Ted Husing. Gordon pursued practicing his radio delivery in the same intense and methodical way as he pursued developing his vocabulary. The practice method that Gordon found most proficient was to imitate Ted Husing while driving alone in his car. His frequent trips to and from Texarkana to visit a girlfriend provided ample opportunity to perfect his announcing style (McLendon, 1969a). Gordon said that he never got to where he could imitate Husing precisely, but he was able to develop his own unique announcing style. And Gordon said in classic understatement that "it seemed to be good enough to carry me along" (McLendon, 1981a).

Gordon did not confine himself to this one method of preparing himself for the career he was planning. He said that he "frequently read whole columns of newspaper copy aloud to attempt to improve [his] blind-reading facility" (McLendon, 1969d, p. 5). Moreover, Gordon began a lifelong quest to develop his mind, to expand the horizons of his own knowledge of the world around him. Whatever he might learn, of course, would have its practical application in Gordon's broadcasting pursuits, but he was imbued with an intellectual curiosity whose fulfillment carried a gratification that stretched far beyond broadcasting.

Gordon simply loved to learn. He also valued education in others, and in later years would point out that a very important measure of a person was his or her education. He underscored that point while speaking to a group of aspiring broadcasters in 1969. How should they prepare for entering the profession? Learning to write and speak well was an obvious prerequisite. But Gordon went on to include a knowledge of such subjects as history, geography and literature. "Read (and reread) the best novels and non-fiction works of America's finest wordsmiths and phrasemakers," advised Gordon. Furthermore, he said, "Do not read these books just once but two or three times at different periods, underlining certain passages that particularly grip you" (McLendon, 1969d, pp. 4–7).

Before leaving high school, Gordon was fortunate to get a taste of what sports announcing was all about. Borrowing a public address microphone and speaker from his father's theater, Gordon created his own makeshift "broadcasting" system to describe the play-by-play action of the Atlanta

Rabbits high school football team (Patoski, 1980, p. 103). There is little doubt that the most excited person attending the Rabbit's football game was Gordon McLendon, and there is little doubt too that his descriptions of the games made them far more dramatic than they actually were.

In a technical sense, of course, public address announcing was not broadcasting. Gordon later recalled that he actually embarked on his broadcasting career during the two summers he spent at debate workshops while in high school. The workshops were conducted at the Texas State College for Women in Denton. While attending these workshops Gordon was able to do some radio announcing, presumably on the campus radio station (McLendon, 1969a).

LIFE AT MILITARY SCHOOL AND COLLEGE

Atlanta High School had provided Gordon with what he described in a 1969 interview as a "marvelous background." So successful was he in his academic pursuits that Gordon completed his high school requirements in three years instead of the customary four, and graduated in 1938.

The following fall, Gordon enrolled at Kemper Military School in Missouri. He was very successful at Kemper, managing the unprecedented feat as a freshman of winning all four of the school's honor awards. But Gordon was not the kind of student for whom a military school is designed. He already had learned self-discipline and rigorous study habits on his own.

So, after a year at Kemper Gordon decided to apply to college. Not just any college would do. Gordon set his sights on the Ivy League. Off went applications to Harvard, Princeton and Yale. Along with those applications for college entrance went applications for scholarships. Gordon later admitted that he really had no business applying for scholarships, since his father was by then doing well in the theater business and certainly had the resources to send his son to any of the Ivy League schools. Nonetheless, Gordon did apply for the scholarships. He was accepted by all three of the universities, and Harvard and Princeton both awarded Gordon scholarships. Gordon insisted that had anyone at Harvard or Princeton investigated his financial situation he would have been found ineligible for any scholarship. He decided that Yale would be the best school for him, since it was the only one of the three not to offer him a scholarship.

Gordon's time at Yale turned out to be more strenuous than he had anticipated. The reason was the major he chose—oriental languages (McLendon, 1969a). This, of course, was by no means an ordinary college major, even for someone with Gordon's linguistic skills. The story behind his choice of the oriental language major may have been stretched a bit, but Gordon said that the major was facetiously recommended by his two roommates during a poker game. Gordon had been consulting them about a possible major that would be easy and that would not take too much time away from his more relaxing pursuits. Gordon said he learned just how much he had been misled when he discovered that he needed more than a twenty-four-hour day just to keep up with course requirements.

Gordon may have exaggerated about the amount of time he devoted to study, because he was able to participate in a number of important extracurricular activities at Yale. He was a member of the Yale tennis team and the Yale debate team. He also served as chairman of the *Yale Literary Magazine* (McLendon, 1969a). Most important to Gordon, though, was the time he spent as a "sports, news and special events broadcaster" for Yale's radio station, WOCD ("Gordon Combines Radio," 1969).

Not all of Gordon's time outside the classroom was devoted to sports or intellectual pursuits, especially after one of his roommates introduced Gordon to a Smith College coed named Gay Noe (Bart McLendon, 1991). Gay was a fellow southerner, from a prominent Louisiana family. Her father, James A. Noe, had even served as governor of Louisiana at one time (Conrad, 1988, p. 607). Gordon and Gay struck up an immediate friendship that later turned to serious dating.

Regardless of whether his pursuits were romantic, athletic, intellectual or otherwise, Gordon realized that there was much to be gained from an association with Yale University. But as much as he learned there, Gordon lamented in later years that he had gotten probably only about 15 percent of what he could have gotten from Yale had he waited a few years to enter the university (McLendon, 1969a).

Gordon had even less time at Yale than he was anticipating. As it happened, he had chosen Japanese and Malayan as the two languages of concentration as required by his major. Before long, Gordon had become reasonably familiar with Japanese, but did not consider himself fluent in the language. His familiarity was sufficient, though, to attract the attention of the U.S. Navy, which, by the time the United States entered the war with Japan in 1941, was eager to enlist persons who possessed any knowledge whatsoever of the Japanese language. Gordon was a junior at Yale by then, and by the fall of 1942—Gordon's first semester as a senior—the Navy had come calling.

The Navy was not the least bit timid in letting Gordon know what it wanted of him. Neither was there any doubt that the Navy would get precisely what it wanted. Gordon said that just before Christmas vacation in 1942, he and about seven or eight classmates were surprised one day during a Japanese language class when in strode a naval officer to notify all male students present that then and there they were being inducted into the U.S. Navy. Although everyone in the class needed one more semester to graduate, the officer told them that arrangements already had been made for them to receive their diplomas once they had been formally sworn in to the Navy (McLendon, 1969a).

LIFE IN THE NAVY

With Yale degree in one hand and induction papers in the other, Gordon was headed toward becoming a Japanese language officer in U.S. Naval Intelligence (McLendon, 1980a, p. 1). His first stop would be at the Navy's Japanese language school at the University of Colorado in Boulder. There Gordon underwent fourteen months of intensive training, where he spoke "literally nothing but Japanese" for the entire time. Next, Gordon was transferred to Pearl Harbor, where he spent about five months interrogating Japanese prisoners and translating captured Japanese documents.

Gordon asked for and eventually was granted a transfer to the forward areas of naval operations in the Pacific. He was stationed at various times on Palau, Saipan, Tinian, Guam and Ulithi. While on the island of Ulithi, located in the Western Caroline Islands, Gordon was able to move back into radio with the Armed Forces Radio Network, or AFRN (McLendon, 1969a). Actually, he had managed to engage in some part-time radio announcing at commercial radio stations in Honolulu while stationed at Pearl Harbor (McLendon, 1981b). There he had broadcast morning newscasts and Honolulu high school football games (Bane, 1982, p. 9).

The chance to broadcast on the AFRN opened a door for Gordon to bring some of his abundant wit to the American forces in the area. In addition to sports and general news announcing, he also created a program of news satire in which he delivered nonsensical commentary using the name "Lowell Gram Kaltenheatter" (McLendon, 1981a). The name was a compound of Lowell Thomas, Raymond Gram Swing, H. V. Kaltenborn and Gabriel Heatter, all famous radio news commentators of the day. Gordon later said: "The idea for the program came because I had so often listened to many commentators, such as Gabriel Heatter, and at the end of the program wondered what they had been talking about" (McLendon, 1957b, p. 1).

The "Kaltenheatter" commentary aired every evening and ran for five minutes. Listeners loved the nonsensical interlude because it was impossible to determine after five minutes just exactly what had been said (McLendon, 1969a). Here is a brief example of one of the infamous commentaries:

> One thing appears to be more certain than anything else in the South Pacific right now, and that is that there is action in the South Pacific tonight. Our troops, in the fast-shrinking hub of the flattening salient, just beyond the sharp tip of the bulging wedge, cannot at this time be either overestimated or entirely discounted. As a result, I believe that I can say that the final result of this battle for the South Pacific may, or may not, depend upon one, or more, of several significant military developments not at this time entirely foreseeable (McLendon, 1962c, p. 2).

However attracted to Lowell Gram Kaltenheatter's commentary the soldiers and sailors listening to it might have been, its attraction hardly measured up to that of the major league baseball games that the AFRN periodically aired. The popularity of the broadcasts caught Gordon's attention. "When the major league baseball games came on, work just stopped," Gordon observed: "I mean even if a kamikaze was coming, they were going to hear that ballgame" (McLendon, 1978).

The idea was firmly implanted in Gordon's mind that listeners eager to hear baseball games during wartime in the South Pacific would be just as eager to hear the games during peacetime in the United States. At the moment that was not possible for much of the country. Only radio listeners who lived in or near cities where major league baseball teams played were able to hear daily games on local stations. Persons living elsewhere, and that included most of the South and West in the 1940s, were confined to listening only to the World Series and the Major League All-Star Game, and occasionally a nighttime baseball game on a powerful distant radio station. Why did this have to be, Gordon wondered. He decided that as soon as the war ended, he would remedy what he viewed as an injustice to baseball fans across the nation. (McLendon, 1978).

Gordon bid the U.S. Navy farewell in October 1945. His entrance to the armed forces had not been at all routine, but once there Gordon had served with distinction. He was even awarded a special commendation prior to his discharge for securing documents from a dying kamikaze pilot that helped break the Japanese code (McLendon, 1969a).

SHORT-LIVED HARVARD LAW SCHOOL STUDIES

A postwar career in radio seemed the most logical path for Gordon, and was one that he indeed shortly would take. However, one detour lay along the way—a detour for which family tradition rather than any burning desire on Gordon's part was responsible. The detour led to Harvard Law School. So, while thousands of ex-servicemen at war's end were eagerly filtering into the broadcasting business, Gordon's considerable broadcast talent was placed on hold for the moment.

There was no doubt that Gordon had the talent for practicing law. His legal career might have been a brilliant one if he had had the heart to pursue it. As it happened, the decision to attend Harvard Law School was described later by Gordon as "a minor disaster." He admitted that he had no business being there and that his decision to study law was prompted entirely by his father's and grandfather's success in their law practices (McLendon, 1969a).

Motivation certainly was a factor in Gordon's eventual decision to leave Harvard Law School after his first year, but sheer fatigue played a part as well. The mental pressures of Yale, followed closely by the mental and physical pressures of the war, required a kind of postwar relief that Gordon's plunge into law studies had not provided (McLendon, 1969a).

There was another reason for wanting to leave Harvard: Gordon by now had a family to raise. He had managed to find time to marry Gay Noe in 1943. What's more, by war's end a daughter, the first of Gordon and Gay's four children (Jan, Bart, Kristen and Anna Gray), had been born to the couple ("Gordon McLendon for United States Senator," 1964).

After Gordon's first and only year at Harvard Law School, he decided to quit and to pursue his first love—radio. And as a bemused Gordon later recalled, "Events have taken place which show that I was on the right track" (McLendon, 1969a). Such was Gordon's gift for understatement.

2 *KNET and KLIF: First Ventures into Radio*

Gordon returned to Texas following his short-lived stint at Harvard Law School. His undivided attention would focus now on radio—a medium that in time would make his name famous among millions of Americans. Considering all that would happen in a relatively short span, Gordon's initial plunge into radio was by no means grandiose. It was modest in every respect.

RADIO STATION KNET

Gordon moved his family to Palestine, Texas in 1946, and with the help of his father purchased one-half ownership of Palestine radio station KNET (McLendon, 1969a). B. R. McLendon's helping hand at this point was a particularly noteworthy gesture. He had wanted Gordon to become a lawyer, but he also had sensed his son's unhappiness during his stay at Harvard Law School. A phone call from B. R. finally had assured Gordon that not only would it be okay to leave law school, but that B. R. would financially support Gordon's entry into the radio business. Gordon, it has been said, spent the rest of his life trying to show his father that he had made the right decision (Odom, 1990).

The theater business and smart real estate investments (McDougal, 1984, p. 18) had by now allowed B. R. the wherewithal to easily loan Gordon the $17,000 needed for his portion of KNET's purchase price ("The Top-40," n.d., p. 18). Johnny Long was the station's co-owner. "He was such a great guy," Gordon later remarked, because he put up "with all my eccentricities" ("The Top-40," n.d., p. 18).

An amusing incident related to the KNET purchase helped cement a lifelong friendship between Gordon and Washington attorney Marcus Cohn. As it happened, Gordon was meeting with a radio engineer in Washington when he mentioned needing a lawyer to help with licensing matters normally associated with purchasing a radio station. The engineer suggested Cohn, who had just begun his law practice, and Gordon paid him a visit. Gordon wasted little time in coming to the point of his visit: he needed someone to represent him in his efforts to buy a radio station in Palestine. Gordon did not say Palestine, Texas, and Marcus Cohn, assuming the Palestine to be the one in the Mideast, told Gordon that he only represented American station owners. Cohn was corrected by a somewhat indignant Gordon McLendon, who nonetheless appreciated the humor of the incident. Cohn thought that he would be losing one of his first clients, but instead he gained both a client and a friend for life (Cohn, 1989). The value of that friendship would be proved time and time again as Marcus Cohn maneuvered Gordon through one legal mine field after another in years to come.

KNET's 100 watts of power carried its signal just far enough to serve Palestine's 12,000 inhabitants. The station, however, did have the good fortune of being the only one in town, and its location 100 miles southeast of Dallas made big-market radio competition minimal.

While there was nothing "big time" about KNET, it did prove to be the perfect place for a young radio executive like Gordon to learn his trade. "There I got a real bath of fire in the radio business," Gordon said. "I saw it from a different side for the first horrifying time. I saw it not from the romantic side next to the microphone but the not-so-romantic side across a desk from advertisers that I had to convince to get on the radio station or else be extinct" (McLendon, 1969a).

Gordon's introduction to the sales and management chores of running a radio station proved right away that his heart was not in that side of the radio business. Gordon's attention was focused squarely on radio's creative side. "Instead of doing what a normal owner would do—work with his sales department . . . meet people as they came in . . . and get out in the community," Gordon admitted, "you'd most [often] find me back in the trenches, either on the air, writing copy, trying to create a constructive commercial for some account . . . even, I remember, sweeping out" (McLendon, 1978). But Gordon said he "never regretted that, because I really got to see . . . how my guys had to work" (McLendon, 1978).

From his early days at KNET it became obvious to those around him that creativity and not money was what Gordon regarded as most important. "The creative act," observed Marcus Cohn in an interview, was the "driving force" that motivated Gordon McLendon (Cohn, 1989). Bill Meeks, who, like so many others, would entrust his fortunes to the McLendon bandwagon, remarked that it was even difficult to talk with Gordon during his early days in radio because his mind always seemed to be racing ahead to a new idea (Meeks, 1990).

Bill Meeks did not work for Gordon at KNET, but did work for him later in Dallas. It was a baseball game that Meeks heard Gordon announcing on KNET that convinced him that one day he would like to work for someone with such talent. Meeks happened to be driving through Palestine with members of a dance band he conducted when he heard Gordon announcing a baseball game. The game was not being covered live; rather it was being re-created in the KNET studios. Practically everything that happened during the game was the product of Gordon's vivid imagination. Meeks later recalled: "It was just interesting as hell. And I wasn't particularly a baseball fan. But we all got to listening and thinking what a great announcer he was; what a marvelous sports announcer" (Meeks, 1990). What Meeks heard was the genesis of what Gordon shortly would mold into an art form.

While Bill Meeks would join Gordon later, there were others who would go to work at KNET and remain with Gordon for many years to come. Bill Weaver was one of these (Meeks, 1990) and so was Edd Routt. Routt's tenure with Gordon began the very day he went to interview the new radio station owner for a *Palestine Herald* newspaper story. Within two hours of that interview, Routt decided to resign from his newspaper job for a position at KNET. He later explained what had so attracted him to Gordon:

> He just was an exciting man. . . . He was just burbling with ideas. And he was going to turn KNET into a real force in the community. . . . I came to work as his news director, and he would not let me deliver the news on the air 'cause I was not yet into that aspect of news broadcasting. But I would write the stuff and he would put it on the air. And this went on for the longest time. And he would work with me at night. We were affiliated with Mutual, and at 10:00 at night we would switch operations to the transmitter. That is to say we'd just feed the network through direct and no longer man the studio. At 10 o'clock he would often meet me down there and teach me how to read news. He'd get into the control room and I'd get into Studio A as we had back in those days, and I'd read a newscast and then he would read it and say, "Now emphasize this." He literally taught me to read news. (Routt, 1989).

Palestine, Texas was meant to be only a stopover for Gordon—a place to earn his wings, so to speak. His stay there perhaps was shortened more than he had anticipated when, quite unexpectedly, the railroad decided to move out of Palestine (McLendon, 1969a).

For a city whose livelihood depended heavily on the railroad, such news caused economic shockwaves. Money would become scarce, and businesses would either close or tighten their advertising budgets. This was not happy news for a business such as radio, which depended entirely on advertising dollars. And while both Palestine and KNET would survive, Gordon

McLendon began marking time until his departure. He also spent time applying to the Federal Communications Commission (FCC) for a license to operate a radio station in Dallas.

Owning a station in Dallas had been Gordon's objective all along. Even during the war he had mentioned to a friend that he wanted someday to own a Dallas radio station (Callison, 1989). He also had important family ties in Dallas by now. B. R. had moved there in 1942 to expand his theater business ("Movie Theater Owner," 1982), and B. R.'s parents had followed their son to Dallas in 1945 ("McLendon Rites Set," 1954).

The FCC granted Gordon a license to operate a Dallas radio station in early 1947. His half interest in KNET was sold back to its former owner at a slight loss, and Gordon headed to the big city (McLendon, 1969a).

RADIO STATION KLIF

Dallas, Texas was, as late as 1940, "still a provincial Southwestern city, strongly characterized by overtones of the Old South," according to one local historian (Rogers, 1965, p. 366). Not until midway through the 1940s did the city's dynamics become supercharged. Dallas had by then "reached a stage that was comparable to achieving the critical mass in a nuclear bomb" (Rogers, 1965, p. 367). The same historian attributed all that Dallas had been and would become to the breed of its inhabitants: "From the first decade, nay, from the first settler, [Dallas] has drawn to itself men and women not only robustly typical of the time and region, but men and women who possessed an independence of thought and action which had a way of making history" (Rogers, 1965, p. 17). Without a doubt, Gordon McLendon and Dallas, Texas were made for one another.

Gordon positioned his new radio station not in Dallas proper but rather a short distance to the southwest, in the suburb of Oak Cliff. Oak Cliff had been named for the abundance of oak trees that grew on the bluffs overlooking the Trinity River, which flowed between Oak Cliff and Dallas (Rogers, 1965, p. 190). And while there was not a single cliff in the vicinity worthy of the term, Gordon would make that part of the city famous by choosing the similar-sounding K-L-I-F call letters for his radio station.

Once in operation, KLIF would broadcast from the Cliff Towers Hotel ("Station KLIF to Take," 1947). Making the station operational—actually constructing it—fell to engineer Glenn Callison. Gordon had met Callison during the war while the two were stationed on Guam. Gordon was a program officer and Callison a program engineer at the time, and both were responsible for feeding programs onto the AFRN. Gordon informed Callison then and there that he was determined to own a radio station in Dallas after the war and asked if Callison would be his chief engineer. "I just thought that was so much Navy talk," said Callison, but "sure enough, in 1947 he called me, and he said, 'Come on down' " (Callison, 1989). So, he went. Not only would Callison put KLIF on the air, but he also would oversee either the construction or modification of every future McLendon Station acquisition (Callison, 1989). The high-quality sound for which McLendon Stations became known throughout the broadcasting industry was the product of Glenn Callison's technical wizardry.

The inaugural broadcast of KLIF was scheduled for 12:50 P.M., Sunday, November 9, 1947 ("Station KLIF Takes," 1947, p. 7: sec. 2). The FCC had classified KLIF as a daytime-only station, with an assigned 1190 frequency on the AM dial and a transmitting power of 1,000 watts. The Trinity Broadcasting Corporation was the business title under which the station operated. B. R. McLendon served as Trinity's president, while Gordon became the company's executive director (*1948 Broadcasting Yearbook*, p. 240). Gordon was off and running at the young age of twenty-six, but he still relied on—and would continue to do so—the business mind and financial clout of his father to keep the McLendon radio enterprise running at full throttle.

Also playing a key role in the McLendon organization was Dorothy Manning. Ms. Manning had joined B. R. as a bookkeeper (and sometimes theater custodian) while still in Atlanta, Texas. She would rise to be the secretary-treasurer of the future McLendon Corporation and eventually would exercise considerable power in the corporation's financial decisions (Manning, 1990). Gordon's son Bart even referred to Dorothy Manning as the "power behind the throne" when commenting on her role in McLendon business affairs (Bart McLendon, 1990). She would become the McLendons' longest-term employee.

KLIF PROGRAMMING

Asked many years later what philosophy of broadcasting he had planned to implement at KLIF, Gordon said he had not given any immediate thought to the matter. What was apparent, said Gordon, was the challenge that lay ahead. He knew that KLIF's programming would have to be unique in order to compete with the other, more powerful and better-established Dallas radio stations (McLendon, 1969a). The Gordon McLendon philosophy of radio developed from this realization. It was his guide for years to come as he and B. R. acquired one radio station after another. The philosophy was simple: Provide as many listeners as possible with the kind of programming they want to hear, and *always* outperform the competition (McLendon, 1969a).

Whether KLIF's first program schedule actually differed markedly from that of other Dallas stations is uncertain. What is obvious, though, was that the eclectic blend of programs that Gordon lined up for KLIF gave the station more the appearance of a network affiliate than a local independent operation (MacFarland, 1973, p. 209). A number of the musical programs, headlined by such well-known personalities as Tommy Dorsey, David Street and Gene Autry, were recorded. Locally, Mrs. Tim Healy hosted a homemakers advice program called "Mrs. Healy At Home." Ann Sterling, operator of a Dallas modeling school, hosted an over-the-air charm school called "How to Be Charming." And Gordon himself revived his Lowell Gram Kaltenheatter character, now to dispense with civilian instead of military "news commentary." Joe Keith hosted a local disc jockey show, as did Red Calhoun and Buster Smith, two Dallas band leaders (Advertisement, 1947), who were "the first black announcers in the Southwest" (Brock, 1971).

Also part of the KLIF announcing staff was Klif the parrot. Named in honor of the radio station that he now would serve, Klif was a bonafide announcer, complete with an American Federation of Radio Artists union card, who had been trained to chirp "K-L-I-F" during station identification breaks. The parrot reportedly had been reluctant to repeat the all-important call letters until he was placed inside a sound studio and subjected to a recording that repeated "K-L-I-F" over and over (Tolbert, 1947). Klif the parrot was the first of many promotional gimmicks that helped make KLIF's presence quickly known throughout Dallas.

The programming and the program talent that Gordon had chosen for KLIF may have been unique among other Dallas radio stations. Certainly, no other station carried a parrot on the announcing staff. But there remained the need to create something that would set KLIF entirely apart from its competitors. What Gordon did that was different was to take KLIF listeners to the ballpark—first to professional football games and then to major league baseball games. This was Gordon's "hidden weapon." Here at last was Gordon's chance to implement an idea that he had conceived during the war: sportscasts every day of the week, with baseball on weekdays and a mixture of baseball and football on the weekends (McLendon, 1969a). Gordon would announce the games himself. He would be KLIF's play-by-play man and color commentator all rolled into one.

Gordon's plans were those of a visionary—one with unlimited wealth. How was it that such a grandiose sports operation would originate from a radio station like KLIF, where money was in short supply? The answer was re-creation, a technique that Gordon already had practiced on a smaller scale at KNET. He would sit in his KLIF studio, receive a running account by wire of the highlights of a particular ballgame, and then re-create that game for his listeners (McLendon, 1969a).

Sports re-creations were by no means a McLendon invention. They were an "honorable practice of the time," and had been around since the earliest days of radio. Indeed, one early practitioner while a young radio announcer in Des Moines, Iowa was none other than Ronald Reagan (Nelson, 1985, p. 143).

Gordon wasted little time in getting straight to the business of re-creating ballgames. His first re-creation on KLIF aired the same day that the station began operation, November 9, 1947. The game was a professional football contest between the Chicago Cardinals and the Detroit Lions (McLendon, 1969a). Highlights of the game were telegraphed to KLIF from the game site, and recorded stadium crowd noises were heard in the background as Gordon described the game action (Tolbert, 1952, p. 57). The re-creations caught on immediately with Dallas radio listeners, most of whom thought that they were listening to game coverage direct from the ballpark (McLendon, 1969a). Gordon's showmanship flair for re-creating sports events was a trademark that would excite and entertain listeners for years to come.

The sense of humor that would become another Gordon McLendon trademark also emerged during his inaugural football game re-creation. Gordon introduced himself as "Gordon McLendon, the Old Scotchman, 83 years old this very day" (Tolbert, 1952, pp. 57–58). Gordon had called himself the Old Scotchman when he re-created his first baseball games at KNET (Meeks, 1990). Now he would get extra mileage from the colorful nickname. "Hallo evvabody evvawhere, this is the Old Scotchman, Gordon McLendon" was the homey way one listener remembered Gordon's introduction to practically every radio appearance he ever made (Hitt, 1979).

The nickname would lead to all sorts of fun and instant celebrity recognition, but why that particular choice for someone whose ancestry probably was more Irish than Scotch (Odom, 1990)? Gordon explained that he wanted to create an on-air nickname for himself that listeners could easily remember. Since the Scottish are a people that practically no one dislikes and since the McLendon family could claim a Scottish lineage of sorts, Gordon decided that the Old Scotchman moniker would be perfect. One more addition to Gordon's on-air image was his claim to being an octogenarian (McLendon, 1969a).

Gordon relished the fun of what he was doing, and how he was doing it. But football game re-creations were just a warm-up for what to Gordon was the main event. Come springtime, KLIF would be airing baseball game re-creations—or so Gordon thought. It was at this juncture that the powerful—and what Gordon would come to regard as the apparently monolithic—force of organized baseball entered the scene. In order to re-create major league baseball games one first had to secure legal permission, or the "rights" to those games. But this was not something that baseball clubs were eager to part with.

Gordon said later that he never had encountered any difficulty in securing the rights to carry professional football games. Moreover, he had paid only a minimal fee for the privilege. Gordon therefore was unprepared for what he faced when attempting to negotiate for the rights to broadcast professional baseball games. What he encountered from organized baseball was a summary rejection toward any efforts to negotiate.

There were two basic reasons for the baseball executives' decision to deny either broadcast or re-creation rights to their games. First, they claimed exclusive territorial control over individual baseball teams' "club networks." Baseball executives did not want competition for those stations that carried the ballgames of teams for whom these exclusive territories had been created (McLendon, 1969a). This, for the moment, was not the most important reason for the baseball executives' decision. However, its importance would increase in due time.

The second and more important of the two reasons for denying Gordon broadcast rights pertained to another kind of territorial exclusivity controlled by minor league baseball clubs. "The minor league owners . . . had a rule prohibiting major league game broadcasts within fifty miles of a minor league park without the owner's consent." As it happened, the minor league Dallas club played its games in a ballpark just a few blocks from the KLIF studios (Tolbert, 1952, pp. 57–58). The "fifty-mile rule," as Gordon put it, resulted from a fear that broadcasts or re-creations of major league games would diminish interest among baseball fans in attending local minor league baseball games (McLendon, 1969a).

Western Union, whose telegraph lines Gordon normally would have used to relay the information necessary to re-create baseball games, also balked at providing the wire service. It appeared that Western Union would not cooperate until Gordon had obtained broadcast permission from major league baseball (Adams, 1950).

But Gordon was, in his own words, "a determined cuss" when it came to having his way (McLendon, 1969a). What he did next was the stuff of legend—a move that made Gordon "a modern-day Texas outlaw, so far as baseball was concerned," according to the *New York Times:*

> He came to New York, rented an office on Lexington Avenue and bought a "TWX" line—teletype service—from the telephone company. Gordon hired a man to listen to Mel Allen's baseball broadcasts over WINS and teletype the play-by-play to him in a studio of his Dallas station. Deep in the heart of Texas, "The Old Scotchman" re-created major league diamond plays only ten seconds behind the actual happenings. The method indeed was a unique triple play. (Adams, 1950).

Thus was Gordon able to broadcast his first re-created major league baseball game, on March 21, 1948. The spring training game was played in Florida between the St. Louis Cardinals and the New York Yankees (Tolbert, 1952, p. 58). From a remote broadcast in Florida the game's description had been transformed into a series of nearly unintelligible symbols in New York, retransmitted to Dallas and then, as if by magic, reassembled in the imagination of Gordon McLendon and broadcast to the KLIF radio audience.

The broadcast was an immediate hit, according to Gordon. But just as immediate were the legal questions associated with the broadcast. Was Gordon infringing on organized baseball's property rights, and was he illegally appropriating program matter that did not belong to him? Gordon's position on both questions appeared to have a reasonably sound legal foundation. He contended that the moment a baseball game was broadcast, regardless of how much time had elapsed since play had occurred, the game became news. Anyone was then free to report on the game or to go so far as to re-create the game in full. Property rights to any part of a baseball game, once broadcast, were then forfeited (McLendon, 1969a).

The powers that be in organized baseball probably did not at all agree with Gordon's position, but they nonetheless were unwilling to force the issue. After only a few weeks into the 1948 baseball season, major league club owners offered to sell Gordon the rights to Western Union's wire service directly from all the major league ball parks, and at a very reasonable fee. "So then," said Gordon, "I became legal, accepted and legitimate for the first time" (McLendon, 1969a).

Gordon's legitimacy came none too soon. He had begun resorting to teletyped game reports from observers perched high atop buildings overlooking ballparks. They observed entire baseball games—reporting on the action as it occurred—through binoculars ("Tribute," 1986).

For the moment, matters appeared settled between Gordon and the major league baseball establishment. However, as events began to unfold, it became obvious that organized baseball's 1948 posture was deceptive. Concern over the broadcast rights issue, though, was diverted for the moment by interest over the number of radio stations that were beginning to carry the Old Scotchman's baseball broadcasts. With little or no fanfare, KLIF miraculously was finding itself the flagship station of a burgeoning new radio network. The story of that network follows in the next chapter.

KLIF SALES AND PROMOTION

Gordon had hired others to fill key management and programming positions at KLIF. Aubrey Escoe became the station's first general manager ("Station KLIF To Take," 1947), while Bud Watson became the first KLIF news and sports editor, and Howard Bogarte was named the station's first chief announcer (Advertisement, 1947). These persons no doubt played important roles in getting KLIF off the ground, but there was no mistaking that Gordon McLendon exercised much greater authority over the day-to-day operation of his station, particularly with respect to creative matters, than the ordinary station owner. "Gordon ran everything, and B. R. was more or less in the background," was the way Bill Meeks viewed the father-son management (Meeks, 1990). That did not mean that B. R. actually played a lesser role in KLIF affairs—quite the contrary. It meant only that Gordon's was the more visible and audible presence at KLIF.

As many talents as Gordon possessed, selling station time to advertising clients was not one of them. A two-person sales staff, comprised of Bill Meeks and Bruce Collier, was entrusted with the task of generating enough advertising dollars to keep KLIF running. Meeks, who had been impressed by Gordon's baseball re-creations at KNET, was leading a band at Dallas radio station WFAA when he heard that KLIF was going on the air. One brief meeting with Gordon soon afterwards convinced Meeks to move his band to KLIF, where he hosted two live musical programs per day. Before long, though, Gordon had convinced Meeks that he could make much more money as a KLIF salesperson than as a band leader.

The Bill Meeks-Bruce Collier sales team had little luck at first in persuading advertisers to buy time on KLIF. "They didn't believe there was such a radio station. And it took, oh, three or four years to get it to where people really recognized that [KLIF] was a valuable property," recalled Meeks in 1990. One of the station's major problems, claimed Meeks, was the failure of the audience rating services to portray KLIF's true audience size. "It took the rating services over a year to really realize that [KLIF] had an audience—a big audience" (Meeks, 1990).

The major problem in ascertaining KLIF's audience size stemmed from the method used by rating services for measuring radio station listening. Rating service representatives merely asked audience survey respondents what stations they listened to. Persons in those days usually responded by identifying the names of their favorite networks instead of the call letters of individual stations. This created a dilemma for independent radio stations whose lack of any network affiliation made call letter identification vital. Gordon and Bill Meeks managed eventually to solve the identification dilemma and to lock the KLIF call letters firmly into the minds of the station's listeners. What's more, these listeners began telling rating service representatives that they tuned to KLIF (Meeks, 1991).

Once word of KLIF's audience size finally reached advertisers, the station took off. Helping the word to spread were the bargain rates that Meeks and Collier were charging for KLIF spot announcements. Meeks said that in order to create a clientele he offered ten radio spots, and threw in a bonus spot, for the same rate that an old-line Dallas radio station like KRLD was charging for a single spot. Hardly able to resist such rates, major Dallas advertisers began moving their accounts to KLIF. "And all of a sudden," said Meeks, "we were beginning to sell all the time and take all the money away from all the other stations" (Meeks, 1990).

Time sales were going so well after a while that Meeks, Bruce Collier and Harold Bertell, a third salesperson who by now had joined the KLIF sales staff, often found themselves with no more time to sell. The three would meet in the mornings, pretend to have a sales meeting and then adjourn to a local cafe, where they would spend the rest of the morning eating biscuits and drinking coffee (Meeks, 1990).

One method of spreading the word about KLIF to potential listeners and advertisers alike was through promotion. Gordon realized early on that if he could get the KLIF call letters before the public as often as possible, then he could beat his competitors (Meeks, 1990). But how could he accomplish this? There was little money to purchase newspaper space to promote the station. And since the major Dallas newspapers also owned radio stations, there was little likelihood of free publicity ("The Top-40," n.d., p. 20).

Bill Meeks suggested a way that actually was born of necessity for using KLIF to promote itself (Meeks, 1990). Commercial jingles had been used since the late 1930s as a way of creating an identifiable sound signature for products advertised on the radio. Since listeners seemed to remember easily the short jingle songs that repeated a product name, why not use similar jingles for radio station identification? The idea already had been tried at one New York station (MacFarland, 1973, p. 135), but KLIF apparently would be the first station in Dallas to air such jingles.

Bill Meeks recalled singing the very first KLIF station identification (ID) jingle ("Radio Jingles," 1987, p. 32) on November 11, 1947, just two days after KLIF had signed on the air (Passman, 1971, p. 160). Meeks and several other singers subsequently produced other jingles of varying lengths on disk recordings ("Radio Jingles," 1987, p. 8). The jingles began catching on among Dallas radio listeners, and, according to Meeks, "had an awful lot to do with making [KLIF] a recognizable station, where everybody knew it" (Meeks, 1990).

There was another more utilitarian purpose for the KLIF jingles. The station had only one studio in its Cliff Towers Hotel basement facility capable of accommodating the musicians and other performers necessary for local live programming. Whenever one person or group moved in or out of the studio there needed to be an on-air cover of some kind to allow for the transition. Jingles, as it turned out, were found to be the perfect cover (Meeks, 1990). What's more, they were constant reminders to listeners that they were tuned to KLIF.

3 *The Liberty Broadcasting System: Halcyon Days*

Whether Gordon McLendon ever intended to create his own radio network is unknown. The best evidence suggests that the network that came to be called the Liberty Broadcasting System, or LBS for short, just happened. The network was named by B. R. McLendon, who liked the patriotic association of the name (McLendon, 1981b).

In a 1969 interview, Gordon described how a successive string of radio stations, each intent on sharing in the popularity of KLIF's baseball broadcasts, joined to form LBS. First, he said, came the manager of a small radio station in Dennison, Texas, who claimed that his station was losing its audience to KLIF whenever the Dallas station broadcast afternoon baseball games. Could the manager pay KLIF a fee and carry the broadcasts locally? Then came similar inquiries from radio station representatives in other nearby Texas towns, such as Tyler, Mount Pleasant, Mineral Wells, and so on. When these stations started carrying KLIF's baseball games, the idea began to spread to other Texas radio stations to do the same. By the end of 1948 some fifty stations had joined the new network (McLendon, 1969a).

And so it went. Week after week more stations joined LBS. At first most of them were in small Texas towns, but gradually, stations in cities like Fort Worth, Houston, Wichita Falls and Lubbock began to affiliate with LBS. Then the network became interstate as radio stations in Louisiana, Mississippi, Oklahoma, Kansas, Arkansas and Colorado joined (*1950 Broadcasting Yearbook*, p. 64). Within three years LBS would have 458 affiliates and rank second in network size only to the Mutual Broadcasting System ("End," 1952, p. 92). Remarking on how LBS had zoomed to such heights so quickly, Gordon could only say, "It just grew like Topsy" (Adams, 1950).

LBS AND PLAY-BY-PLAY BASEBALL BROADCAST RIGHTS

LBS was "founded . . . as a sports network," Gordon said during a 1981 interview. "That's all we ever wanted to be at the start" (McLendon, 1981a). And baseball, of course, was the sport from which the network derived greatest acclaim. Gordon would not have had it otherwise. Baseball was his favorite sport, and he had, after all, prepared himself since childhood to be a baseball announcer. Gordon's enthusiasm for the game was shared by millions of other Americans, many of whom could be counted among the most ardent LBS listeners. There was an implicit excitement about baseball that attracted fans, to be sure, but baseball's immense popularity on the radio also owed to its position among other sports. Baseball "just didn't have the competition sportswise in broadcasting" that it later would have, noted Gordon. In late 1940s America, baseball simply "was *the* game" (McLendon, 1981a).

Another factor that made LBS successful was scarcity. Until the network began broadcasting its "Game-of-the-Day," most of the nation was limited in what baseball broadcasts were available. In fact there was only one "inner area" of the country—confined mostly to a small corner of the Northeast—where baseball games were broadcast daily (Nelson, 1988). Why here and nowhere else? Because organized baseball rules (the same rules mentioned earlier with which Gordon had to contend) limited broadcast of major league games to a well-defined territory surrounding the franchise location of each major league team. The radio stations whose owners held rights to broadcast the home club's games were all within a fifty-mile radius of a line stretching precisely from home plate of a particular baseball club's ballpark (Smith, 1987, p. 114). To live beyond the reach of radio stations in these territories was to live in a land devoid of radio's version of the sport. Baseball fans throughout the nation annually were treated to national network broadcasts of the World Series and the Major League All-Star Game, courtesy of the Mutual Broadcasting System, but "during the regular season, these folks were out in the cold" (Smith, 1987, pp. 112, 117).

Sportscaster Lindsey Nelson, who began his network career with LBS, explained in the following terms the territorial situation of major league baseball that greeted the Liberty network's arrival:

> Don't forget, this was before expansion and before established teams started shifting around. If you looked at the major-league map, the existing teams were all clustered in ten cities—the upper right quandrant of the country—and the area that they covered was from Boston only as far as St. Louis to the west, and Cincinnati and Washington to the south.
>
> That being true, it was only a matter of time before someone got the golden idea: "Gee, whoever brings baseball to these folks on radio—people, remem-

ber, panting to follow big-league games—is going to make a whale of a lot of money." All it took was to look at a map. (Smith, 1987, p. 112).

And look at a map Gordon McLendon most certainly did. Buoyed by his local success in Dallas and encouraged by the way in which LBS had developed so rapidly, Gordon decided to stretch his coverage even more. He "simply moved in and took over the West Coast, the Southwest, and the South, where he and his network soon became better known among sports fans than far more famous announcers and far more solid networks" (Nelson and Hirshberg, 1966, p. 31).

LBS had an abundance of listeners—between sixty and ninety million. What they heard usually exceeded what listeners in major league baseball cities heard. After all, LBS treated its audience to games from every team in both the American and National Leagues. A radio station in a major-league city carried only the games of that city's team. Lindsey Nelson remarked that the LBS baseball broadcasts "made for coverage like no sport has ever had—day in, day out, team in, team out—and it created just a storm of baseball enthusiasm. . . . I don't think interest in non-major-league areas has ever been as high" (Smith, 1987, pp. 115–116).

Here, then, is where Gordon McLendon and his Liberty network stood as the 1949 baseball season began winding down. The network was enormously popular, but its programming still centered on sports re-creations. It hardly compared with networks such as NBC or CBS in terms of programming variety. And LBS remained regional, albeit a gigantic region, in nature; it had yet to assume both the reach and the image of a full-fledged national network. LBS, was, as Gordon later attested, still perhaps better described "as being more of a hook-up than a network" (McLendon, 1981b).

Topping off all this was Gordon's still tenuous relationship with organized baseball. He was allowed to re-create major league games, it was true, but there were few among the baseball club owners who were comfortable with this arrangement. Events that occurred in October 1949 were to better define the situation, however. Along with the improved definition there also came a dramatic change in the Liberty network's entire complexion.

BASEBALL RELAXES RULE 1(d)

To better understand those events of October 1949 and why they occurred, some perspective is necessary. Justice Oliver Wendell Holmes, writing for the majority in the U.S. Supreme Court's 1922 *Federal Baseball* decision, declared that organized baseball was not by its nature interstate commerce and therefore was exempt from federal antitrust law (*Federal Baseball*, 1922).

From that early date baseball's antitrust exemption had held secure, until 1948, when the U.S. Justice Department began a probe of the major league's practice of awarding baseball game broadcast rights. The investigation was initiated by a complaint from radio station WARL in Arlington, Virginia (Crater, 1948, p. 21). Owners of the station had sought permission to carry games played between the New York Giants and the Brooklyn Dodgers, but were prevented from doing so by Clark Griffith, owner of the Washington Senators baseball club. Griffith argued that WARL's broadcasts in nearby Arlington would diminish the value of his Washington team's broadcast rights ("Baseball Ban," 1947).

By 1949 eight other station owners, including Gordon and B. R. McLendon, had filed similar complaints. What the Justice Department concluded in August 1949 did not bode well for organized baseball. According to *Broadcasting* magazine, high department officials felt that organized baseball indeed might be in violation of antitrust laws, particularly in the way that World Series broadcast rights were awarded to only one network (Crater, 1949, p. 23).

Commissioner of Baseball Albert B. Chandler was compelled to meet with Justice Department officials in order to avert the government's filing an antitrust suit against organized baseball. The two sides in the dispute held conferences on April 7 and June 2, 1949. Both conferences focused on major league baseball's Rule 1(d), which prohibited the broadcast "of any major league game in any city without the consent of all major and minor league clubs in that city and within 50 miles" (Crater, 1949, p. 23).

Rule 1(d) had been adopted officially in December 1946 (U.S. Congress. Senate, 1953, p. 13) and added to the complex set of rules and agreements governing the operation of all U.S. major and minor league baseball clubs (Neville, 1947, p. 208). Ford Frick, baseball commissioner at the time, asserted that the rule was necessary because of the effects that broadcasting of major league baseball games had when carried into minor league territories. Said Frick:

> Carried to the ultimate it would destroy the minor-league club, and the minor-league club destroyed would eventually destroy the major leagues, and the major leagues destroyed would destroy what we believe is a terrific American institution that is called baseball, which extends far beyond the major leagues and minor leagues: that which goes into the sandlots, into the lives of our young people. (U.S. Congress. Senate, 1953, p. 11)

Gordon McLendon had locked horns with Rule 1(d) when he first attempted to re-create baseball games at KLIF. Owners of the local minor league team in Dallas refused him permission to carry major league games. It was then that Gordon stationed someone in New York to relay play-by-play information to Dallas to accommodate his re-creations. The success of Gordon's method finally had persuaded major league baseball owners to allow him "legally" to carry their games by paying five hundred dollars monthly to the owners of the Dallas minor league club. However, once the Liberty Network began spreading across the United States, Gordon found that many of the network's affiliates in such places as New Orleans, Memphis and Los Angeles were denied the right to carry LBS baseball games due to the pressure of local minor league teams (U.S. Congress, Senate, 1953, pp. 95–96).

Lawyers representing Commissioner Chandler insisted that Rule 1(d) protected minor league baseball clubs from loss of fan support in the event that major league games were broadcast in minor league franchise areas while minor league games were in progress. Justice Department officials were unconvinced, though, and claimed that Rule 1(d) clearly violated antitrust laws by placing restraints on interstate broadcasts (Crater, 1949, p. 23).

Commissioner Chandler obviously could see that the Justice Department was prepared to press its case to the ultimate conclusion. Not wanting to totally abolish Rule 1(d), he instead agreed to amending the rule. Several amendments were announced in October 1949. The one that most affected radio broadcasters allowed local minor and major league teams, during home games, to object to broadcasts of any other major league baseball games by radio or television stations located within the local team's home territory. As before, "home territory" extended for a radius of fifty miles around a baseball club's home ballpark ("Baseball Probe," 1949, p. 23).

The Justice Department seemed satisfied with amended Rule 1(d), at least for the moment. The department's investigation was suspended until some evaluation could be made of the amended rule's effect. Feelings among broadcasters were mixed, however. Some were satisfied, but others felt that by its approval of Commissioner Chandler's resolution of the matter, the Justice Department had given its blessing to what continued as a restraint of trade. Some broadcasters, in fact, were displeased enough to be still contemplating antitrust action ("Baseball: Opposition Mounts," 1949).

LBS GROWTH AND EXPANSION

The somewhat touchy situation proved a boon for Gordon McLendon and LBS. Taking full advantage of organized baseball's relaxed rules, Gordon signed contracts with both American League and National League officials for the rights to carry a minimum of 210 major league baseball games—some 8 per week—during the 1950 season (Osbon, 1950, p. 15).

The popularity of the LBS sports package already had attracted numerous affiliates: 40 by early 1949; 71 by the fall of 1949 and 150 by February 1950 ("LBS Expands," 1950). Now that the 1950 baseball exhibition season was about to begin, a steady stream of queries from local radio station owners began appearing about how they might affiliate with LBS ("LBS Plans: Network," 1950). Expansion of the network by now had reached into the

Southeast and the Atlantic Coast states, and included the entire West Coast. Key affiliate stations in the west were located in major markets ranging from Seattle to San Francisco to Los Angeles. The only region yet to be penetrated by LBS was New England ("Liberty Web," 1950).

Amidst this network expansion, Gordon and B. R. moved their business offices to downtown Dallas, at the corner of Commerce and Central Expressway (Vaughn, 1989). A triangular building located nearby on Jackson Street that once had been a Magnolia Oil and then a Mobil Oil service station was soon purchased to house LBS facilities (Meeks, 1990). KLIF one day would move into the Jackson Street building and turn it into a Dallas landmark. For the present, though, KLIF remained housed at the Cliff Towers Hotel (Odom, 1990).

Most of the LBS programming was fed over network lines from the new Jackson Street location, though much of the network's musical programming originated from other Dallas locations. Some of it came from Jim Beck's recording studios, and at least one program featuring western music came from the Dallas Sportatorium. All of the LBS baseball re-creations originated from the KLIF studios (Meeks, 1990).

By March 1950, LBS had expanded to 160 local station affiliates and had begun airing a daily five-hour program schedule. The usual baseball game broadcasts were included in these five hours, but nonsports programs now had become a part of the LBS program fare ("LBS Plans: Network," 1950). Gordon explained that programs began growing around the baseball broadcasts. First, there was a sports roundup preceding the game; then a wrap-up following the game; and then other programs adjacent to these two naturally evolved (McLendon, 1981b). One of the first nonsports LBS programs was "Musical Bingo"—a quiz program offering money, trips and appliances to contestants ("Liberty Expands," 1950).

By June 1950, LBS boasted of 241 station affiliates spread among 33 states. The network's program schedule had increased to seven hours, and a Hollywood office now had joined an LBS New York office ("Liberty Expands," 1950). New York City radio station WMGM at last formed a cornerstone for Liberty's venture into the New England states (Vaughn, 1989). With the making of a national network now that northeastern radio stations were joining the fold, Gordon moved quickly to establish LBS as a competitive enterprise alongside such other radio network giants as NBC, CBS, ABC and Mutual.

Announcement of Liberty's plans to expand from regional status to national network status came in September 1950 ("LBS Plans: Expands," 1950, p. 25). *Time* magazine noted of the occasion that the existing radio networks now "were beginning to take serious notice . . . of a bustling new rival" ("The Old Scotchman," 1950). Liberty's inaugural broadcast as the nation's fifth radio network aired on October 2, 1950, at 7:45 A.M. Ironically, the initial program originated not from Dallas but rather from Washington,

D.C. Programs originated later in the day from Dallas, New York and Hollywood. Radio station affiliates in all of these cities were to serve as LBS origination sites on a regular basis ("LBS on the Air," 1950, p. 25).

"Good programming," asserted Gordon, "is the key to Liberty's success or failure" ("LBS Plans: Expands," 1950, p. 25). LBS was created to accomplish two goals: providing counterprogramming to the competing networks, and providing programs that local LBS affiliates could not produce themselves. Gordon cited the need for LBS to provide its affiliates with network programs that would attract local advertisers to buy time from the local affiliate stations ("LBS Plans: Expands," 1950, p. 25).

Programs that were scheduled for LBS were chosen for qualities that were said to be unique. One of these was the "Liberty Minstrels," a daily one-hour show fashioned around "old-fashioned minstrel lore" ("LBS Plans: Expands," 1950, p. 59). The "Liberty Minstrels" aired on weekday mornings and apparently was one of the Liberty network's longest running and most popular programs. The show consisted of a master of ceremonies, a twelve-piece band, a gospel quartet and a "blackface act," recalled former LBS music director Tom Merriman in a 1990 interview. The show's ambiance "was very Southern, very Southern humor," said Merriman. The master of ceremonies also interviewed program guests, in a way similar to today's television talk show host. A noontime musical show, two afternoon variety shows (Merriman, 1990), a listener participation crossword puzzle game show called "Cross Words and Sweet Music," and a daily one-hour program called "Disc Jockey Roundtable," which showcased the various styles of guest disc jockeys from around the country, were some of the programs that filled out the LBS program schedule ("LBS Plans: Expands," 1950, p. 59).

A number of the musical programs were recorded for replaying on the weekend, but practically all of the musical programs airing on weekdays were live. Not all of them were rehearsed either, according to Tom Merriman. There simply was not enough time. Brief notes on a "lead sheet" indicating what tunes would be played oftentimes was all the advance notice that musicians had for the music they were to perform (Merriman, 1990).

Bill Meeks served as the first LBS music director. He left that position when Gordon requested his help in boosting KLIF's advertising sales. Bill's brother, Charlie, then took over the music director's post (Meeks, 1990). Charlie Meeks was succeeded in 1951 by Tom Merriman, whom Charlie had hired only a short time before as a musical arranger (Merriman, 1990).

Gordon had resisted the idea of soap operas on LBS, but that resistance eventually gave way, and a series of soap operas and mystery programs moved onto Liberty's daily schedule. All of these were written and performed by an LBS repertory company that consisted only of four or five persons. Fortunately for this group, none of its shows was aired live. The shows instead were produced at the Maple Street Theater, where they were recorded for later network play. Remarking on the amount of work required of this repertory company to produce one show after another, Tom Merriman said: "They just turned it out like we turned out the music—by the pound" (Merriman, 1990).

LBS also aired six daily newscasts from Washington. The network's reporting staff was anchored by Arthur MacArthur and George Campbell. Daily weathercasts from the U.S. Weather Bureau in Washington were provided to LBS listeners, along with the daily celebrity reports from Omar Garrison in Hollywood and Eloise McElhone in New York ("LBS on the Air," 1950, p. 89). All of this programming, combined with LBS sports coverage, amounted to a sixteen-hour broadcast day for the new network by the end of 1950 ("Watch Liberty Grow," 1951).

The Liberty network had grown to 431 affiliate stations by August 1951, thus surpassing all but Mutual in network size ("Watch Liberty Grow," 1951). A 1952 map showing the location of all LBS affiliates indicates just how extensive the network had become. The greatest cluster of stations was found in the Southwest, Midwest and along the Pacific Coast. Texas and California had the most LBS affiliates among the individual states. Hawaii and Alaska, not yet states, nonetheless had LBS affiliates. Alaska, in fact, had six. Only five states (Maine, Montana, New Hampshire, North Dakota and Vermont) were without any LBS affiliate stations. Most important, though, was that LBS affiliates were found in every major metropolitan area in the country, from New York City to Los Angeles to Chicago to Miami ("Liberty Broadcasting System, Inc.," 1952, p. 57).

LIBERTY NETWORK SPORTS

The focus of LBS programming, regardless of whatever else the network might have scheduled, was sports. Sportscasts were the LBS trademark. Baseball and football broadcasts, in particular, had been there from the beginning and remained the network's bread and butter. As LBS evolved into a national radio network, its sports department and announcing staff grew both in size and reputation.

Gordon had carried the sports producing and announcing load by himself in the early days of LBS. But by 1951 he had created the position of director of sports, and filled it with Jerry Doggett. As director of football, Gordon recruited Lindsey Nelson ("Liberty Broadcasting System, Inc.," 1952, p. 56). Nelson was just beginning a sportscasting career that would bring him considerable fame (Smith, 1987, p. 184). Here at LBS, though, he was making his break into network broadcasting, and received a modest salary of $125 per week (Nelson, 1985, pp. 145–146). Nelson described the requirements of his new LBS position:

> It meant that I would call a college director of athletics or a pro general manager, offer the least possible amount of money, procure the broadcast

> rights, then get on an airplane, and proceed to broadcast the game myself. For a fellow who liked to broadcast football games, it was a pretty nearly perfect arrangement. (Nelson, 1985, pp. 153–154)

The football schedule overseen by Lindsey Nelson was extensive. Six games—four college and two professional—usually were broadcast on LBS every weekend. University of Miami games were aired on Friday nights, followed by a Saturday afternoon game featuring an Eastern college, and then one featuring a West Coast college. Coverage of Louisiana State University games on Saturday night rounded out the LBS college football schedule. Two National Football League games were featured on Sunday. The first game originated from New York, and the second originated from Los Angeles (Nelson and Hirshberg, 1966, p. 41).

Once the football season ended, LBS began making its transition to baseball coverage. All of the baseball game broadcasts aired by the network were re-creations, until the 1950 baseball season. From that time forward, approximately half the games were re-created and half were live (McLendon, 1981c). By 1952 practically every major league baseball team had granted LBS coverage rights, and practically every major league ballpark had facilities providing LBS live origination capabilities (Nelson and Hirshberg, 1966, p. 39).

The network's broadcast schedule for baseball was even more rigorous than that for football. Lindsey Nelson later commented on just how extensive Liberty's major league baseball coverage had become by 1951:

> We started off only broadcasting games in the afternoon and then we got smart. We'd have a "Game of the Day" from a Wrigley Field, starting at two-thirty Eastern Time, and then a few hours later, we'd do a "Game of the Night" from Philadelphia. And there wasn't any tape delay; to the audience, even on re-creations, we seemed *live*. (Smith, 1987, p. 115).

Nelson said that in case of rain LBS always was ready with a Western Union link to a standby game in another city. On rare days when LBS scheduled only one game and that game happened to be cancelled because of rain, the network would supply affiliates with re-created games from the earliest days of baseball—many of them even predating radio's coverage of the sport (Smith, 1987, p. 115).

THE ART OF BASEBALL GAME RE-CREATIONS

Re-creating notable sports events from the past was Gordon McLendon's real love. "Great Days in Sports" was an LBS regular program specially created so that Gordon could showcase his talent. Tennis matches, boxing matches and ballgames of every sort from years past were re-created on

"Great Days in Sports" (Tolbert, 1952, p. 58). The program had its practical side, as suggested above by Lindsey Nelson. It served as a filler in case a scheduled ballgame was rained out. A faithful audience developed, since LBS listeners knew for certain that the network would air sports of some kind—modern or ancient (Harper, 1986, p. 45).

The program had another side to it as well. Gordon's genuine affection for the game of baseball attached itself to every aspect of the sport, particularly its history. His thorough research and attention to detail for every old-time baseball game that he re-created were appreciated by LBS listeners (Harper, 1986, p. 45). Lindsey Nelson described Gordon's "Great Days in Sports" as an "invention . . . which was a sure-fire hit everywhere" (Nelson and Hirshberg, 1966, p. 33).

Gordon turned his ability to re-create sports events into an art form. Whether ballgames were of ancient or modern vintage, Gordon brought a flair, an excitement and a sense of reality to them that became legendary among listeners and fellow announcers alike. "He had lived such a life with sports," said LBS audio engineer Les Vaughn, "that he knew what a baseball game should have been like. Whether it was actually that way or not out on the field was beside the point, but he made it that way" (Vaughn, 1989). Not surprisingly, the McLendon re-creations came to be more popular than the live baseball broadcasts aired on competing radio networks ("Tribute," 1986). Not surprising either was Gordon's later admission that he preferred re-creating ballgames to announcing them live from the ballpark (McLendon, 1981c).

What was it about the re-creation process that so enamored Gordon? What was there about the process that fit so well his natural creative ability? The sport of baseball itself was one key element. Lindsey Nelson said that there was "no radio sport better than baseball to do stream-of-consciousness—the slow pace, the time to improvise. . . . You just let yourself roam. And you're the entire show—you paint the picture" (Smith, 1987, p. 191). What was even better with baseball game re-creations, though, according to Nelson, was that there were "no limitations" (Nelson, 1988). The announcer was in control; his imagination was free to wander wherever he pleased.

Gordon took full advantage of his own mental inventiveness to construct the kind of event that he felt necessary to sustain the listener's interest. Les Vaughn remarked that Gordon was not the first to re-create ballgames, but he was the first to dramatize them. Gordon had a tremendous source of images immediately available to him, said Vaughn, "by just reaching up in that gorgeous mind of his ("Tribute," 1986).

Gordon once described his baseball game re-creations as providing him an "enormous . . . element of satisfaction":

> I was able to paint a picture there. No picture that is shown on television could be possibly as vivid as the picture I painted in my own mind of a baseball

game. To me . . . those players were far bigger than life, and Ebbetts Field, even though there were 3,000 people there if you were actually broadcasting from the field, was always in my mind's eye crowded with 35,000 people. The walls were a thousand feet tall that those home runs were hit [over]. . . .

So, I could take and in the re-creations spin from my own imagination, coming out with the right facts—that is, balls and strikes being correct and the final score being accurate—I could come out with a far more vivid picture than any that I could have ever painted from the baseball park itself. (McLendon, 1981c).

Two of the necessary ingredients in painting the kinds of pictures described by Gordon were, of course, an effective vocal delivery and a mastery of the English language. Gordon possessed both in abundance. He had a baritone voice that was said to be similar to that of his childhood idol, Ted Husing. And Gordon was entirely free of a Texas accent (Tolbert, 1952, p. 57).

Having a natural radio speaking voice was one thing, but Gordon injected something extra into his delivery that made his baseball re-creations so exciting. He wanted his listeners to feel that they actually were listening to a live broadcast. Gordon said that much of the illusion of reality had to be created vocally by the announcer's use of inflection. The announcer had to be enthusiastic about the game, had to feel that he was there at the ballpark, and had to enjoy what he was doing (McLendon, 1981a).

The information coming over the Western Union telegraph wire was all that broadcasters re-creating ballgames had in terms of hard facts to pass along to listeners. That information was minimal at best, and it was encoded in a special telegraphic language. Lindsey Nelson provided this brief description of the language:

For example, "B1" meant "ball one," "S1-C" meant "strike one called," "F1" meant "Foul," and so on. The positions were numbered by standard scoring procedure, with the pitcher 1, the catcher 2, the first baseman 3, the second baseman 4, the third baseman 5, the shortstop 6, the left fielder 7, the center fielder 8, and the right fielder 9. Thus, "4-3," on the wire meant that the batter was out, second baseman to first baseman. Or "F-9" meant the batter flied out to the right fielder. (Nelson and Hirshberg, 1966, p. 30).

What was absent here was the color that added life to a baseball broadcast. And it was in the addition of that color, that spark, to the ballgame that Gordon McLendon's reputation as a showman was made. Either by his own hand or by that of some assistant hired for the task, Gordon constantly invented epigrammatic phrasing to flavor his on-air commentary (Nelson and Hirshberg, 1966, p. 36).

One McLendon assistant, Mitch Lewis, told of writing similes for Gordon to be incorporated in the word pictures he used to describe the progress of a baseball game. Describing a player who had just gotten a base hit as being "happy as a cow in a Quaker Oats factory" was an example of the

Lewis touch. And when a baseball team was down on its luck, Gordon might say, "So far, this team has been colder than an igloo's basement." Weaving such figurative language into the flow of his delivery was a McLendon specialty. Gordon, of course, was able to think about the words he would use for a while longer than normal, since a brief time elapsed between the re-created game and the actual event ("Tribute," 1986).

Gordon knew the difference between the ordinary and the extraordinary in how he chose to call a baseball game. He no doubt was aware of the impact his words had on listeners. But he hardly could have expected the kind of homage paid him by writer Willie Morris in his autobiography, *North Toward Home*. Morris wrote of his youth in the Mississippi Delta town of Yazoo City. In one passage he gave this lyrical account of a daily ritual during a Yazoo City summer:

> By two o'clock almost every radio in town was tuned in to the Old Scotchman. His rhetoric dominated the place. It hovered in the branches of the trees, bounced off the hills, and came out of the darkened stores; the merchants and the old men cocked their ears to him, and even from the big cars that sped by, their tires making lapping sounds in the softened highway, you could hear his voice, being carried past you out into the delta.
>
> The Old Scotchman's real name was Gordon McLendon. . . . He had a deep, rich voice, and I think he was the best rhetorician, outside of Bilbo and Nye Bevan, I have ever heard. Under his handling a baseball game took on a life of its own. . . . [H]is games were rare and remarkable entities; casual pop flies had the flow of history behind them, double plays resembled the stark clashes of old armies, and home runs deserved acknowledgement on earthen urns. Later, when I came across Thomas Wolfe, I felt I had heard him before, from Shibe Park, Crosley Field, or the Yankee Stadium. (Morris, 1967, p. 109).

In similar fashion, Dallas newspaper columnist Dick Hitt said of Gordon McLendon, "he was Shakespeare writing on his feet," and added that "it was sheer inventiveness and bald gall that enabled [Gordon] to transport millions of listeners to fantasyland as he recreated play-by-play broadcasts of major-league baseball games, using only a flimsy sheet off the Western Union ticker to transform these dry words into elegant and dramatic pageantry" (Hitt, 1986a, p. A–8).

The baseball announcer's role was important, but there had to be additional ingredients present to create the realism that Gordon wanted. These ingredients included the various sounds associated with the ambiance of a ballgame. Gordon was as meticulous in creating the proper sound effects as he was in honing the proper words.

The technique of mechanically re-creating a ballgame, whether baseball or football or basketball, was rather simple. Over the voice of the announcer there had to be superimposed periodically either recorded sound effects or sound effects produced live in the studio. Sometimes both were required simultaneously. Gordon said that besides the Western Union telegrapher, only two persons usually were necessary to re-create a baseball game: himself and a sound effects engineer. "We used to broadcast seven-hour doubleheaders," Gordon remarked, "and there would just be the engineer and myself, not even a color announcer. We didn't know anything about statisticians or crews. . . . We had to do all that for ourself" (McLendon, 1981a).

Three or four turntables were kept spinning throughout the re-created games with disks containing the various crowd noises always cued on one or more of the turntables. Gordon incorporated three styles of crowd noise in his re-creations. There was the continuing "general murmur" that is normally heard during moments of inactivity. Then there was the "more pronounced crowd enthusiasm" that occurred during a hit. Finally, there was the excited crowd sound that usually accompanied a big play such as a home run (McLendon, 1981a). A creative audio engineer could meld these crowd noises together—selectively increasing or decreasing volumes of each—to manufacture a very realistic sound. Gordon's audio engineer, Les Vaughn, was among the best. Vaughn, whose formal title was director of production (Vaughn, 1989), was a primary contributor in giving a Gordon McLendon baseball re-creation "the theater of the air drama that it had" ("Tribute," 1986).

Les Vaughn recalled how Gordon signaled him as to what play was about to occur so that the proper sound effect could be readied. Gordon sat in a separate studio from Vaughn, so all signals had to be silent. Hand signals sometimes were used—a finger to the right meant a hit, to the left meant a foul ball, and both hands straight up meant a home run (Blackwell, 1986, p. 6C). After awhile, though, Vaughn often required nothing more than Gordon shifting his head in a certain way as a sound effect cue (Vaughn, 1989).

What would be distinguishable above the crowd noise every so often would be a vendor hollering out the name of a sponsor's product. Special tape loops (an oddity at the time, since the use of audio tape was still in its infancy) were created by Glenn Callison to allow for easy insertion of LBS sponsors' messages during the flow of a game (Vaughn, 1989).

Gordon's passion for realism and accuracy led him to send an engineer to record every ballpark sound that a radio listener might expect to hear. Glenn Callison recorded many of the sounds at Burnett Field in Dallas (Callison, 1989). Les Vaughn also helped with some of the recording, but what probably was the most important recording task fell to Craig LaTaste. Gordon sent LaTaste to every major league baseball stadium in the country to record sounds identified with each particular stadium (Vaughn, 1989). This even included the national anthem. Thus, when Gordon introduced a particular organist playing "The Star-Spangled Banner" from Forbes Field in Pittsburgh, it was a recorded version of the real thing (Nelson and Hirshberg, 1966, p. 32).

Gordon even accounted for game-day weather conditions during his re-creations. If a weather report indicated rain during a game that was scheduled for re-creation, then Les Vaughn periodically had to insert a thunder clap sound effect. And to be playfully realistic, Gordon sometimes would delay the game momentarily, claiming that lightning had caused a power failure (Vaughn, 1989).

Gordon's penchant for realism spread his re-creation productions beyond the immediate studio control room. In order to create the muffled sound of the stadium public-address announcer, Gordon placed someone from his staff in the men's room just a few feet from the studio. The echo effect that resulted from the "men's room" announcer was captured on Gordon's open microphone and sounded uncannily like the real thing. Gordon often passed on information to his listeners that purportedly had just been picked up from the public-address announcer (Nelson and Hirshberg, 1966, p. 35).

There was a quintessential sound effect—the crack of the bat on the ball—necessary to create the greatest degree of realism for any baseball game re-creation. Gordon said that everything was tried to create the effect, but nothing sounded like the real thing. Finally, someone discovered that the sound Gordon wanted was most easily manufactured by striking a baseball bat near its handle with a "nickel pencil" (McLendon, 1981a).

All of this production activity originated, of course, from the KLIF basement studios in the Cliff Towers Hotel (McLendon, 1981a). Regardless of how authentic a re-creation Gordon and his staff could manage from this location, the absolute key ingredient to making the re-creations work was the information supplied by the Western Union telegrapher. Heavy reliance was placed on this distant data source. And as sometimes happens with mechanical systems, breakdowns would occur. Failed transmission lines required that re-creation announcers resort to a special reservoir of ingenuity and fortitude to cover whatever span of time there might be before transmission could be restored. Gordon recalled having to "kill as much as an hour-and-a-half" during some transmission interruptions (McLendon, 1981a). What devices did he resort to for such emergencies? Foul tips were good, for a starter. Responding to a question about how many foul tips might be necessary, Gordon said with a smile:

> Probably seventy-five. . . . And the number of times that a loose dog was out on the field was incredible. . . . It just went on, and on, and on. . . . There was no way of knowing how long the Western Union line would be out. . . . Interminably, until the Western Union line came back, there were several other things that we did along about that time. We would have a fight start in the stand. And this fight would go on for 30 minutes. Of course, any thinking listener would have wondered why the police by that time had not broken

> up the fight. . . . When we figured that somebody must be getting murdered, we'd have four or five more people join the fight. (McLendon, 1978).

A Western Union breakdown was not always required for Gordon to inject some whimsical element into his re-creations. He drew from his language experience one time to announce the entire last half inning of a Brooklyn Dodgers ballgame in Japanese. The game's lopsided score had made it boring, so Gordon decided that if it had to be boring it might as well be incomprehensible too ("The Top-40," n.d., p. 20).

Gordon had a particular knack for carrying on in this manner. It required a certain linguistic flair, to be sure, but it also required unbridled loquaciousness, coupled with a genuine sense of humor. Gordon possessed both. They were prerequisites to a flamboyant style of broadcasting that would forever after characterize the Old Scotchman.

Gordon freely admitted to the flamboyance, and claimed that he owed at least some of it to his early association with baseball great turned announcer Dizzy Dean (McLendon, 1978). Gordon and Dizzy became acquainted while Dean was living in Dallas. Dizzy would later develop a reputation as a CBS baseball announcer for his irreverence toward the English language and his less-than-serious attention to preparation and game details. In short, Dizzy Dean was known for verbally demolishing the game of baseball. Some say that his announcing antics were not always happenstance, but were planned in advance. Whatever the case, his fans loved them and even came to expect them, "and Diz aimed to please" (Smith, 1987, pp. 132–133).

Dizzy Dean's reputation as a baseball player was well known, but it may have been one brief announcing stint on the Liberty network that led to his reputation for disassembling a ballgame. The account of Dizzy's introduction to the LBS audience was one that Gordon often was asked to repeat. The story, ironically, centered not on baseball but rather on football, and occurred during the Liberty network's first year. Gordon was re-creating a game between the New York Yankees and the Cleveland Browns, of the now defunct All-American Conference. He decided it would be fun to invite Dizzy to his Cliff Towers studio to "assist" in the re-creation. Gordon would do the play-by-play, and Dizzy would do color commentary. Here is how Gordon described the occasion:

> I didn't realize that Dizzy didn't know whether a football was oblong or round. He didn't. And about the end of the third quarter, Dizzy leaned over to me and said during a lull, "I've about had enough of this here color announcing; I'd like to do some of that play-by-play that you're doing." I said, "Well, okay." And with my heart in my mouth and rightfully so, I gave him the first sheet of paper that the telegrapher handed me for the beginning of the fourth quarter. It said, "Marion Motley," who was the big fullback of the Cleveland Browns, "goes around right end 60 yards for a touchdown."

> Dizzy's description of that was a small classic. It went like this: "All right folks," he says, "Now here is this big Motley, and that fella's standing way back there behind the line of scrimmage just looking around and he gets that ball, and there goes that Motley around right end. . . . He's just running like hell." He says, "He's up to the 40, the 45, the 50, the 55, the 60, the 65."
>
> And then I just kicked the fool out of Dizzy. . . . And then suddenly it hit him. He said, "Oh, no fans." He says, "Here's this Motley; he's back at the 50, and here he comes again." ("Tribute," 1986).

Dizzy Dean never could understand entirely that part of re-creating a ballgame was the illusion of reality that the announcers had to create. One of the most important unwritten rules of broadcast re-creation that announcers had to follow was acting as though they were at the scene of the event being re-created. Dizzy constantly broke the rule. Glenn Callison laughingly recalled one example of Dizzy's breaking that rule during the seventh inning stretch of a baseball game that he and Gordon were re-creating. Gordon turned to ask Dizzy how he liked the game so far. "Great," Dizzy replied. "I wish I were there!" (Callison, 1989).

Tom Snyder, former McLendon Station announcer and later host of his own NBC television program, once asked Gordon how LBS affiliates reacted to mistakes of the Dizzy Dean variety. Gordon replied that although he made every effort to be a good broadcaster, he certainly was not immune to making mistakes. However, he said, Liberty network affiliates were willing to tolerate the errors because they were so happy to be receiving Liberty's sports coverage (McLendon, 1978).

Some of the LBS mistakes probably endeared the network and its programming to radio listeners. After all, mistakes showed the LBS announcers to be real people who in the course of describing an exciting ballgame were apt to make an error now and then. That added to the realism that Gordon tried so hard to create and sustain.

Gordon wanted realism, but he did not want to deceive his listeners into thinking that re-created ballgames were the actual thing (McLendon, 1981a). In fact, he announced both before and after every re-created ballgame that the games were not being broadcast live. But that meant nothing to the audience, said Lindsey Nelson. "Everything sounded so realistic that people forgot the announcer was in a studio in Dallas instead of on the scene. Besides, so many broadcasts actually were live that I'm sure most listeners assumed they all were" (Nelson and Hirshberg, 1966, p. 34).

Gordon's efforts toward creating realistic re-creations were not universally appreciated. Roy Hofheinz, president of Houston radio station KTHT, even went so far as to file a complaint with the FCC in 1950, alleging that the manner in which LBS re-created its ballgames was a deliberate effort to deceive listeners into thinking that coverage actually was originating from the ballpark. Gordon's only comment on the charge was to criticize Mr.

Hofheinz for misspelling "McLendon" ("Baseball Re-Creation," 1950). The FCC apparently viewed the complaint with little seriousness, since nothing more came of it.

Did anyone from Liberty's vast listening audience feel deceived? There is no evidence that anyone ever did. As a matter of fact, quite the contrary seemed more likely—a genuine affection for the Old Scotchman, and for the Liberty Broadcasting System in general. Take, for example, Chuck Woods, who listened to the LBS "Game-of-the-Day" while a youth in western Nebraska. He remarked on how the broadcast "was very important" to him and his father:

> We . . . planned our work schedule to a certain extent around "Game-of-the-Day". We lived on a farm, and Dad and I would urge my mother to plan dinner at about one o'clock in the afternoon, which is when the "Game-of-the-Day" started. And we could at least listen to an hour or so of the game . . . while we ate. Then . . . we sold our old noisy tractor and bought a newer one that ran quieter. As a result of that, we were able to buy a radio, and we mounted the radio on the fender of the tractor and . . . then we could listen to the whole game.
>
> I really didn't know that these games were [re-created] at the time. . . . I remember thinking a few times that this man that sold Coca Cola seemed to be the same person with the same voice in St. Louis, Cincinnati, or New York—wherever they might happen to be. But, I really didn't think too much of that. ("Tribute," 1981).

Liberty network "Game-of-the-Day" re-creations caught the imagination of others in similar fashion. Willie Morris described his own experiences listening to the broadcasts. In his case the LBS re-creations provided grist for some adolescent mischief that he recalled with great delight in his autobiography.

As it happened, Morris had stationed himself before his father's shortwave radio set while listening to the Old Scotchman re-create a baseball game between the New York Giants and the Brooklyn Dodgers. Morris did not at that time realize that the game indeed was a re-creation. During a lull in the action, he began twisting the radio dial to other stations and happened upon a broadcast of the same game he had been listening to only minutes before. The big difference, to Morris's amazement, was that the game he now heard over the Armed Forces Radio Network was four innings ahead of the one he had heard on the Liberty network station. A close listening to the final innings of the LBS version of the game revealed the Old Scotchman's end-of-game announcement that it had been re-created. "Instead of being disappointed in the Scotchman," Morris said, "I was all the more pleased by his genius, for he made pristine facts more actual than actuality, a valuable lesson when the day finally came that I started reading literature. I must add, however, that this appreciation did not obscure the realization that I had at my disposal a weapon of unimaginable dimensions" (Morris, 1967, pp. 109–112).

Willie Morris began recording in a notebook the events of baseball games as described during the AFRN broadcasts. He would then call friends who were listening to the re-creation of the same game broadcast by a local LBS affiliate and in oracle fashion predict hits, strikes, errors, and so forth that soon would happen. Morris's ruse came to an end, though, when his father demanded that he reveal his method of prophecy. For a short time Morris and many of the persons he had fooled with his "predictions" listened to the live AFRN baseball broadcasts on their shortwave receivers. But, gradually, they all returned to the Liberty network re-creations. "I believe we all went back to the Scotchman," remarked Morris, "not merely out of loyalty but because, in our great isolation, he touched our need for a great and unmitigated eloquence" (Morris, 1967, pp. 112–119).

Gordon was once asked what particular sportscast he would choose as his most outstanding. He deferred that choice to the opinion of others, who said that his live broadcast of the third game in a best-of-three series of the 1951 National League pennant play-off games was Gordon's best. Pitted against one another in the play-offs that year were the New York Giants and the Brooklyn Dodgers. "I thought I did a good job that day, and I thought probably it was one of the better games I'd ever broadcast—not the best, maybe—but one of the better games," Gordon later said with some modesty (McLendon, 1981c).

Lindsey Nelson told of sitting entranced in the LBS Dallas studio as he and fellow announcers listened to Gordon's broadcast from New York. "It was one of the most dramatic sports broadcasts I have ever heard," Nelson said. "Gordon's opening line was something like, 'From the Bay of Tokyo to the tip of Land's End. . . . *this* is the day.' From then on he pulled out all the stops" (Nelson and Hirshberg, 1966, p. 40).

The game ended when Bobby Thomson's home run won the pennant for the Giants (Nelson and Hirshberg, 1966, p. 40). The roar of the crowd was too much for any radio announcer to overcome. But, when the noise began to subside Gordon made a comment that summed up both his and the fans' emotion, and that would endear him to broadcasters from that time forward: "Well, I'll be a suck-egg mule!" he intoned (Hitt, 1986a, p. A–8).

For his announcing achievements Gordon was voted *Sporting News* magazine's 1951 Outstanding Football Announcer. Gordon was certain that the award was meant as an apology for the publication's failure to recognize his contributions as a baseball announcer, especially considering his recent stint covering the National League play-offs. After all, Gordon always freely admitted that although he could excite his listeners when announcing a football game, he really had little expertise in the sport (McLendon, 1969a).

Gordon's string of awards, honors and recognitions for professional achievements had just begun. No sooner had the *Sporting News* bestowed its award on him than the U.S. Junior Chamber of Commerce had named Gordon one of the "ten outstanding young men of 1951" (Tolbert, 1952, p. 60).

LIBERTY NETWORK STATUS REPORT

Things could not have been more upbeat for the Liberty network as it entered its second full year as a national radio network. The network was paying more than a million dollars for coverage rights to the various sports events it broadcast (Tolbert, 1952, p. 57).

And Liberty's audience, estimated at ninety million (Tolbert, 1952, p. 56), was said to be everywhere. One writer noted just how ubiquitous Gordon's presence had become: "Many afternoons during the baseball season, the voice of Gordon McLendon can be heard, literally, throughout the land. Say your car radio isn't working, you can still keep up with the 'Game of the Day' by driving slowly past the filling stations in the little towns. You stop in roadside cafes and his voice follows you" (Tolbert, 1952, p. 58).

Lindsey Nelson spoke of his amazement over Liberty's impact and how he had been reminded of it constantly. Nelson said that even as late as the mid-1980s, he would meet people who commented on having listened to him when he worked for LBS. The comments were all the more surprising, said Nelson, because he only worked at the network for two years (Smith, 1987, p. 116). Nelson also spoke with amusement of the time when he was attempting to rent a car in Los Angeles. He was then working for NBC and showed his NBC employee's card to the rental agent for identification. The NBC card was unacceptable. As Nelson fished around in his billfold looking for more identification, the agent spotted his Liberty network employee's card. Nelson was asked if he had worked for the network. When he said that he had, he got his car (Nelson, 1988).

The success that LBS was having defied logic in some respects. It happened at a time when the power brokers on Madison Avenue had declared that "television was king and radio was dead" (Nelson, 1988). Indeed, the long-established broadcast networks were turning their attention toward television and away from radio. Radio, the older medium, was dying, or so network executives reasoned (Nelson and Hirshberg, 1966, pp. 33–34). Even radio networks not connected with television, as were NBC, CBS and ABC, were feeling the economic pinch of television's competition for the advertising dollar (Tolbert, 1952, p. 56).

But Gordon McLendon was betting on some important points that still favored radio networks. One was the absence of live television programs in large areas of the country where network television had yet to penetrate. Another was the expense of a television set, which made its presence in many American households of the early 1950s only a luxury (Nelson and Hirshberg, 1966, p. 34). A final point was Gordon's contention that television would "settle down as an after-dark entertainment" medium. "In the daytime, millions of radios are going on all over the country and being listened to even by people at work," he said (Tolbert, 1952, p. 56). Gordon saw radio as a daytime medium, and that's where he concentrated LBS programs (Tolbert, 1952, p. 56).

That he proved himself right, at least for the moment, was something that Gordon cherished. "He just *loved* it, creating something the big guys had called impossible," Lindsey Nelson said (Smith, 1987, p. 115). Gordon's enthusiasm for what he did was contagious. The Liberty network was a "fairy tale come true" for sports announcers. Dozens of applications flooded LBS from sportscasters and would-be sportscasters from across the nation. Here, after all, was a network where sports was king (Nelson, 1988).

4 *The Liberty Broadcasting System: Finis*

Gordon McLendon remarked to an interviewer in 1952 that LBS would be the "No. 1 radio network in the daytime, both as to coverage and programming" by 1953 (Tolbert, 1952, p. 56). He genuinely may have felt that way, but he must have realized that major obstacles first would have to be overcome. The first of these centered on network finances.

TROUBLING FINANCIAL TIMES AT LBS

Gordon's role in creating the Liberty network had been that of a visionary. He had been and would remain an "idea" person, a promoter. Lindsey Nelson said that Gordon had tried to promote LBS every way he could. Gordon had a new idea every minute about promoting the network, and the LBS staff tried them all. Some worked; some did not. Nelson remembered telling Gordon at one point that his "good ideas were making LBS rich and famous, but his bad ones were driving the network to bankruptcy" (Nelson, 1988).

Gordon's management style was not that of a typical broadcasting executive. His attention was planted firmly in the product his network turned out—not in how the network made its money or how much money it made. Indeed, for someone destined to become a millionaire and to be called a "financier and businessman" (Porter, 1980, p. 1-M), the Gordon McLendon of the early 1950s seemed slightly ill at ease in dealing with financial matters. This particular personality trait would remain with Gordon throughout most of his career in broadcasting (MacFarland, 1973, p. 269).

The real financial brains behind the Liberty network was B. R. McLendon. Gordon "leaned heavily on the backing of his father," and in a financial sense "was sort of protected or sponsored by his father," recalled Tom Merriman (1990). While there is little doubt that Gordon's creativity built the Liberty network's popularity, there is little doubt, either, that B. R.'s money put the network on the air and kept it flying (Meeks, 1990).

The financial status of the Liberty network appeared strong at the time it became a full-fledged national network in 1950. Its commercial sales policy, in addition to its affiliation compensation policy, appeared sound. Both policies actually were quite unique in view of the customary network practices. Stations that joined the Liberty Network were assessed an affiliation fee based on a standard formula. The formula, for the most part, considered station market characteristics and audience demographics ("LBS Plans: Expands," 1950, pp. 25, 59). Monthly fees for LBS affiliates in accordance with this formula ranged from a minimum of $450 to a maximum of $10,000 (Adams, 1950).

The Liberty network was responsible for paying all line charges for AT&T telephone lines that connected local station affiliates with the network. Glenn Callison, whose responsibilities included overseeing all technical operations related to feeding network programs and connecting or disconnecting network affiliates, said that LBS generally paid a monthly AT&T line charge bill of $25,000 to $30,000 (Callison, 1989).

By late 1950, LBS was said to be gearing up a sales force to sell commercial time on the network to national advertisers. Income from such time sales would be shared in part with LBS affiliates carrying the network programming in which the national advertisers' commercials appeared. The objective here was to generate so much national advertising revenue that the affiliation fee that local radio stations normally paid LBS would be offset by the advertising fees paid by the network to each affiliate. A sales feature that was meant to be particularly attractive to national advertisers was the ability to buy commercial time on a regional rather than a full-network basis. Thus, an advertiser like General Motors could choose to air a commercial on LBS in one or more of six regions of the country ("LBS Plans: Expands," 1950, p. 59).

This regional system actually resulted from major league baseball territorial exclusivity rules. Since LBS was prohibited occasionally from broadcasting baseball games into certain regions, the network had to be designed to bypass these "blacked out" regions while still carrying network programming to all other regions. Glenn Callison referred to the procedure as "breaking apart" the network (Callison, 1989).

The Liberty network appeared to be riding high in 1951—so high, as a matter of fact, that Gordon decided to raise the network's advertising rates. This proved to be a major error. Falstaff Beer, one of Liberty's chief sponsors, immediately switched its advertising account to Liberty's main competitor, the Mutual Broadcasting System (Nelson, 1988).

Loss of the Falstaff account, said by one source to be worth a million dollars annually (Cullen, n.d.), was a "desperate blow," recounted Bill Meeks in 1990. "I wasn't there when the man cancelled on Gordon, but I understand that they almost had to pry the phone out of his hand," Meeks added. The departure of Falstaff meant more than just the loss of the Liberty network's biggest advertising client. There was no other national advertiser to take Falstaff's place. The loss was a symbolic blow as well. It revealed the ineffectiveness of the LBS sales effort. The network's growth simply had outdistanced its ability to structure a sales staff capable of penetrating the national marketplace. "Our sales staff was just weak," confided Bill Meeks (1990).

TROUBLING TIMES AT LBS–POLITICS

The Liberty network already was beginning to feel financial pressure from its rapid expansion even before the loss of its major advertiser. Ironically, B. R. McLendon had turned down a $250,000 offer to buy a tenth of Liberty's stock in 1950 (Tolbert, 1952, p. 56), but by 1952 the McLendons were looking for an infusion of outside capital to shore up the network's faltering economic situation. Coming to the rescue was Hugh Roy Cullen, an independent oilman from Houston who was rumored to be "possibly the wealthiest individual in Texas in the decade following World War II" (Carleton, 1985, p. 69).

Evidence indicates that Gordon and Hugh Roy Cullen had not met formally prior to August 1951. Cullen had learned of Liberty's financial plight at some point in 1951 and had even asked that a Houston associate investigate the wisdom of investing in the network. The investigation was cancelled as a result of Gordon's and Cullen's August meeting. So impressive were Gordon and the case he made for investing in LBS that Cullen gave him the money he was seeking then and there (Nelson, 1988). The total amount handed to Gordon came to a million dollars, $400,000 of which Cullen agreed to invest in LBS and $600,000 of which he agreed to lend the network. Gordon initially had offered Cullen a 51 percent share of LBS in return for his financial assistance, but Cullen agreed only to a 50 percent share (Carleton, 1985, p. 92). With his half interest in the Liberty network, Hugh Roy Cullen now became a co-chairman, along with B. R. McLendon, of the LBS board of directors. Gordon remained the network's president ("Liberty Broadcasting System, Inc.," 1952, p. 56).

Gordon was struck immediately by Cullen's faith in him and LBS. "He bought 50 percent of the network from me without ever looking at the books," Gordon said (1969a). Cullen's attorneys indeed had advised that he look at the LBS books before giving Gordon any money, but Cullen rejected their advice, saying, "I'm not bettin' on his books; I'm bettin' on this young man" (Cullen, n.d.).

The relationship shared by both men grew into a strong friendship in later years. Gordon admitted to having much admiration for Cullen and to being greatly influenced by him (McLendon, 1969a).

Gordon's admiration appeared genuine. He was no doubt impressed with Cullen and appreciative of his financial support. Whether LBS would have survived much longer without Cullen's rescue is unknown. Given the problems LBS would face from other quarters in early 1952, the network's financial survival actually became a moot issue. Nonetheless, Hugh Roy Cullen's association with LBS was accompanied by criticism from certain corners claiming that he carried some major political liabilities to his new position. What these were and what bearing they had on the Liberty Network require some explanation.

"In his time Hugh Roy Cullen of Houston was perhaps the biggest of the Big Rich," remarked writer James Presley (1983, p. 212). The foundation for Cullen's enormous fortune lay in his entrepreneurial skills as an oil wildcatter during the Texas oil boom period from 1917 to 1920 (Presley, 1983, p. 213).

Hugh Roy Cullen's reputation as a philanthropist was nearly unparalleled. He was called the "champion Texas oilman-philanthropist," and his gifts to various charitable causes, hospitals and educational institutions amounted to nearly $200 million, or about 90 percent of his entire wealth (Presley, 1983, p. 350).

Besides devoting time to the oil business and to philanthropic pursuits, Hugh Roy Cullen was a political activist. "While one of the motives behind Cullen's political activities was probably the protection of his own wealth and its related prerogatives," noted one observer, "his sincere belief in the creed of the self-made man also underpinned his actions. He believed that self-help and hard work could solve any problem better than government" (Carleton, 1985, p. 89).

There was no mistaking Hugh Roy Cullen's politics. He most assuredly was a conservative. And in response to the political complications of postwar America and the Korean War, Cullen's political views had moved several notches to the right of simple conservatism. By the early 1950s many were calling him a "right-winger" or ultraconservative. And it was the ultraconservatives whose allegations of Communist infiltration into U.S. public institutions had been so instrumental in creating what later would be called the Red Scare in America. Regarding Hugh Roy Cullen's role in such matters, one critic said that Cullen "contributed substantial public rhetoric and money, which helped create and sustain the Red Scare at the national and local levels" (Carleton, 1985, p. 89).

Cullen nurtured political friends with beliefs similar to his own. One of these friends was author John T. Flynn (Carleton, 1985, pp. 117–118). Cullen had purchased and mailed around the country over two million copies of Flynn's anti-New Deal book *The Road Ahead* during the 1950 political campaign season (Carleton, 1985, p. 92). It was, as a matter of fact, Flynn who called Cullen from New York with information about the Liberty network's financial difficulties. Flynn assured Cullen that Gordon McLendon was a good conservative and advised him that an investment in LBS had the potential of providing the ultraconservative cause a national radio voice. Taking his friend's advice, Cullen was said to have accompanied his LBS loan and investment with the stipulation that the network " 'further the principles of free enterprise' by featuring radio commentaries by such people as his good friend John T. Flynn" (Carleton, 1985, p. 92).

To what extent did Gordon acquiesce to the wishes of the Liberty network's new part-owner and co-chairman of the board? Moreover, to what extent did Cullen influence LBS programming policies? The answer to the first question is cloaked with uncertainty. According to one source, John T. Flynn was placed in charge of LBS news broadcasts and the setting up of a network news bureau. That same source—*The Nation* magazine, a noted liberal publication—also said that Flynn's "official mission is to make certain the news is no longer given what he calls a 'leftist' slant" (Husserl, 1951, p. 370).

The installation of Flynn as an LBS news executive was cited as the reason for the resignation of well-known network news commentator William Shirer. Shirer, Raymond Gram Swing, Joseph C. Harsch and John Vandercook, all recognized as top-flight news analysts and all associated with LBS, clearly added prestige to the network's news operation. However, Swing had left LBS for the Voice of America shortly before John T. Flynn's arrival. Now, with Shirer's resignation, John Vandercook and Joseph C. Harsch were the last of the big four names to remain with the Liberty Network as 1951 drew to a close (Husserl, 1951, p. 370; "The Shape," 1951). *The Nation* referred to the two men as "liberalism's precarious survivors in a set-up which once held promise of providing a haven for commentators of proved integrity and independence" ("The Shape," 1951).

William Shirer's departure may have been premature. There was little if any evidence suggesting that John T. Flynn induced a noticeable ultraconservative slant in LBS news. Comments appearing in *The Nation* even gave grudging confirmation to that fact:

> In fairness to McLendon it should be said that Liberty has not wholly succumbed to the Cullen-Flynn axis. John Vandercook maintains that he is still "free and uncensored," and McLendon professes not to understand what is meant by "the new set-up" under Flynn. There is no question of McLendon's sincerity, but the fact that John T. Flynn is director of news certainly indicates that a new set-up exists. (Husserl, 1951, p. 371)

Several years after his departure from the Liberty network, Joseph C. Harsch was questioned about his experience at the network. He also had no recollection of any Flynn influence on his LBS commentaries (Glick, 1979, p. 134, n. 32).

Apart from Hugh Roy Cullen's success with placing John T. Flynn at LBS, there is no indication that he made any additional effort to involve himself in network program matters. Gordon said so himself. While insisting that he "would have had no objections to Mr. Cullen's objectives as to the network because they were much the same as my own" (Dugger, 1964, p. 8), Gordon nonetheless was sensitive to problems that Cullen might have caused LBS. And at one point Gordon emphatically stated that Cullen "never tried to foist his very far right political views on the listeners of the network" (McLendon, 1969a).

Hugh Roy Cullen himself also confirmed his limited role in Liberty network affairs. Although plainly stating his fear that some "radical element" might have acquired LBS had he not helped the McLendons when Gordon came calling, Cullen said that he had played no direct role at the network once he became its part owner. He said that Gordon occasionally did consult with him by phone and sometimes in person (Cullen, n.d.). His biographers attached an entirely altruistic motive to Hugh Roy Cullen's interest in LBS: "He conceived of a gigantic 'American forum of the air' in which all views on current topics could be presented, and the American people could make up their minds which views to follow" (Kilman and Wright, 1954, p. 299).

Whatever happened at the Liberty network during late 1951 and early 1952 with respect to politics should be placed into proper historical context. It was a time in our nation's history when whispered rumors called into question the patriotism of friends and colleagues. That the Liberty network, in view of its role as a leading communications medium, would not be tinged by some of the political excesses of the time is doubtful. To what extent Hugh Roy Cullen and his particular brand of politics succeeded in politicizing LBS remains for future historians to determine. It would appear, though, that the allegations regarding Cullen's influence probably far exceeded the reality of that influence.

LBS AND THE MUTUAL BROADCASTING SYSTEM

The Mutual Broadcasting System (MBS) led LBS as a radio network in number of affiliates during 1950–1952. The fact that both networks prided themselves on their baseball broadcasts made competition inevitable. MBS even adopted Liberty's "Game-of-the-Day" concept after Mutual's affiliates complained that it and not LBS should be the network of choice when listeners wanted to hear baseball games (Smith, 1987, p. 116). The network already carried exclusive coverage of major league baseball's World Series and All-Star Game. In 1949, MBS began broadcasting its own "Game-of-the-Day" live from major league ballparks. The decision not to re-create games, as LBS was sometimes doing, was seen by MBS personnel as a sign of superiority (Smith, 1987, pp. 117–118).

The decision to broadcast all its games live often brought Mutual into direct competition with LBS when the two aired the same game—but, in Liberty's case, via re-creation. In those areas where baseball fans had access to both a Mutual and a Liberty station they could switch from one station to another to make comparisons. "When the game was dull or the live crowd apathetic, Mutual suffered," Lindsey Nelson recalled. "They couldn't make excitement where there wasn't any, but we could. They couldn't anticipate what might happen, either, but we weren't afraid to anticipate anything that seemed logical" (Nelson and Hirshberg, 1966, p. 38).

Besides its decision to broadcast baseball games live, Mutual's broadcasting policy had two other facets that would prove very important to the network in the future. Mutual, at the urging of organized baseball, had decided not to broadcast night games and not to broadcast games played on Sunday (Smith, 1987, p. 117).

LBS AND MINOR LEAGUE BASEBALL

Baseball game attendance for both major league and minor league games had set postwar records. The trend actually had begun during the war. In 1943 paid attendance figures for major league games stood at approximately eight million. By 1944 the figure was nine million and by 1945 it was eleven million. Attendance jumped markedly in 1946 to approximately nineteen million. The figure would jump by a million for each of the next two years. But from 1949 through 1951, attendance dropped by about one million per year. A similar trend was seen for minor league paid attendance. From an approximately six million figure in 1943, attendance jumped by nearly three million in 1944. Another jump to nearly thirty-three million occurred in 1946. An attendance peak of approximately forty-two million was reached in 1949, but then minor league game attendance dropped by nearly seven million in 1950. Another drop of seven million occurred in 1951 (U.S. Congress. House, 1951, p. 1616).

Diminished attendance meant, of course, a loss of gate receipts. Hardest hit were the minor league teams, none of which had been very profitable anyway. The 24 triple A minor league teams that had showed net profits of varying amounts from 1946 through 1949 showed a total net loss of nearly $1.5 million in 1950. The 146 teams in the A, B, C and D minor leagues also recorded sizable losses for 1950. Only the 15 double A minor league teams showed a net profit that year (U.S. Congress. House, 1951, p. 1625).

Persons in the major and minor league baseball establishment viewed with alarm what they perceived as a setback for "America's pastime." They pegged broadcasting as the primary reason for falling game attendance. They saw television as somewhat a problem, but viewed radio as the most significant threat to organized baseball's livelihood. Minor league officials in November 1950 cited both the Liberty and Mutual networks as the cause for the

1950 minor-league attendance drop. The officials' immediate solution was to suggest to baseball commissioner A. B. Chandler that he pare down the number of major league baseball broadcasts allowed in minor league areas ("Baseball Outlook," 1950, p. 23).

The assertions of minor league officials were partially supported by a lengthy study that analyzed sports attendance over the last several years ("Baseball's Gate," 1950, p. 19). The study's author, Jerry N. Jordan, looked in particular at baseball attendance in 1950, and concluded that the numerous broadcasts of major league games during the year, on television as well as radio, were responsible for lower minor league game attendance. Jordan did concede, however, that such factors as weather and team performance also contributed to the 1950 attendance slump ("Baseball's Gate," 1950, p. 32).

Gordon McLendon responded to the Jordan study by pointing to the declining attendance at theaters owned by him and his father as an indication that the entire entertainment industry was suffering an attendance slump. Minor league baseball was not alone in its inability to attract a crowd. Economic conditions and not the Liberty network, claimed Gordon, should be blamed for the minor leagues' woes. Gordon also criticized the minor league establishment for not acknowledging all the free publicity it had received from the Liberty network's baseball broadcasts (Beatty, 1950, p. 91).

Gordon's reasoning notwithstanding, the National Association of Minor Leagues adopted a proposal at its December 1950 meeting asking that officials at the upcoming major league baseball meeting curtail the awarding of broadcast rights to networks that aired a considerable number of games into minor league territory. The minor league officials did not cite LBS specifically as the network they considered most bothersome, but the implication was clear when the officials went out of their way to praise the Mutual Network for its self-imposed game coverage limitation ("Baseball: Broadcast," 1950).

The minor league proposal was informally discussed during the December 1950 major league meeting, but it never formally became an agenda item. The ouster of baseball commissioner Chandler by major league club owners took priority over other business during the meeting ("Baseball Coverage," 1950, p. 25). The minor league proposal, however, would not be forgotten. Its residue eventually would wreak unremitting havoc on the Liberty Broadcasting System.

RULE 1(d) REDUX

Organized baseball's territorial rights and broadcasting's coverage rights came into conflict once more only five months after major-league officials chose to sidestep the issue. As had been the case in 1949, the U.S. Justice Department had received enough complaints alleging that organized baseball had unreasonably restrained certain radio and television stations from broadcasting major league baseball games to order an investigation of the situation. The investigation would extend beyond baseball to include professional and college football and other professional sports ("FBI Probes," 1951, p. 25). As discussed in the previous chapter, a revision of organized baseball's Rule 1(d) in 1949 had halted the Justice Department's original investigation of the territorial rights versus broadcast rights matter. At the heart of the rule was the exclusion of major league baseball broadcasts in minor league territories. Minor league officials insisted this was necessary, and major league officials agreed. This arrangement, nevertheless, remained legally questionable, particularly from the antitrust angle.

By late May of 1951, enough broadcasters had complained of the adverse effects of Rule 1(d) that Attorney General J. Howard McGrath once more prepared to interject the federal government into organized baseball ("FBI Probes," 1951, p. 25). However, Justice Department intervention was forestalled in October 1951 when major league baseball officials made a surprise announcement that all territorial restrictions on baseball game broadcasts had been lifted. From then on broadcasters could negotiate directly with individual major league teams rather than with league officials for coverage rights. Rule 1(d) now was essentially a relic of the past.

Minor league officials reportedly were not contacted in advance of the major league officials' change of direction. Whatever minor league protection there might be from major league broadcast competition now rested squarely in the hands of the senior league (Beatty, 1951, pp. 25, 105).

As the announcement was made that baseball's Rule 1(d) was suspended, reporters turned their attention to Gordon McLendon and the impact of the rule's suspension on LBS. The greatest impact, said Gordon, was that the Liberty network for the first time would be able to air games in the major league cities of the Northeast, East and Midwest where the network heretofore had been excluded (Beatty, 1951, pp. 25, 105).

THE END OF LBS

The weather in Dallas during the first weeks of 1952 would have been perfect for Gordon McLendon had it been cold and dreary. What better way to usher in the kind of year that awaited him and the Liberty network.

The year started well enough as LBS signed contracts to carry the baseball games of the Brooklyn Dodgers, Chicago White Sox and Cincinnati Reds during the 1952 season. Contracts with three other ball clubs supposedly were pending with no announcement about contract talks with any remaining major league clubs. The network was offering advertisers a fifty-two-week All-Sports Package that it called "unprecedented in scope and completeness." Included in the package would be coverage of a whole range of sports activities, including major league baseball games, college basketball games and both college and professional football games. Broadcasts that were part of the package were scheduled to begin on March 8 with the opening of major league baseball's spring exhibition season. An unnamed oil company was rumored to be interested in buying the entire package ("Sports Package," 1952), but it appears that LBS never struck a firm deal.

The optimism that surrounded the announcement of Liberty's 1952 All-Sports Package veiled some major misgivings about the network's future. The financial picture was grim at best. Hugh Roy Cullen's assistance had brightened the situation briefly, but 1952 brought new financial woes. The pullout of the Falstaff Brewing Company as a prime Liberty sponsor was a serious blow. Lindsey Nelson went so far as to call it "the beginning of the end" for LBS (Nelson and Hirshberg, 1966, p. 43). On top of losing such an important means of income, the LBS expansion into a full schedule of nonsports programming was turning out to be more expensive than anticipated. The biggest financial blow, however, came from the increased fees charged to LBS for the rights to carry major league baseball games. The two major leagues that had charged Liberty $1,000 per season in 1949 for carriage rights had upped that fee to more than $225,000 by 1951. With individual baseball clubs negotiating their own contracts with LBS by 1952, carriage rights fees were certain to rise again (*Congressional Record*, 1952, p. A3745).

The Brooklyn Dodgers, Cincinnati Reds, Chicago White Sox and Boston Braves previously had signed contracts with Liberty that ran through the 1952 season. The first three agreed to honor their contracts, but the Boston Braves did not (Glick, 1979, p. 135, n. 39). Owners of the other twelve National and American League teams simply refused to budge. They effectively were shutting out Gordon McLendon from their ballparks, withholding from LBS access to the very product it needed most to survive. "Without the product Liberty had been founded on, how could there be any Liberty?" questioned Lindsey Nelson. "It was all over, curtains" (Smith, 1987, p. 134).

Gordon and B. R. attempted to compensate for the loss of advertising income coupled with rising expenses by upping the fees charged LBS affiliates who carried the network's baseball games. The original fee had been ten dollars per game, but now it would be doubled (Smith, 1987, pp. 113, 133). The already frustrated and angered LBS affiliate station owners might have been more understanding of the network's financial plight had there been anyone at LBS headquarters besides Gordon with whom they could talk. But the network appeared to revolve around its president ("Liberty Suspends," 1952, p. 93), and he oftentimes was nowhere near Dallas. Gordon's constant business trips were making him a more and more infrequent sight around the home office (Merriman, 1990). The result of all this was the loss of over 100 LBS station affiliates by early 1952 ("End," 1952, p. 94).

Gordon reacted to this chain of events now plaguing his network by filing a twelve-million dollar suit against the thirteen major league teams that refused him a broadcasting contract, charging them with violations of the antitrust laws. Named as co-defendants in the suit were Commissioner of Baseball Ford Frick, National League President Warren Giles and American League President William Harridge. Former Commissioner of Baseball Albert B. Chandler and National Association of Minor League Teams President George N. Trautman were named in the suit as co-conspirators but not as defendants.

Gordon's suit, filed in U.S. District Court in Chicago on February 21, 1952, alleged that the defendants were acting in concert to monopolize the broadcast rights to both minor and major league baseball games. If LBS were only given the opportunity, claimed Gordon, the network would be willing to outbid any other radio station or network for those rights ("Baseball Suit," 1952).

Why did the major league baseball owners take such drastic means of locking out LBS from coverage of their games? Two theories were advanced on the matter. One held that each ball club wanted to protect its own local or regional network from LBS competition (Smith, 1987, p. 134). That was reasonable, but on the same day that Gordon filed his antitrust suit, Mutual announced that it just had acquired broadcasting rights to carry the games of nine major league teams on its "Game of the Day" ("Baseball Suit," 1952). Why would a team wishing to protect its own network of stations from Liberty's competition act so quickly to sign a contract with Liberty's chief rival? Gordon argued that it was because Mutual was not attempting to compete in the major league club network areas, was not broadcasting at night, was abiding without question by the former Rule 1(d) fifty-mile dictates, and in general was "playing a complete patsy and stooge to baseball" (*Congressional Record*, 1952, p. A3745).

Another theory was more likely the correct one, and the one that Gordon at least publicly professed to believe. This theory grew from the continuing minor league problem. As they had done in 1950, minor league baseball officials once more asked major league club owners in 1951 to restrict broadcasts of major league games in minor league territories. The minor league plea apparently was more forceful this time, because it proved successful ("Liberty Network," 1952). The restrictions that were requested unfortunately came entirely at the expense of the Liberty Broadcasting System.

Reaction to Liberty's suit was not long in coming. Fred Saigh, owner of the St. Louis Cardinals, said that he was considering a countersuit and that the Liberty suit was an action taken "to improperly coerce baseball." He contended that baseball club owners held all rights to any broadcast of their teams' games and that they could choose to dispose of these rights however they pleased. Moreover, said Saigh, the Liberty suit lacked any foundation, since monetary damage could not be proved by LBS owners, who often had claimed that the network was losing money on its baseball broadcasts ("McLendon May Be," 1952).

There was yet one more obstacle to add to Liberty's woes. As had happened when Gordon began his LBS re-creations, Western Union now was refusing to provide him the necessary baseball game play-by-play wire service. Gordon responded to the company's refusal by amending his original suit against organized baseball to include Western Union as yet another co-defendant. Gordon's objective here was to seek a restraining order and then a temporary injunction that would remain in effect until a decision could be rendered in his suit. The legal maneuver, if successful, would force Western Union to provide Liberty with play-by-play accounts that the network could use to re-create the games of baseball teams whose live coverage rights Gordon could not acquire. These re-creations, added to the live broadcasts of the three teams with whom Liberty did have contracts, would keep the network's remaining affiliates supplied with baseball coverage and make them, for the moment, less likely to bolt the network ("Liberty Seeks," 1952).

Liberty's motion for a restraining order against Western Union was heard by Judge John P. Barnes in Chicago Federal District Court on April 14—one day prior to the official start of the 1952 major league baseball season ("Liberty Seeks," 1952). Judge Barnes issued a very terse statement denying Liberty's motion. The ruling was based on several "conclusions of law," key of which were the following: (1) baseball club owners have property rights in the games played in their baseball parks and in the "news, reports, descriptions and accounts" of those games: (2) each club owner has the right to place "restrictions and limitations upon persons entering [his] park with respect to the transmission of news, reports, descriptions or accounts" of the baseball games played there; and (3) Western Union's contract with baseball club owners legally restricted the telegraph company to providing its play-by-play accounts only to persons or organizations approved by the club owners (*Liberty Broadcasting System*, 1952, pp. 2166–2167.)

Judge Barnes's decision was a nearly mortal blow, but despite the setback Gordon stated publicly that the Liberty network would continue broadcasting baseball games throughout the 1952 season ("Radio Plea," 1952). Gordon attempted valiantly to live up to his promise, although the odds against Liberty's survival mounted daily. The network had to suspend its efforts to attract national advertisers as a result of uncertainty over what baseball games it would air and the number of local affiliates remaining with Liberty. A rumor began to circulate in May that the network would soon file for bankruptcy. The network, of course, said the rumor was groundless ("LBS Official," 1952).

The first real hint of Liberty's trouble came to network affiliates during a May 6 closed-circuit address by Gordon. He told affiliates that there no longer existed the "solid family feeling" that once characterized the network. Then he noted that "for the most part during the last two years . . . the story of Liberty has been a story of money lost, hard work lost, fighting a huge monopoly" ("Liberty Suspends," 1952, p. 25). Gordon apparently spared details on the network's financial losses, which reportedly were in the neighborhood of $66,000 monthly. Hugh Roy Cullen had even lent Gordon an extra $175,000, but had warned that no more loans would be made ("End," 1952, p. 94). Cullen by now had begun to question Gordon's ability to oversee the Liberty network's financial affairs. "We've got to have a man who knows the radio business as business manager," Cullen said when questioned about the network's future (Cullen, n.d.).

The major program-related announcement that Gordon made during his May 6 closed-circuit remarks was that Liberty was cutting its service in half—from sixteen to eight hours a day. The reason given for the cut was the high cost of telephone line charges necessary to carry the LBS signal to individual affiliates. Prior to the cut in service, LBS had managed to broadcast 50 baseball games. Some 103 live game broadcasts and 38 re-creations remained on the LBS schedule. The total of 191 games planned for all of 1952 was said by Gordon to be a "pitifully inadequate list" of authorized games for the Liberty network ("Liberty Suspends," 1952, p. 25).

The service cut was either a real effort by LBS to regroup and continue broadcasting, or simply a stalling tactic. Regardless of the motive, it delayed by only one week the inevitable. On Thursday, May 15, 1952, at 1 P.M. (EDT), all LBS affiliates were notified that Gordon would make a major public address on the network at 7:45 P.M. (EDT) that night. All affiliates were urged to carry the speech ("Liberty Suspends," 1952, p. 25).

When time arrived for the broadcast, Gordon was primed for what would be his last remarks on the Liberty network. This was a speech of about fifteen minutes that bristled with anger and frustration. Shortly into the speech, Gordon stated his main point: "Tonight, as a direct result of the United States Government's failure to enforce our laws against monopoly, the Liberty Broadcasting System must suspend operations" (McLendon, 1952, p. 1).

Gordon then told of how the U.S. Justice Department, with "full and documented proof of the monopoly and conspiracy" that was dealing the deathblow to LBS, failed to act against organized baseball. He next reviewed the suit that he had filed against the several baseball clubs and baseball officials, calling it "one of the most momentous steps in the history of broadcasting and free speech." The suit, Gordon noted, was aimed directly at those persons in organized baseball—chiefly, the club owners—who conspired "illegally to restrict the broadcasts of baseball to the fans of this nation." On that point he became more emphatic:

> These men at the top of baseball, posing as a public institution, propose to deny broadcasts of this great game of baseball to the blind, the aged, the sick,

> the disabled veterans and the people at large. Baseball is a game rooted deep in the heart of America. The diamond dictators propose to turn our national pasttime into their private monopoly. I do not propose that they shall go one inch further. It is no good any longer to fight them with words and pleas and compromises. That would be like taking aspirin to cure cancer. They have not listened before, and they will not listen now. In combination and conspiracy, they have said to you, "We have decided that you may hear baseball when we tell you, where we tell you and how we tell you." I fought, for one, too long overseas to come back home and submit to dictatorship here. I'd rather fight again. (McLendon, 1952, pp. 1–2).

Gordon next gave listeners examples of how organized baseball had fought his efforts in the distant and recent past to broadcast baseball games nationally, and of the controls club owners had attempted to exert over what announcers could say about the various baseball teams. All of this was the owners' way of exercising monopoly control, charged Gordon. "If Liberty succeeds in its fight to bring you unrestricted baseball broadcasting," he said, "baseball will lose that economic monopoly and all of the trade restraining, price fixing, and other unlawful advantages that go with a monopoly" (McLendon, 1952, pp. 3–5).

In closing, Gordon thanked his listeners and assured them that they "will again hear the voice of the Liberty Broadcasting System" (Mclendon, 1952, p. 6).

Gordon had promised at the outset of his radio address that he would be "as explicit as possible" (McLendon, 1952, p. 1), and he kept his promise. This was the speech of a political orator, perhaps even a preview of the style that listeners would come to expect in later years as Gordon actually entered the political arena. Someone viewing the speech analytically probably would have criticized its all-too-apparent and all-too-frequent resort to demagoguery. But, considering the emotional strain of knowing that all that he had worked years to accomplish would be gone forever in just a few more moments, the tone of Gordon's remarks was understandable.

LIBERTY NETWORK BANKRUPTCY AND BEYOND

The Liberty Broadcasting System ceased operation at 10:45 P.M. Dallas time, on Thursday, May 15, 1952 ("LBS to Quit," 1952, p. 1). Two weeks later, the network agreed to involuntary bankruptcy proceedings. With no means of paying its debts, Liberty had little other choice. Gordon noted that Liberty's twelve-million-dollar antitrust suit pending against organized baseball, if successful, would provide enough money to pay all network debts ("Liberty Agrees," 1952).

By early June of 1952, federal bankruptcy referee D. M. Oldham had named Dallas attorney William J. Rochelle, Jr. as receiver (or trustee) for the bankrupt Liberty Network. Some 450 Liberty creditors had filed claims in Oldham's court that totaled $1,400,880. Liberty's assets were listed as only $507,489. As a means of settling Liberty's debts, referee Oldham ordered that attorney Rochelle "diligently prosecute" the network's antitrust law suit. In the event that LBS won its suit or settled with the defendants within the next ninety days, said Oldham, "Liberty could go right on operating as before" ("Lawyer," 1952).

Referee Oldham's ninety-day limit on legal proceedings relating to a hoped-for LBS resuscitation was by no means met. In fact, the legal wrangling over the Liberty antitrust suit stretched on for more than two-and-a-half years (Maule, 1955b).

Perhaps realizing the protracted nature of the suit, LBS creditors bowed to the inevitable and ordered that trustee Rochelle set July 15, 1952, as the date to liquidate the Liberty network's physical assets—its radio equipment and office furniture—valued at $85,000 ("Liberty Properties," 1952). At the conclusion of the liquidation sale, the Liberty Broadcasting System ceased to exist; the end for "the country's second largest radio network" arrived, as Edwin Glick described it, "in somewhat ignominious fashion" (Glick, 1979, p. 131).

Tom Merriman remembered that the Liberty network's demise did not come as a great surprise. LBS personnel had been hearing B. R. McLendon say for quite a while that the network was going out of business. Merriman, in fact, felt that it was B. R.'s and not Gordon's concern over Liberty's precarious financial condition that finally convinced him that there was no alternative to bankruptcy (Merriman, 1990).

Les Vaughn recalled that news of the pending decision to close down the Liberty network came sparingly to lower-echelon personnel. When it did come it usually arrived through the rumor mill. Vaughn said that Gordon showed little outward emotion, certainly no depression, when the network came to an end (Vaughn, 1989).

Marcus Cohn said that Gordon's appearance was deceptive. On the inside he was emotionally drained. Gordon "did not take defeat well at any time. The idea of defeat was an abominable idea. He had to be above defeat," said Cohn (1989).

Actually, although LBS was legally defunct, Gordon was not yet ready to lay the idea for a sports radio network to rest. At least two shortlived efforts were made to revive such a network. The first came only days after LBS had announced the close of its operation in mid-May 1952. Two regional radio networks were in formation, said Gordon and B. R., that would include a number of former West Coast LBS affiliates and a number of former Texas and Louisiana LBS affiliates. The West Coast network would be headquartered in Los Angeles and would be named the Liberty Radio Network. Some forty radio stations in California, Washington and Oregon were said to be committed to joining the new network, though no affiliation contracts had been signed. The Texas-Louisiana network, which was yet to be named, would consist of McLendon-owned KLIF in Dallas, KLBS in Houston and KELP in El Paso. Stations KNOE in Monroe, Louisiana and WNOE in New Orleans, owned by Gordon's father-in-law, James A. Noe, would also join the network. Network headquarters would be either in Dallas or Houston. Both the West Coast and Texas-Louisiana networks were to begin service in June 1952 with a mid-afternoon program schedule of public domain baseball game recreations, newscasts and news commentaries ("LBS Successors," 1952).

There is no evidence that either of these two regional networks ever became operational. Despite this setback, Gordon kept to the task of forming another regional network in Texas that would become operational in April 1953. The Knickerbocker Network (named for its chief sponsor, Knickerbocker beer) would broadcast major league baseball game recreations throughout the 1953 season. Approximately 118 games were scheduled for broadcast during weekday evenings (U.S. Senate, 1953, pp. 129–133). Gordon would be handling the announcing chores. Several stations were said to be interested in affiliating with the new network, but as of sign-on day, only the McLendons' own KLIF and KLBS were "in the fold" ("Re-Creations," 1953).

The Liberty case, for the moment, was in a state of limbo. Defendants in the twelve-million-dollar suit had filed answers to the suit the previous year, on November 17, 1952. As expected, they denied violating antitrust laws and conspiring to illegally restrict broadcasts of major league baseball games. Moreover, the defendants said that LBS had agreed to sign contracts with major league baseball clubs for as many as five years, so if a conspiracy did exist, then LBS "was a part of it and enjoyed its benefits" ("Major League," 1952).

The trial date for the Liberty suit, set originally for January 19, 1953, was postponed and reset several times ("LBS-Majors," 1953). The last date set for the trial was April 18, 1955. Prior to that date, on January 10, 1955, Will Harridge, American League president and representative of the organized baseball defendants, offered a $200,000 settlement for dismissal of the suit. The offer was made to LBS trustee William J. Rochelle, Jr., who filed application in U.S. Bankruptcy Court in Dallas for its consideration. Settlement of the suit was suggested by U.S. District Judge Julius J. Hoffman, in whose Chicago courtroom the Liberty suit would be tried. Judge Hoffman said that the settlement would "save the court and the parties the time and expense of a protracted jury trial," which was expected to require at least three months. Gordon McLendon called the settlement offer a victory, but rejected the $200,000 figure ("Majors Seeking," 1955, p. 14). He and B. R., and presumably Hugh Roy Cullen, preferred continuing the suit (Dugger, 1964, p. 7).

Bankruptcy referee D. M. Oldham would make the final decision on whether or not to accept the settlement offer. To assist in his consideration he called a meeting of all Liberty network creditors on January 25, 1955, in Dallas. Trustee Rochelle favored pressing forward with the suit, but said that in addition to the $50,000 that already had been spent in preparing Liberty's case, another $25,000 would be necessary. Only $42,977 remained available to the network for fighting the case. If the $200,000 settlement were accepted, legal fees and other expenses deducted from that amount would leave only about $100,000 to be spread among 209 creditors. Rochelle added that while Liberty's Chicago attorney felt certain that the network could establish violation of antitrust laws, there remained some doubt over the amount of damages the court might award in the event the network did win the suit. Trustee Rochelle felt that the award might not be any more than the $200,000 settlement now being offered.

Altogether LBS creditors had entered claims amounting to about $1,100,000. Ironically, the two biggest claims filed against LBS were from its two owners, B. R. McLendon and Hugh Roy Cullen. B. R. was asking for $158,235 and Cullen was asking for $600,000. Referee Oldham found it peculiar that the two could not underwrite Liberty's lawsuit themselves without using what little money remained for that purpose, if indeed the lawsuit were continued. Gordon supplied the reason: "I told them not to throw good money after bad" (Maule, 1955a). Only about half the creditors present at the meeting favored continuing the suit. The others were willing to accept what trustee Rochelle termed the "disappointingly small" settlement offered by the major-league baseball interests (Maule, 1955a).

Referee Oldham deliberated for twenty-four hours on his decision. On January 26 he ordered that LBS trustee William Rochelle, Jr. accept baseball's settlement offer (Maule, 1955b).

Once the offer was officially accepted, Judge Hoffman formally dismissed Liberty's twelve-million-dollar antitrust suit on February 8 (Glick, 1979, p. 132). Rochelle filed a final report with Oldham on November 13, 1956, indicating final disbursement of remaining LBS funds to the network's creditors. In the end most creditors received only about thirty-one cents for each dollar in debts owed them by LBS (Dugger, 1964, p. 8).

The dissolution of the Liberty Broadcasting System now was complete. Actually, Judge Hoffman's dismissal of the Liberty suit on February 8, 1955, had marked the formal end of the network.

Lindsey Nelson once said that Gordon had created LBS "with a minimum of cash and a maximum of nerve, ingenuity, enterprise, and imagination" (Nelson and Hirshberg, 1966, p. 30). Would Gordon care to see if that combination might work again? Yes, but most certainly not with the reincarnation of a radio sports network. Losing LBS had been quite a blow, Gordon later said. "I had to get in, and turn my life around, make a new future . . . which was still going to be in radio, but it could no longer be in sports" (McLendon, 1969a).

Continue in radio Gordon most certainly did. And his success with the medium in later years would be legendary. But Gordon was already a legend by the end of his Liberty Broadcasting System career. Few would deny that Gordon McLendon had earned himself a place among the elite of sports announcers. Lindsey Nelson claimed never to have heard a "better play-by-play announcer than Gordon" (Nelson, 1988). Even sportscaster-turned-President Ronald Reagan once had remarked to former McLendon employee and future Dallas Mayor Wes Wise how much he had admired Gordon's work (Drape, 1986, p. 10A).

Regardless of his many achievements in later years, Gordon always regarded his sportscasting days as among his finest. Asked in 1981—after the close of his broadcasting career—what was his most exciting time in the business, Gordon replied without hesitation, "For me, from '47 to '52 when I was actively involved in broadcasting play-by-play sports" (McLendon, 1981b). It was, he said, his most "personally satisfying" time in broadcasting (McLendon, 1981b). Waxing more poetic during a moment of reminiscence about his Liberty Broadcasting System, Gordon said: "All those years have long since passed into oblivion. They were years of a young man's springtime. And I cherish nothing but warm feelings about baseball, and I still love it" (McLendon, 1978).

5 *KLIF and Top 40 Radio*

The demise of the Liberty Broadcasting System left Gordon McLendon with a need to redirect his life. "I realized all the king's horses and all the king's men couldn't put Humpty Dumpty back together again," Gordon lamented later about the effort to revive LBS (Porter, 1972, p. 13E). There were choices to be made at this point. Gordon was still in his early thirties and could have had his pick of several sportscasting jobs being offered by the major networks. But someone had to run the radio stations that Gordon and his father were beginning to accumulate. Besides KLIF in Dallas, the McLendons now owned stations in El Paso—KELP, purchased in 1951—and Houston—KLBS, purchased in 1952 (*City of Camden*, 1969b, pp. 431–432).

Gordon took the station ownership route. "Whether that was the right road to take for my own happiness, I don't know. But, that's where I went," Gordon later would say (McLendon, 1981a).

CHANGING TIMES FOR RADIO

There is little surprise that Gordon chose to stay in radio. He loved the medium. Speaking to a group in Chicago in 1962, Gordon remarked: "Radio, the eighth and perhaps greatest wonder of the world, is still today the most enveloping means of communication in the universe. It will remain so, probably, until the last sound of recorded time" (McLendon, 1962f, p. 1). Gordon's love for radio hardly had diminished when in 1977 he confided to a Dallas audience that "radio . . . just the word alone still creates within my body the greatest thrill I have ever known. Radio is beautiful" (Routt, McGrath, and Weiss, 1978, p. x).

Gordon's decision to remain in radio might have appeared unwise at first. After all, the industry that he would devote most of his future to was undergoing dramatic changes. The whole dynamics of broadcasting in the early 1950s were quite different from the time in 1947 when Gordon had broken into radio. Part of the broadcasting industry—that part associated with the new *wunderkind*, television—was thriving. That part of the industry associated with radio, however, while projecting a healthy appearance, was struggling. Many industry observers felt that radio could not compete with the newer, more glamorous medium and that, as comedian Fred Allen said, television was trying to "get radio to pucker up for the kiss of death" (Elliott, 1978).

World War II had delayed television's introduction into the consumer marketplace, but by 1946 the medium was poised to take off and to compete with radio for consumer attention. Eleven television stations had begun operation by 1947; that number had jumped to 354 by the end of 1954 (Sterling and Kittross, 1978, pp. 254–255, 511). The number of television stations taking to the airwaves was being driven in large part by the American consumer's embrace of the new medium. Only ten thousand television receivers were in American homes by 1946; by 1949 that number had jumped to a million. By 1952 the number had zoomed to nearly sixteen million and by 1954 the number had reached nearly twenty-seven million.

All of these television receivers in American homes meant that people were devoting more and more leisure time to watching television programs. A measurement of viewing in 1950 showed that individuals were spending an average of just over 4.5 hours a day in front of the television set. That figure rose by one-half hour in 1955 (Sterling, 1984, p. 216).

What did these figures mean to the radio industry? For one thing they meant that radio's loyal audience—those persons who had spent as much time listening to radio in the past as they now were spending watching television—was eroding. Radio listening time dropped from a per-person, per-day average of over four hours in 1950 to little more than two hours by 1955 (Sterling, 1984, p. 220). The most dramatic listener decline occurred during radio's evening prime-time hours. By the early 1950s radio's prime-time audience had dropped by nearly two-thirds when compared with pre-television figures (Fornatale and Mills, 1980, p. 7).

Most profoundly affected by the shifting of audience interest to television were the radio networks. At its peak in 1947, when 97 percent of all commercial U.S. radio stations were affiliated with one of the four national networks (NBC, CBS, ABC or Mutual), national network affiliation had dropped to 53 percent by 1954 (Sterling, 1984, pp. 12–13). The decline was attributed to the mass desertion of network radio talent, management and technicians for television. Moreover, these people were taking with them the programming that had popularized the radio networks in the first place (Fornatale and Mills, 1980, pp. 6–7). And although radio networks would continue to exist once the radio-to-television exodus was complete, their conceptual role would change and their importance would diminish considerably.

The position of the U.S. radio industry as a whole was linked with the plight of the radio networks. The industry was struggling for some precise direction, certainly, but there was every indication that radio's vital signs were good.

Statistics proved the point. The number of radio stations (AM and FM) on the air had zoomed upward from just over a thousand in 1946 to over three thousand by 1952. The growth rate was not as dramatic during the remainder of the 1950s, but it nonetheless continued (Sterling, 1984, p. 6). And while total radio revenue dropped substantially in 1954, revenue figures had risen steadily every year prior to 1954. What's more, two years after the 1954 decline, radio revenues were higher than ever (Sterling, 1984, p. 107).

Another measure of radio's popularity is radio receiver ownership figures, which climbed continually throughout the early 1950s. The number of radio households had increased by anywhere from one to two million per year from 1946 through 1953. The increase fell to only 300,000 in 1954, but by 1955 the earlier trend had resumed. Most phenomenal was the growth in car radios. By 1955, 60 percent of all automobiles were equipped with radios (Sterling and Kittross, 1978, p. 533).

Radio obviously was destined to hang on in the new competitive world that television had created. The question then revolved around what form that survival would assume.

KLIF AND TOP 40 EMERGE IN DALLAS

Gordon McLendon admitted during a 1969 interview that the minions of organized baseball "put me out of business before I had a chance to waste another five years of my life in hard and non-productive effort" (McLendon, 1969a). The wasted time that Gordon was spared, of course, would have been manifested in his efforts to sustain a radio network at a time when radio networks were becoming nearly extinct. So, losing LBS was as much good fortune as bad in view of the circumstances. Adding to the good fortune, Gordon and B. R. still commanded three radio stations, most important of which was KLIF and its talented staff, and the McLendons were willing to do whatever was necessary to assure radio's survival.

Actually, KLIF was surviving quite well. The station had progressed from daytime-only to programming a twenty-four-hour "round-the-clock" schedule by February 1950 ("KLIF to Start," 1950). The McLendons also moved KLIF from its Cliff Towers Hotel location to its permanent home in the familiar downtown Dallas triangular building on Jackson Street. The station would share facilities with LBS until the latter no longer existed (Odom, 1990).

KLIF carried the entire Liberty network program schedule, and originated much of it. But apart from network programming, KLIF aired a very popular assortment of local programs for its Dallas listeners (Meeks, 1990). Using a "block programming" approach that was quite common among radio stations in the 1940s, KLIF aired music arranged in specific time periods or blocks to allow for different musical styles and tastes throughout the broadcast day. By 1950 Jimmie Jefferies, Buddy Harris and Johnny Murray took turns disc jockeying some of the program blocks, most of which consisted of contemporary popular music. But in order to please as many listeners as possible, KLIF even scheduled a country-western block hosted by Al Turner (Advertisement, 1950), while Buddy Harris occasionally hosted a rhythm and blues program (Meeks, 1990). The only other program fare that occupied a substantial chunk of the KLIF schedule was coverage of local minor-league baseball, college football and basketball games.

This, then, was the KLIF programming that listeners grew accustomed to hearing at least until there no longer was a Liberty network (Radio Program Schedule, 1950a, 1950b, 1951). Promotion still consisted primarily of station ID jingles, which had become a part of KLIF's sound signature by the early 1950s.

Gordon's request for more elaborate jingle productions soon pushed Tom Merriman to record vocal and instrumental backgrounds in an abandoned church—the only facility big enough to handle the band that Merriman had assembled. Not only were the productions for KLIF becoming more elaborate, but after other radio station owners from across the country heard the KLIF jingles, they began asking Gordon to record similar jingles for their own use. Merriman set to work filling the orders by using one basic instrumental sound track—one that already had been recorded for KLIF—combined with a vocal track tailor-made for any customer station. As a result, Merriman remarked, for years afterwards,"if you said to anybody, 'Sing the jingle, sing the call letters of any radio station,' they would sing it to the tune of the KLIF logo" (Merriman, 1990).

Tom Merriman and Bill Meeks both later developed very successful jingle production companies, independent of any McLendon connection but nevertheless owing to Gordon's original station jingle syndication idea. Like so many other radio industry trends, trends that Merriman swore Gordon could spot before they happened (Merriman, 1990), station ID jingles would become a familiar fixture in the repertoire of radio programming.

The mark that KLIF was making in Dallas as the station moved into the 1950s was coming not so much from the Liberty network programming it carried but from the music it aired, according to Bill Meeks. Music was also a better means than the sports-heavy programming that LBS had relied upon for building KLIF's revenue base. Programming built around records simply was easier, cheaper and more reliable for carrying commercials than was programming based on seasonal sports. In fact, Meeks was convinced that KLIF would not have been so successful and perhaps would not have survived at all if it had continued to carry the LBS schedule. Most ironic, though, was Meeks's contention that the publicity generated from the Liberty network's bankruptcy worked in KLIF's favor. "It [KLIF] just got bigger and better," he said (Meeks, 1990).

What Gordon had learned about programming at KLIF, other radio station owners also were beginning to learn in the early 1950s. Local radio had to appeal to local tastes in music and in turn provide local public service. Station programming could be and indeed had to be targeted to specialized audiences, such as teenagers, who heretofore had been overlooked or neglected by radio.

Finding what the listener wanted most required experimentation with what came to be called program "formulas" or "formats." Format radio

> involved methodology rather than content. Stations no longer left things to chance. . . . They developed rules that would give each station a definable personality to its listeners. These rules might include: Playing X number of songs an hour, identifying the station X number of times by its call letters, and specifying where to do the commercials. (Fornatale and Mills, 1980, pp. 13–17)

By far the most successful format to emerge in the early 1950s was Top 40. How Top 40 actually was born may be more apocryphal than true, but it makes for a good story. Radio station owner Todd Storz and his assistant (and future McLendon station employee) Bill Stewart were said to have conceived the Top 40 concept after observing how bar patrons repeatedly played their favorite tunes on the jukebox. Storz and Stewart decided that the jukebox idea of allowing repeated play of the most current popular hits from a limited selection or playlist might work for radio (Hall and Hall, 1977, p. 167). Storz incorporated the idea into the programming of his Omaha radio station, KOWH. And even though Top 40 had some distance to go before its recognizable format would emerge, its infant version started paying almost immediate dividends. By 1953, KOWH had zoomed from last to first place among six rated Omaha stations.

Bill Stewart took the programming idea next to New Orleans in 1953 to test it at Todd Storz's newly acquired WTIX. Here was a major market radio station where Storz could let Stewart loose to create the classic Top 40 format. Within a year WTIX had become a number one station in New Orleans (Eberly, 1982, pp. 199–200). It was at this point that Gordon McLendon picked up on the Storz-Stewart idea and is said to have "opened up the second main branch of 'Top 40' at KLIF, Dallas" (Passman, 1971, p. 160).

It was Gordon's contributions to the fundamental Top 40 format that would make his brand the most popular nationwide. Gordon also indirectly accounted for the name "Top 40," according to his one-time associate Chuck Blore. The name, which evidently never was formally applied but rather evolved over time, was said originally to have come from the forty-record playlist that Todd Storz used at KOWH. The forty records supposedly had derived from the forty slots on the standard jukebox (Curtis, 1987, p. 43). But Chuck Blore claimed that the forty-record playlist actually derived from the number of records that each KLIF disc jockey was allowed to play. Blore said that Gordon did not want his disc jockeys repeating any music during their four-hour on-air shifts. So, it was decided that they would play ten different hit tunes every hour for a total of forty hit tunes per shift. Thus, each disc jockey played the "top 40" hit records. Added to the popular hit tunes played every hour were two "oldies" and a Glenn Miller single. The hourly dose of Glenn Miller was ordered by Gordon, who happened to prefer that brand of music. Disc jockeys later were allowed to substitute their own "pick hit" choices of the oldies.

Since the top forty tunes were based upon local record store sales, Chuck Blore said that some of the so-called hits that fell near the end of the Top 40 list were anything but hit records. But, since there had to be forty records on the Top 40 playlist, "digging the bottom of the barrel" sometimes was necessary in order to complete the list (Blore, 1990).

The essence of Top 40 was the meticulous craftsmanship of station owner and staff in their ability to fine-tune the format. The key to the format, noted Philip K. Eberly, "was a basic management understanding of the importance of nuances—nuances of timing, of sound reproduction, of listener empathy. Nothing was left to chance. Top 40 Radio was quality-controlled all the way" (Eberly, 1982, pp. 202–203).

And what were the basic ingredients of Top 40? Long-time McLendon associate Edd Routt said that the format

> consisted principally of music, light chatter, and news. Promotions in which money, merchandise and services were awarded listeners were a vital part of the over-all plan. Disc jockeys were selected for their sexiness, their voice, their ability to communicate excitement. Basic service consisted of time and temperature checks. Any idea of doing anything more than entertain the listener was out of the question. (Routt, McGrath, and Weiss, 1978, p. 61)

Routt maintained that the "Top 40 idea became a commercial success partially because audience rating services such as Hooper and Trendex began to publish results of surveys. Soon, the idea that we're 'NUMBER ONE' attracted time-buyers at advertising agencies, and the race was on" (Routt, McGrath, and Weiss, 1978, p. 5).

Top 40 station owners—the serious ones, at least—continually tinkered with their stations' programming mix in an effort to discover what listeners most wanted to hear (Freedgood, 1958, p. 124). And what listeners wanted in precise terms meant what young listeners, many of them teenagers, wanted. That usually meant rock 'n' roll. One reason for the close association of this style of music with Top 40 was the reliance by Top 40 station program directors on local record sales for determining playlists. Since "teenagers bought more records than adults, they determined what would be on the air. In the mid-1950s most of those records were rock 'n' roll" (Fornatale and Mills, 1980, p. 37).

Among the other crucial ingredients making Top 40 radio a success, perhaps none was more crucial than the disc jockey (or deejay). Here was the one ingredient of the Top 40 format that pulled all the others together. The disc jockey introduced and played the records; read the news, commercials and public service announcements; and participated in station promotional campaigns.

Within the parameters set by the format and nurtured by management, the Top 40 disc jockey had considerable creative freedom to develop an on-air identity. A gift for gab and rapid-fire vocal delivery helped. The ultimate trick, though, was to blend personality with music. Unifying the two was the key to a successful Top 40 performance (Eberly, 1982, p. 273).

A disc jockey was free to develop his own talent, but he had to remember that Top 40 radio would never allow a personality to develop independent of the music. The same eventually was true of station promotion. The disc jockey as personality was responsible for promoting his radio station, and in doing so he became linked with the stunts and gimmicks and contests that were to become as much a trademark of Top 40 as the music.

The champion at program promotion undeniably was Gordon McLendon. This is where he made his real and lasting mark on Top 40. Some would say that he invented Top 40 by himself, but he never took credit for it. Gordon always gave full credit to Top 40's rightful inventor: friend and fellow radio entrepreneur Todd Storz (McLendon, 1969a). "But when it came to the Compleat Top 40, Top 40-cum-Pizz-Zazz, Top 40 Pure and Undefiled," noted Eberly, "Gordon McLendon whipped up the *chef d'oeuvre*" (Eberly, 1982, p. 207).

KLIF RISES TO THE TOP

Gordon's intentions never were simply to assist radio in its survival but rather to make the medium better than it ever had been. Only a few others among the fraternity of radio station owners shared both the motivation and the skills to see radio through its transitional years. The roles played by this band of entrepreneurs were underscored most notably by a 1962 article in *Sponsor* magazine. "Less than 10 years ago," read the article,

> when the future of radio was gravely in doubt, there appeared on the horizon a handful of innovators—broadcasters who made headlines with their ideas about "formula" operations, who charted courses toward rating dominance that shook the very foundations of the radio industry. Of this small band of revolutionaries, Gordon McLendon, Todd Storz and the Bartell brothers—Jerry, Lee and Mel—were unmistakably the giants, and they became, almost within months, the fathers of modern radio. ("Earlybirds," 1962, p. 35)

All of these men were said to be a special breed of radio devotee "who lived, ate, breathed, and slept radio" (Hall and Hall, 1977, p. 15). All were young and bright, and all had entered the radio business at nearly the same time (MacFarland, 1973, p. 260). Their management philosophies were similar in that programming matters preceded sales matters. And they all believed that "management should be thoroughly involved in the development of the programming which actually reached the audience" (MacFarland, 1973, pp. 264–265).

Collectively, this group gave the U.S. radio industry a new direction. Individually, these men fashioned a new brand of radio that headed in a singular direction and carried an excitement all its own. In so doing, the fraternity shared ideas. But Gordon McLendon was unique among his radio brethren in that he contributed far more than he took from that pool of ideas (MacFarland, 1973, p. 215). In fact, KLIF was credited by industry observers as having had "more programming innovations than any other American radio station" during the years when Gordon controlled it (Blackwell, 1986, p. 1C).

Gordon often made light of his effort to push KLIF to the top. "By and large, running a radio station is kind of like death by drowning—a really delightful sensation when you stop struggling," Gordon remarked to a 1957 Dallas gathering (McLendon, 1957b, p. 1). Perhaps he was saying that running KLIF finally had become fun. Certainly it had become rewarding; Gordon announced at that same 1957 gathering that KLIF was "the top-ranked radio station in the world today, a distinction of which Dallas may justly be proud" (McLendon, 1957b, p. 2).

How had Gordon achieved such great success? He created programming that went far beyond the ordinary. It had an excitement about it that made "people afraid not to listen" ("Zany," 1961, p. 124). Even at a time when other radio stations in the same market were copying the KLIF format, Gordon had the knack for pulling in the listeners. "The music and news format we use is much like soap," Gordon would say. "We all can buy the same records, play them on the same type of turntable, and we can all hire someone to talk. The difference in radio is like the difference in soap—it depends on who puts on the best wrapper" ("Zany," 1961, p. 124).

Gordon had only recently finished fashioning his own version of Top 40 before he was being recognized by his peers as an industry leader. More stations would be added to the McLendon Station group in the 1950s and 1960s, until there were few areas of the country not somehow touched by the McLendon brand of broadcasting.

Gordon's influence was felt in other ways as well. His contributions toward the careers of future radio station owners, managers, programmers and disc jockeys was unparalleled. Moreover, many of these "McLendon disciples" would go on to become radio industry leaders (Hall and Hall, 1977, p. 17).

Bill Stewart, who was Top 40 radio's chief tactician, once said of Gordon that he "recognized—either instinctively or somehow, I don't know—what the people needed, or wanted. . . . And without doubt, Top 40 wouldn't be the success it is today without Gordon McLendon, because he had the guts to risk his radio station, to put it on the line" (Hall and Hall, 1977, p. 169). The risk that Stewart spoke of reflected the business community's lack of respect for Top 40 when it first appeared. Gordon and Todd Storz were seen as rebels by many fellow broadcasters. "It was very illogical to the old-line radio people. They couldn't believe what we were doing. We were sort of upstarts in the industry," said Stewart (Hall and Hall, 1977, p. 166). But, respectability was not high atop the McLendon agenda when Top 40 was introduced at KLIF. "Gordon never let anything deter him from taking a good idea and heading for the goal line. And he usually scored with it, too" (Hall and Hall, 1977, p. 169).

How and why Gordon chose to embark on the Top 40 route is not in dispute, but exactly when he introduced Top 40 to KLIF listeners is open to question. Gordon himself set the earliest Top 40 arrival date at 1952 (McInnis, 1979, p. 5). However, *Sponsor* magazine pegged 1953 as the year that KLIF "burst into national prominence with its formula of music and news plus razzle-dazzle promotion" ("Earlybirds," 1962, p. 35). Another source suggested that Gordon perhaps was tinkering with the Top 40 idea "in the early part of 1953" but was "using a top 25-record playlist (updated daily)" (Hall and Hall, 1977, p. 31). But one other source said that by mid-1953, Gordon still had not settled into a particular Top 40 programming scheme (MacFarland, 1973, p. 213). The latest time (and probably the closest to being correct in view of the evidence) for KLIF's transition to Top 40 was said by Bill Meeks to be 1954 (Meeks, 1990).

Memories sometimes fail to recall specific dates for specific events. That appears to have happened here. There is another reason for the confusion as well. Unlike the virtual overnight transition to Top 40 that Gordon later would make at some of his newly acquired stations, Top 40's implementation at KLIF occurred not all at once but rather very gradually (Routt, 1989). There is good evidence that Gordon was making some adjustments in KLIF's programming as early as 1953 that gave the station perhaps the essence of Top 40, although the official format name might not yet have applied. There also is evidence that at least by May 1953, Gordon was promoting a programming change for KLIF that would move the station in the direction of full-blown Top 40. Nonetheless, a perusal of the KLIF program schedule for June 1953 showed that Gordon was airing programs in a block style quite similar to what he had been doing for several years. Morning programs included "Coffee Capers," "Sunny Side Up," "House Party" and "Hillbilly Roundup." "Luncheon Music," "Bandstand" and "Lullaby in Rhythm" were the afternoon programs. The evening KLIF programs included "Mellow's the Mood," "Candlelight and Gold," "Tops in Pops" and "Harlem Hit Parade" (Radio Program Schedule, 1953).

One year later, the KLIF program schedule had taken on a decidedly different look. Gone were most of the program titles, along with their potpourri of music. In their place were time slots identified by disc jockey names—names that would become famous in the annals of Top 40 radio. Kenny Sargent led the pack with a mid-morning show, followed by Bruce Hayes from late morning to early afternoon. Kenny Sargent returned after the Hayes shift, and at mid-afternoon Bill Stewart came aboard. His shift ran until just past 6:00 P.M., when Gene Edwards took over (Radio Program Schedule, 1954). That schedule did not change appreciably through mid-1955. The only differences came with the addition of three new disc jockey names to the KLIF family: Don Keyes, Larry Monroe and Jim Randolph (Radio Program Schedule, 1955).

Somewhere around late 1954 and early 1955, then, all of the ingredients necessary for Top 40 appeared to be coming together at KLIF. The real catalyst in the development of a true Top 40 format at KLIF was Bill Stewart and the ideas that he brought to the station from his earlier association with Todd Storz. Don Keyes recalled that Stewart

> came in knowing what he was doing. And that's when he really tightened the playlist. That's when we really went Top 40—hard Top 40. Then we took off something fierce. We were still number one prior to that. But, if I had a record I liked, I'd play it. If the other disc jockey didn't like it, he didn't play it. It was kinda loosey goosey. We had jingles and contests and promotions, but it wasn't a rigid Top 40. And Bill came in and firmed up that music policy, and away we went. (Keyes, 1989)

The chemistry of whatever was happening at KLIF was beginning to have noticeable impact within the Dallas radio community. KLIF's station ratings—foremost indicators of a station's well-being in the marketplace—were indeed impressive. "Within weeks after implementing Top 40, KLIF jumped from a 2 percent share of the market to 45 percent," noted one source ("Pioneer," 1984). Another said: "In its titan days, KLIF . . . had ratings as high as 52" (Hitt, 1979). Bill Stewart remembered that the station "went from tenth or eleventh in the market to No. 1 in 60 days" when Top 40 was introduced (Hall and Hall, 1977, p. 162). Gordon himself described KLIF's position in April 1954 as "the leading metropolitan independent in the United States in share of morning audience, third in the afternoons, fourth at night and undeniably first on Saturdays" (MacFarland, 1973, p. 215). Hooper Ratings showed the station in June 1954 to be number one in the Dallas market in every time period (MacFarland, 1973, pp. 215–216).

There was no doubt that KLIF was knocking the socks off the competition. But how was it doing it? The Top 40 format was only the product of a very keen intuition about what kind of radio programming people wanted to hear. Once you have ascertained what your audience wants, Gordon felt, then give it to them. On that point, Gordon once wrote:

> Time and again—without exception—successful broadcast operators have proved that in order to survive and prosper financially, any radio station must provide a programming service of utility to a meaningful segment of the potential listening audience. Neither sales nor general administration nor engineering comes first. Programming does. The station failing to provide some service of unique programming utility to one or another reasonably large demographic element of the population is doomed. (Routt, 1972, Foreword)

The programming-ahead-of-sales philosophy was really Gordon's broadcasting credo. "You can have the greatest sales staff and signal in the world and it doesn't mean a thing if you don't have something great to put on the air," he would say ("Gordon McLendon," 1980). If he kept his eye on the programming, Gordon assumed, station advertising sales would take care of itself. And, of course, he was usually right.

Programming at KLIF "received the constant attention and monitoring of its owner—to the station's obvious benefit" (Patoski, 1980, p. 167). Gordon was convinced that much of his programming success stemmed directly from all of his attention to every detail (McLendon, n.d., Letter to Joe Roddy).

Gordon was forever fine-tuning his Top 40 format, while other station owners watched and followed suit. "People were coming to Dallas and monitoring KLIF, leaving with a briefcase full of tapes and going back to their hometown and doing likewise," noted Don Keyes (1989). It was not long before KLIF would become "America's most imitated radio station" (Patoski, 1980, p. 167), and with good reason. When asked what kind of audience he was programming KLIF for, Gordon replied rather matter-of-factly: "I geared it toward what I would like to hear. I assumed the audience to be interested in what I would like to hear" ("The Top-40," n.d., p. 24).

That was not altogether true, of course, since Gordon's reading of the marketplace might very well have told him the listeners liked something that he did not. If so, his listeners got whatever they, not Gordon, wanted. Gordon's son Bart even said that his father "knew nothing at all about music and cared nothing at all about music" (Bart McLendon, 1990). And there is no record of Gordon ever speaking favorably of rock 'n' roll. Nonetheless, he was among the first radio station owners "to appreciate its commercial potential and to mold it into a salable package" (Patoski, 1980, p. 101).

Whether any buyers were available was another matter. Al Lurie, then working as an account executive at a Dallas advertising agency, told of his clients' initial reluctance at buying advertising time on KLIF. They preferred to wait and see how the station performed, but Lurie "realized the impact KLIF was making . . . in Dallas" and persuaded them to take a chance. The "gamble certainly paid off," commented Lurie, "because KLIF went right to the top and got terrific results" ("Tribute," 1986). Edd Routt recalled his days as a KLIF sales representative having to overcome initial advertiser reluctance because of the station's young audience. "Nobody listens to that kid's stuff," the advertisers would say, and even the other Dallas radio stations "looked down their nose at us" (Routt, 1989). But the low regard from fellow broadcasters did not matter once KLIF's Top 40 became popular. "We were just killing them," Routt said of the competition. "We were just programming rings around them, outselling them" (Routt, 1989).

Gordon's ability to deliver listeners to his advertising clients was tied closely to his incessant need to program KLIF so that all who could would listen. As the McLendon stable of radio stations grew, Gordon spread among them his philosophy of filling the listener's need to be entertained and informed. "For to me," he once said, "the only thing that matters in radio is the size of the audience. . . . If . . . programming is the most important single factor in radio, we feel that we must have a continuing measurement of our audience, or lack of it. . . . We program by our ratings" (McLendon, 1958a, pp. 2–3).

Keeping KLIF's ratings high required feeding the musical needs of its listeners. And keeping in touch with the musical tastes of listeners was not done in a very scientific way, according to Gordon. "The very first way I remember," he said, "was we just called the local record stores and asked them what their top sellers were and would they number them. From that we came up with a consensus Top 40 and we weighed that against Billboard, which was the big magazine in the field at that time" ("The Top-40," n.d., pp. 21–24).

From an unscientific method of monitoring what records listeners were buying, Gordon developed a very specific music policy—"the first music policy in the history of man," asserted Chuck Blore (Hall and Hall, 1977, p. 180)—which indicated to disc jockeys just what types of records they could play on the air. Some latitude was given as to specific record titles that could be played, but all records had to be chosen from a playlist prepared by the KLIF program director. Certain types of records, such as classical, opera and country-western, were banned altogether. One of Bill Stewart's contributions to the KLIF Top 40 sound, as noted earlier, was to tighten considerably the record playlist so that disc jockeys had less and less freedom to air music of their own choosing (MacFarland, 1973, pp. 298–300).

The importance of the KLIF playlist could be seen in particular whenever the station chose to air a "pick hit," as a newly released record with a potentially good sound came to be called. "If a record was played on KLIF it was almost assured of being a smash hit all over the nation," said KLIF national operations director Ken Dowe (1989).

The one concession made to Bill Stewart's playlist control happened as a result of KLIF's determination to reach a more adult audience. Don Keyes saw a need for the station to back away from its rock 'n' roll music during the important 3 to 6 P.M. hours in order to attract the "homeward-bound traffic audience." Keyes therefore approached Gordon with a request that he be given the late afternoon announcing shift and allowed to program it the way he pleased. The 3 to 5 P.M. portion of the shift still would carry light rock music to accommodate teenagers returning home from school, but the 5 to 6 P.M. portion would be programmed for adults. The idea was a spectacular success. Keyes picked up 50 percent of the audience during his "drive time" shift, the highest share for any Dallas radio announcer to that point, and he was having a terrific time in the process. "I was having so much damn fun," said Keyes, "that when payday rolled around it always struck me as a surprise. I get paid, too? Gee whiz!" (Keyes, 1989).

Subtle changes in music policy continued to occur as years went by so that KLIF could adjust for listener needs and wants. By the 1960s the station's music had moved more toward what later would be called "adult contemporary" (Dowe, 1989).

The disc jockeys who played the music, who really were the spark or catalyst that made the programming work, had to be the best; Gordon insisted on that. KLIF "jocks" were undisputably in a class by themselves. Don Keyes, Kenny Sargent, Bruce Hayes, Bill Stewart, Gene Edwards, Larry Monroe and Jim Randolph have been mentioned already as having formed the vanguard of Top 40 disc jockeys who would lend their efforts toward building KLIF into America's leading radio station. Many others would follow, and each would carve a niche for himself in KLIF history. Most of their real names never were known to KLIF listeners, but their radio names ("noms de radio") were famous throughout Dallas. Among them were Charlie Brown and Irving Harrigan, who teamed up as Charlie and Harrigan; Johnny Dark, Jim O'Brian, Deano Day, Jimmy Rabbitt and Russ Knight, the Weird Beard ("KLIF DJs," 1970).

These disc jockeys more often than not were bigger than life. In many respects they did not just make KLIF, they *were* KLIF. Identities of person and station were inseparable. The same was true for disc jockeys at other McLendon Stations where Top 40 had been installed. Disc jockeys who had the good fortune to work at a McLendon Station took great pride in that fact. "We were all young fellas with young families, and we were all walkin' tall and walkin' proud," said Don Keyes (1989). There was "great esprit de corps" among McLendon Station disc jockeys, Keyes added (1989). Ken Dowe recalled that to be a KLIF disc jockey "was sort of like being a celebrity movie star" (Dowe, 1989).

To become a KLIF disc jockey was the dream of many Top 40 disc jockeys eager to make a name for themselves. Don Keyes told the story of his days as McLendon station national program director when he kept a roster of potential KLIF disc jockeys (called the "farm club") then working at other stations around the country. Many of the roster names came from tapes, called "air checks," that disc jockeys had made of their on-air performance and had sent to KLIF. Keyes said he listened to each tape and made notes about what he had heard. Keyes also traveled extensively to listen to on-air performances and to talk with disc jockeys about joining the KLIF team. His presence oftentimes caused quite a stir:

> When they heard Don Keyes was in town monitoring . . . they fell all over themselves to have a cup of coffee with me and be interviewed and keep them on my list, 'cause when the break came, I'd draw from the farm club. "It's time, it's time to come to Dallas to be on KLIF. . . . " It was obviously a promotion financially. But these little young egos, these 26 year old disc jockeys, it was a move up. Boy, in the industry to come to KLIF—that was heavy, heavy stuff. (Keyes, 1989)

Once a disc jockey worked at a McLendon Station, assuming he performed his job successfully, he generally had little trouble moving on from there whenever he chose. Edd Routt recalled how a disc jockey in KLIF's glory days could "run an ad in *Broadcasting* or *Sponsor* magazine, and he'd say 'McLendon-trained morning man seeks employment' and give a phone number. No problem. 'If he's McLendon-trained, we want him' " (Routt, 1989).

Gordon attempted to exact a pledge from any newly hired disc jockey that he would not work at a McLendon Station, taking advantage of the training and name recognition that he would receive, and then resign to pursue a job at a competing station (MacFarland, 1973, pp. 533–535). The pledge probably worked reasonably well, although some McLendon Station disc jockeys moved to competing stations and worked under different names. And McLendon Station disc jockeys regularly moved to stations in other markets. Chuck Blore, for instance, persuaded Bruce Hayes and Art Nelson from KLIF and Elliott Field from KILT to leave McLendon employment to help build the fortunes of KFWB in Los Angeles (Blore, 1990).

Other McLendon Station disc jockeys moved on to gain fame in television as well as radio. Gary Owens, for example, worked at KLIF, KILT and KTSA in the late 1950s before moving to Los Angeles and his role as the hand-cupped-behind-the-ear announcer on "Laugh-In" (Owens, 1990). Tom Snyder worked at the McLendon's Milwaukee station WRIT before eventually moving on to host a late-night talk show on NBC television (McLendon, 1978). And Rod Roddy, later to become the announcer for television's "The Price Is Right," also began his broadcasting career at KLIF. In fact, Roddy began working at the station in the late 1960s doing a talk show. Gordon shortly wrote Ken Dowe, then the KLIF program director, a memo commenting on Roddy's talent. "Dear Ken, regarding Rod Roddy," the memo read, "he is the most awful talk show personality I have ever heard, but I'll give you this. He is consistent in that he gets worse every day. Do something about him" ("From #1," 1987, pp. 8–9). Roddy did improve and ended up remaining at KLIF for two or three more years ("From #1," 1987, p. 9).

Besides himself and such right-hand persons as Don Keyes, Gordon sometimes dispatched other employees to search out and interview budding on-air talent. These station envoys were Gordon's "arms out reaching for people he wanted," said Les Vaughn (1989). Gordon never gave specific instructions on what to look for (Vaughn, 1989). Those qualities that made a disc jockey a potential McLendon Station employee never were spelled out in precise terms. But, Don Keyes felt that the characteristics of a McLendon Station disc jockey had to include "sophistication in a number of areas: the ability to ad lib, basically a good voice . . . not necessarily deep, preferably on the heavy side, but it didn't rule you out if you had a light voice and you were a good communicator; if you came out of that speaker like a real warm person, that was fine" (Keyes, 1989). Art Nelson was one such KLIF disc jockey who fit the McLendon style perfectly, according to Keyes:

> His voice came right out of the speaker at you. He was a fun companion to listen to as you drove along in your car. He was pleasant. He was happy, cheerful—never too much so, a pleasant companion, always the smile in the voice. I used to watch Art when I was a young jock starting out. Art would sit in a control room when a record's ending. He'd get up next to the mike and have his hand on the mike switch . . . a smile would break his face. And he cracked the mike [and] said, "This is KLIF in Dallas. . . ." And you could hear the smile in the voice. (Keyes, 1989)

While Gordon may not have indicated specific qualities he was looking for in McLendon Station disc jockeys, once inside the station, disc jockeys became well aware of Gordon's expectations. A 1955 written station policy at KLIF, for instance, reminded disc jockeys that the "first order of the day" was to "be brisk and bright":

> Don't laze along and be listless—sound peppy and alert and on the ball. . . . Sounding brisk and lively may call for saying things *faster*. Keep whatever you

> have to say short and informative. . . . Your last words can be overlapped by the music and vice versa. If you sound in a hurry, that's okay. (McLendon, 1955)

Other policy statements of this sort were to follow, some of them providing extensive details on disc jockey requirements and performance "do's and don'ts" (Keyes, 1961a). One in particular, issued by Gordon in 1959, bore this definition of a KLIF disc jockey:

> A KLIF disc jockey is: informative, or humorous, or he merely introduces the records. He *prepares* his show—and he prepares the material for his show. . . . The KLIF disc jockey is a *personality* disc jockey—an entertaining disc jockey—because he is *not* mechanical, he *does* have something to say, he *has* prepared, he is conscious of what the tradition of KLIF disc jockeys has been. . . .
>
> A KLIF disc jockey prepares—he reads the morning and afternoon newspapers, some magazines and books, comments briefly upon what he's reading and seen, or has something amusing to say—in short, he is *interesting* to listen to. (McLendon, 1959g)

Preparation was mandatory with Gordon. He insisted that his disc jockeys spend at least one hour preparing for every hour they were to spend on the air in order to "acclimate the mind to the program material," said Gary Owens (1990). Gordon also believed in rigorous critiques of on-air performances, especially those of his disc jockeys with morning shifts. Whoever held the morning post held the key shift of the programming day, in Gordon's view. "As far as the radio station was concerned," Ken Dowe said, Gordon "thought as the morning show went, so went the rest of the radio station and so went the ratings" (Dowe, 1989).

One idea that Gordon had become fascinated with for morning programming was a two-man disc jockey team. He and Don Keyes had picked up the idea from listening to air checks of a morning show on New York's WNEW featuring a two-man team. Gordon wanted to copy the show on KLIF. So, with disc jockey Ron Chapman donning the name Irving Harrigan and Jack Woods donning the name Charlie Brown, the "Charlie & Harrigan" show was launched (Keyes, 1989). The date was sometime in 1959 (Drape, 1986, p. 10A). In order to fashion precisely what it was that "Charlie & Harrigan" should be, Gordon required that Don Keyes record the program every morning. As soon as Chapman's and Woods's shift ended at 9 A.M., both of them along with Keyes listened to the recording and critiqued what they heard—"polishing, honing, distilling the show down to the ultimate" (Keyes, 1989). The result, said Keyes, "was a dynamite two-man morning show. It just owned the market" (Keyes, 1989). Others attempted to copy the program, but the chemistry that developed between Ron Chapman and Jack Woods and the wry, topical humor around which the "Charlie & Harrigan" show was based was not easily transferred to other markets (Keyes, 1989).

"Charlie & Harrigan" had run its course by the mid-1960s when Bill Stewart, who by then was KLIF program director for a second time, convinced Gordon to let Ken Dowe take the morning shift as a solo act. Dowe, however, would carry to the air with him a comic alter ego character named "Granny Emma," whose voice he would supply. Gordon agreed to the idea, and Ken Dowe took over the reins of the 6 to 9 A.M. weekday shift on KLIF. Following the same routine that Don Keyes had developed but without a tape recorder, Bill Stewart and Ken Dowe met in a local cafe just after nine o'clock every morning to critique Dowe's performance. From that very thorough critique, Ken Dowe said that Bill Stewart "taught me to be morning show guy. It was largely through his instruction that not only did we continue the ratings the morning show had held, but we actually had bested them" (Dowe, 1989).

KLIF PROMOTIONS

KLIF disc jockeys helped set the station apart from its competitors in the market. Even more important in establishing KLIF's own identity, though, were its promotions. Bart McLendon said that his father

> always thought that all radio stations of the same format played basically the same music. That was 90 percent of their product. And therefore it was the other 10 percent that would differentiate one radio station from another. And if you did a better job with that other 10 percent than any other radio station, the other 90 percent basically being equal, then you're the winner. (Bart McLendon, 1990)

That other 10 percent meant station promotion, a programming ingredient for which Gordon developed a mastery (McLendon, 1990). Many of his promotions would extend far beyond the ordinary: "they were stunts, entertaining shows in their own right" (MacFarland, 1973, p. 311). The promotions allowed all McLendon Stations to be "seen" as well as heard, and, after all, what better use of one of the best advertising media ever invented than in advertising itself ("Radio in Transition," 1957, p. 40).

The value that Gordon saw in station promotion, especially the contests and giveaways, were that "first, they stimulate *talk*, and second, lend an atmosphere of excitement and sparkle to the station" (McLendon, 1957a). However, Gordon felt that "a promotion was useless unless the product that you were trying to attract people to was a good one" (MacFarland, 1973, p. 392).

The initial idea to promote KLIF as well as other McLendon Stations did not spring directly from the genius of Gordon McLendon; rather the idea came from C. E. Hooper of Hooper Ratings fame. During a conversation between the two, Gordon recalled Hooper telling him that he was doing everything right at KLIF with one exception: "You're not promoting correctly. You've really got to keep promotions going all the time" ("The Top-40," n.d., p. 24).

So, once the promotions started, said Gordon, they ran "as fast as we thought of them" (Weiss, 1982, p. 15A). Don Keyes recalled that promotions were running "constantly." McLendon Station program directors "were expected to have a major promotion in the wings and a minor promotion at all times," said Keyes (1989). The barrage of promotions met its objective quite well. They were always attention-getters, and they always stimulated talk about the McLendon Stations (McLendon, 1978).

One of Gordon's first big promotional giveaways was the KLIF Great Treasure Hunt. The object of the hunt was to find a $50,000 check that had been signed by Gordon and buried in a soft drink bottle with only the bottle cap showing. Gordon had paid Lloyds of London $1,250 for insurance that required payment by Lloyds of 90 percent of the check's value if found. A local insurance company was paid to bury the check. The contest commenced in December 1956, and clues were read on KLIF twice daily as to the possible whereabouts of the check ("Return," 1956). Gordon said that he did not know where the bottle was buried himself and did not care to know.

The odds against the bottle and the check being found were infinitesimal, according to Gordon, primarily because the clues to their location were intentionally bad (McLendon, 1978). Nonetheless, someone indeed did find the bottle and check. Gordon said that he would never forget when and how the discovery was made. Miserable weather greeted the final day of the contest. Thunderstorms were drenching the Dallas area, and Gordon felt reassured that no one would be outside treasure hunting. But he was wrong. He was notified during an afternoon phone call that the $50,000 had been found. Gordon's response: "Oh, you've got to be kidding" ('The Top-40," n.d., p. 24). KLIF gained the distinction not only of being the first U.S. radio station to conduct a $50,000 treasure hunt but also of being the first to give the money away ("Earlybirds," 1962, p. 35).

Regardless of the loss of money—more from Lloyd's of London's pockets than from Gordon's—the Great Treasure Hunt paid off with spectacular publicity dividends for KLIF. A by-product, however, was some negative publicity about overzealous treasure seekers who were digging up lawns all over Dallas. Gordon said that "stories about the damage that was done were a bit exaggerated" and besides, announcements had been made on KLIF at various intervals indicating that the buried treasure was not on hospital grounds or private property or places that KLIF would not want disturbed (McLendon, 1978).

An even earlier promotion gimmick was the Money Drop giveaway. This involved no contest; all the giveaway recipients had to do was to wait for balloons to be dropped from a window of the Adolphus-Baker Hotel in downtown Dallas. Dollar bills were attached to 250 of the balloons. One week prior to the drop, five announcements per day were aired on KLIF promoting the event (Picture caption, 1954). The announcement simply told "listeners to gather at Elm and Akard streets at five o'clock on Good Friday and 'watch the skies' " (Patoski, 1980, p. 167). Some two hours before the "official" balloon drop time, a crowd that later grew to about ten thousand persons began gathering on the street corner. The resulting traffic disruption and the need to maintain order soon brought the event to the attention of a sizable force of Dallas policemen (Picture caption, 1954). Bill Stewart, instigator of the balloon drop stunt, said that he had to sneak out of town to avoid being arrested (Patoski, 1980, p. 167).

Don Keyes told of another successful promotion—the School Spirit Contest—that nonetheless had an unintended result. The contest's objective was to solicit petitions signed by Dallas area high school students. The high school submitting the most names to KLIF was declared to have the most school spirit and was awarded a free record hop hosted by KLIF disc jockeys. Trouble was, students became so excited about the contest that efforts to seek petition signers resulted in disrupted classrooms. The Dallas school superintendent finally called KLIF to ask that the contest be stopped. It was stopped, but the record hop prize still was awarded. And, of course, resulting publicity gained the station far more mileage out of the promotion than it ever expected (Keyes, 1989).

Contests were especially effective promotions. And the most popular type of contest appeared to be the mystery contest. A collection of McLendon promotion campaign files stored at Texas Tech University's Southwest Collection contains sixteen separate files describing mystery contests that either ran or were at least considered at one time for running on one or more of the McLendon Stations. Titles of some of the sixteen include "Mystery Caller," "Mystery Hi School Hero," "Mystery Location," "Mystery Neighbor," "Mystery Street," "Mystery Telephone Number," "Mystery Teen," "Mystery Voices" and "Mystery Walker."

Winners of McLendon Station contests could expect to receive either a normal prize, such as money, or something a bit more unusual that Gordon and his staff would invent. For example, KLIF once gave away "radio's biggest prize," which turned out to be a mountain—one acre in size—in the Texas hill country (Weiss, 1982, p. 15A). That, of course, probably carried some real estate value. And all the free pizzas, tickets and record albums awarded by the station also carried some value. But there was no monetary value, just laughs, in the "South Sea island" (which was actually a papier-mâché version of paradise), and a "live baby" (which turned out to be a live baby pig) that KLIF dispensed to amused listeners (Patoski, 1980, p. 167). And in a reverse twist KLIF once offered twenty-five words or less to listeners who sent the station $125,000 in cash ("Zany," 1961, p. 131). The most astounding prizes offered by the McLendon Stations were tickets to the moon. The tickets were awarded in 1959 and were redeemable on March 15, 1987. Sure enough, when the 1987 redemption date rolled around, ticket holders for the moon flight began appearing to collect on their prize ("Radio Days," 1987, pp. 1, 22).

Gordon generally unloaded a promotional barrage on listeners whenever announcing the format change of a newly acquired McLendon Station. Promotions for the first few weeks of the new format's unveiling were planned well in advance and with precise instructions as to their time and method of implementation (MacFarland, 1973, pp. 470–472).

In the same manner that he announced the arrival of a new format, Gordon also used his promotional ingenuity to publicize the arrival of new KLIF disc jockeys. Jimmy Rabbit, for example, was welcomed to Dallas by overturned cars alongside the freeways with "I flipped for Jimmy Rabbitt" painted on the bottoms. "Everyone coming into town—or leaving—got the message. Rabbitt was a celebrity before he even hopped past the city limits sign" (Hall and Hall, 1977, p. 135). In another stunt,

> a man appeared on a Dallas street corner giving out one and five dollar bills, and occasionally a ten or a twenty. Local newspapers featured stories of the "eccentric millionaire." He made the news on TV. You can imagine how embarrassed the newspaper and TV reporters were when the "millionaire" announced live on TV that he was the new disk jockey for the morning show on Gordon McLendon's KLIF. (Hall and Hall, 1977, p. 135)

Other KLIF promotions only had as their objective getting the station's call letters before the public, albeit in a unique and sometimes offbeat manner. A "beautiful blond in a shocking pink swimsuit" was hired to sit in a lounge chair under a huge KLIF billboard and to wave at automobile passengers as they sped past on busy Central Expressway. Gordon used that same stretch of highway to hire a KLIF sign carrier whose objective (apart from promoting the station) was to break the long-distance walking record. However, "the man's feet gave out long before he approached the record" (Tatum, 1984). Another promotion took a jab at the tiny space given the KLIF program log in the Dallas newspapers. Listeners were asked to write the station explaining why they liked the way the logs were listed. Writers of the top fifty letters selected received magnifying glasses "to help them locate the program logs" ("Seek," 1955).

One promotion stunt that Bill Stewart claimed was quite possibly the most effective one ever attempted at KLIF was the "Oops, sorry" newspaper apology (MacFarland, 1973, p. 393). The genesis of the apology came as KLIF personnel were attempting to learn how best to air on-the-scene reports from the station's new mobile news units. One evening in early

January 1954, Stewart and newsman Dick Smith were traveling in one of the units monitoring the police radio when they heard a call for police assistance for an armed robbery. Stewart and Smith sped to the scene and were able to get a live, on-the-scene account of what happened from the robbery victim. The victim told his story in a highly excited manner complete with several expletives that were taboo for radio.

Radio listeners hearing such language normally would have been expected to light up the KLIF telephone switchboard, but the station received only six calls of complaint. Stewart, surprised at the low number of calls, decided to take advantage of the live coverage mishap in such a way as to promote KLIF by piquing interest in what was happening at the station (MacFarland, 1973, pp. 393–397). So, he ran the following in the local Dallas newspapers:

> OOPS, SORRY
>
> KLIF wishes to offer this apology for the unfortunate language used on an interview during an on-the-scene broadcast of an armed robbery Friday night at 8:44 p.m. To all of the many people who called the station, KLIF would like to say that we're sorry. But in covering news on the scene as we do, the remarks of a witness, who may be in a highly emotional state, can not be governed. However, in all humility—KLIF tenders this apology. (Advertisement, 1954)

As a result of the "Oops, Sorry" item, Bill Stewart claimed, some six thousand people called KLIF asking what kind of indiscretion had occurred. "And that was what made the station. Overnight," Stewart said. "That was *the* thing that made the station" (MacFarland, 1973, p. 395).

Speculation arose as to the veracity of the "Oops, sorry" claims, especially after another KLIF "Oops, sorry" apology appeared in the *Dallas Morning News* in September 1959. Coincidentally, nearly identical "Oops, sorry" apologies from McLendon Stations were to appear in Louisville (WAKY), San Antonio (KTSA), Shreveport (KEEL) and Houston (KILT) newspapers within the following six weeks. Managers of all the stations swore that an on-air indiscretion really had occurred ("Fanfare," 1959), but it appeared more likely that the "Oops, sorry" apologies were really McLendon promotional gimmicks that consistently attracted plenty of attention whenever and wherever used.

Not all of Gordon's promotional efforts were designed to come on like gangbusters. Many were quite simple in their design and appeal. One such variety of promotions came to be called "sparklers." Don Keyes described sparklers as "little things that gave a sparkle to the format" (Keyes, 1989) and that ingratiated a radio station to the community. Sparklers also served a commercial purpose, as illustrated by the "secret word" campaign, in which names of Dallas business persons whom the KLIF sales staff wanted as advertising clients might be identified as KLIF's "secret word" every hour for an entire day. The idea was that persons whose names were aired would hear about it so much from their friends that they would be convinced of KLIF's reach within the Dallas market and therefore would be receptive to buying time on the station. The ploy usually worked extremely well. "It costs you zero, and the impact at the end of the day is incredible, particularly when you're playing games with a client, having a tough time selling him," said Don Keyes (1989). The "secret word" sparklers paid other dividends as well. They helped convince the business community that not just teenagers listened to KLIF. Adults also were listening (MacFarland, 1973, p. 417).

Gordon never tired of creating unique promotions for KLIF. Some did not work, and some were never tried. One of the unworkable promotions was occasioned by KLIF's boosting its power to 50,000 watts on February 9, 1959. This was the maximum power allowed by the FCC and would extend KLIF's daytime coverage to most of north-central Texas (McLendon, 1959c). To celebrate the power increase, Gordon asked Dallas Mayor R. L. Thornton to name a city street after the station (McLendon, 1958e). The mayor replied that naming or changing the name of Dallas streets was done only by petition of property owners on that street. And since Gordon's promotion campaign announcing KLIF's increased power would begin in January, Mayor Thornton did not believe that there was time to initiate any new street naming effort (Thornton, 1959).

Constant McLendon Station promotion had its cost. Anywhere from $3,000 to $4,000 a month was spent on KLIF promotions alone during the first few years of Top 40 radio (Weiss, 1982, p. 15A). By 1961, Gordon was estimating that promotion expenses were running from 5 to 10 percent of the three to four million dollars in gross revenues of the seven McLendon Stations ("Zany," 1961, p. 131).

Most promotion ideas, especially for KLIF, were Gordon's. Sitting at his desk with his ever-present yellow legal pad, Gordon would sketch out the promotion idea and how it was to be implemented and then let his staff produce it (Keyes, 1989). Others were free to contribute promotion ideas, and some of the better ones came from creative minds like Bill Stewart's (MacFarland, 1973, pp. 416–417). As the McLendon Station group expanded, Gordon initiated a newsletter in which station managers and program directors, who were required to create local promotion campaigns, could share their ideas with other station personnel within the McLendon family (Keyes, 1989).

McLendon Station promotions often became controversial, and in some instances even raised questions as to their propriety or legality. McLendon Station attorney Marcus Cohn said, for example, that he sometimes would receive three or four phone calls a day related to McLendon promotion matters—generally as to whether or not some idea was acceptable (Cohn,

1989). Along with the positive publicity that most often resulted from a promotion campaign, there sometimes also resulted some negative publicity. Unfortunately for Gordon, news of promotion campaigns gone awry most often reached the FCC. And when other Top 40 stations around the country copied the problematical promotions, as was often happening, the FCC's glare became even more intense.

Through the early to mid-1960s the FCC had received complaints about various station promotions. "Among the adverse consequences of some contests and promotions which have come to our attention," read a 1966 FCC policy statement, "were: alarm to the public about imaginary dangers; infringement of public or private property rights or the right of privacy; annoyance or embarrassment to innocent parties; hazards to life and health; and traffic congestion or other public disorder requiring diversion of police from other duties" (*Contests and Promotions*, 1966, p. 464). The FCC statement emphasized "that the carrying of contests and promotions which adversely affect the public interest cannot be condoned" (*Contests and Promotions*, 1966, p. 464).

The FCC's actions deflated much of the enthusiasm that Gordon had had earlier for station promotions. This single factor probably more than any other brought the rip-roaring days of Top 40 radio promotion to an end (MacFarland, 1973, p. 436). Radio promotion itself would not end, of course. But what listeners were subjected to henceforth would be diminished numbers and milder versions of earlier promotion campaigns.

KLIF AND LOCAL NEWS

Gordon's success with Top 40, especially with the promotional accent he had given the format, likely would have left an ordinary person contented. But Gordon was not satisfied. "The formula was hardly a secret in a few months," he remarked. "What was to prevent imitation? What would happen when the public was surfeited with stunts and ballyhoo and giveaways and the frill of promotion?" ("Earlybirds," 1962, p. 36).

"We thought we had the answer—and we did," said Gordon. While "promotion by means of giveaways or stunts was . . . one way of bringing excitement and vivacity to a radio station . . . news, properly done, could lend the same sort of sparkle. Colorful coverage of a continuing news story," suggested Gordon, "could produce more stimulation among listeners than the biggest contest or stunts" ("Earlybirds," 1962, p. 36).

Gordon later underscored the above, saying: "Our objective at KLIF was to create a station of such sparkle and immediacy that you couldn't turn away. . . . We concentrated heavily on local news. . . . It was no gimmick by any means. We were reporting pretty solid news" (Weiss, 1982, p. 15A). Don Keyes said that Gordon was very proud of the KLIF news department "because it gave a lustre of respectability to a jukebox" (Keyes, 1989).

Some even have said that news programming was Gordon's "major contribution to Top 40 and radio in general. . . . He realized early that radio could capture an immediacy in news that television, at that time, could not compete with" (Hall and Hall, 1977, p. 17). Thus, the KLIF promotion mill created the following station ID, extolling radio's virtues over television: "This is KLIF . . . news while it's news and not newsreels" (McLendon, 1957b, p. 2).

Other KLIF promotional announcements for news were meant to emphasize the station's superiority not only to television but to newspapers as well. Note in particular the following abbreviated announcement that aired in 1955:

> When you take the time to read the front page of your newspaper, do you have the feeling that you've heard all that news before? Well, it probably *is* old news to you—you've heard it on radio, and we hope on KLIF. News on KLIF is many hours ahead of any newspaper. By listening to KLIF, you truly get tomorrow's newspaper now. (McLendon Corporation, 1955)

Gordon seemed far less concerned about competing with television than about competing with the print media. He was particularly chagrined at the role that many of his brethren in the radio business had allowed themselves to play with regard to their newspaper competitors. "Too many radio station owners are themselves more impressed with the power of the printed word than with their own spoken medium, which can be even more powerful," Gordon told a group of broadcasters in 1957. He continued:

> Some have shied away from the battle for fear of personal attack, not thinking that they themselves have a medium of defense if needed. But for whatever reason . . . radio has refused to take up the responsibilities of adulthood, refused the exciting challenge of newspapers, has allowed its shining future to drain away into a jukebox, and has contented itself with nourishing the most absurd and monumental inferiority complex ever to perplex an inanimate object. (McLendon, 1957c, pp. 1–2)

Gordon was realistic enough to know that KLIF was not going to run Dallas newspapers out of business, but he felt the station's news coverage at least had reduced newspaper readership. And whenever KLIF news personnel could, they were instructed by Gordon to stick a little competitive barb into their newscasts, such as "Tokyo—here's a story that you won't read in the newspapers for 24 hours" (McLendon, 1957b, p. 3).

Moreover, said Gordon, "Whenever we find in either of the local newspapers a story of any real local interest which has not appeared on KLIF hours or a full day before, our Managing Editor's job is in jeopardy" (McLendon, 1957b, p. 5). The heavy emphasis placed on local news coverage was something that Gordon felt was KLIF's greatest achievement. Even the faraway *New York Post* had taken note of that fact, reporting at one point that "KLIF in Dallas has better local news coverage than all New York radio and television stations combined" (McLendon, 1957c, p. 5).

Such highly touted local news programming obviously had a public service value. But there were other values as well. News of the sort carried by KLIF was, after all, the Top 40 station's one program element that was most certain to attract adults (MacFarland, 1973, p. 481). Gordon had said that his idea in changing KLIF's format originally was not only to play Top 40 music, but also to "capture the audience up to age 39 or 40" (McDougal, 1984, p. 19). News afforded him that opportunity. News actually was one of the few sure links that Gordon felt KLIF had with adults. Teens, he felt, mentally tuned out during newscasts (McLendon, 1962g).

Another value that came with having a respected news operation was "in the prestige and *believability* which competent news coverage lends to your station. If you do a top news job, listeners are just naturally and instinctively going to feel more confidence in your station and in the advertisers that they hear on your station," Gordon asserted (McLendon, 1957c, p. 6).

Gordon referred to his "aggressive news policy" when talking about KLIF news coverage (McLendon, 1956, p. 81), and the punch that his newscasts carried followed through on this aggressive theme. "The news had to be exciting," and KLIF "had to be first" with the breaking stories. "Get it first, get it fast, try to get it right, make it dramatic, which is exactly what television does today," said Edd Routt (1989). The newscast lead-in was itself produced to make the listener sit up and take notice. One observer described the lead-in as "often more exciting than the news itself" (Hitt, 1979). Edd Routt called it "bombastic." It was made to sound as though the approaching newscast were "the second coming. 'You're about to hear KLIF local news. For god's sake, listen!' " was the lead-in's message, said Routt (1989).

From the lead-in there followed four and one half minutes of news, which Gordon decreed would contain no fewer than twenty stories (Weiss, 1982, p. 15A). This "new idea in radio news," inaugurated at KLIF in December 1953, meant that the station aired news at the top of every hour, with a one-minute news headline supplement on the half-hour (Sigma Delta Chi, 1954, pp. 2–3). But once other Dallas stations began airing news at the same time, Gordon adopted the "20/20 News" concept, in which newscasts aired both at twenty minutes after and twenty minutes before the hour. Gordon eventually would try the "20/20 Double Power News" concept, where two newspersons took turns "reading reports at breakneck speed" (Patoski, 1980, p. 167).

News was not a "rip and read process" at KLIF. Gordon wanted his news staff to be qualified reporters (McLendon, 1957c, p. 7). And there was little doubt that KLIF reporters were up to the task of competing with news personnel from any of the other Dallas media. That was true for other

McLendon Stations as well. San Antonio's KTSA and Houston's KILT, for instance, both had very active and very capable news departments (Keyes, 1989).

During the early years, Edd Routt served as the KLIF news department's managing editor. Under his supervision was a staff comprised of "two desk men, and three outside leg men," as Gordon described them (McLendon, 1956, p. 80). Other managing editors and news directors followed Routt's lead, and eventually the news staff grew to include all station personnel, regardless of department. That was "SOP—standard operating procedure," said Routt. "Everybody was expected to keep up with things. If you ran across a two-car collision anyplace in Dallas, call the station, and we'll get something on it" (Routt, 1989).

Gordon himself was, of course, in direct charge of the KLIF news department (Sigma Delta Chi, 1954, p. 3). He made his journalistic presence known not just in setting station news policy but as KLIF's editorial voice. Gordon in fact pioneered the delivery of daily radio editorials following the FCC's decision allowing broadcasters that privilege. So extensive and important were the many editorials that Gordon wrote and voiced through the years that a later chapter of this book has been devoted to them exclusively.

Syndicated news commentaries of Harry Flannery, John T. Flynn and Drew Pearson, along with the Hollywood gossip commentary of Jimmy Fidler, were inserted into KLIF newscasts during the 1950s (Sigma Delta Chi, 1954, p. 3). Gordon was particularly enamored of gossip material. At one point every KLIF newscast had to end with a Hollywood gossip story. Gordon hired a writer to do nothing but to scan all the gossip magazines and scandal sheets and to write a thirty-second "kicker" story highlighting the most scintillating gossip tidbits of the day (Routt, 1989).

Among his contributions to coverage of local news and public affairs, Gordon chalked up an impressive array of firsts or near firsts. Besides leading the way in broadcast editorials, he saw to it that KLIF was "the first station in Dallas to offer sustained coverage of election returns; the first to do continuous coverage of breaking news events; and the first outlet to send out mobile news units" (Eberly, 1982, p. 208).

The KLIF mobile news units deserve more than just passing mention. The idea for equipping a vehicle with a two-way radio to allow on-the-scene reports from remote locations originated with Les Vaughn (Vaughn, 1989). The first such mobile news unit created by Vaughn was a 1954 fire-engine-red Ford V8 Courier combination van/station wagon that contained nearly four thousand dollars of short-wave radio equipment (Sigma Delta Chi, 1954, p. 4). The KLIF mobile unit "gave the station a visible presence around town. Since many stations watched and imitated McLendon, news trucks, news vans, and news cruisers became the rage, especially in the Midwest" (Fornatale and Mills, 1980, p. 98).

KLIF eventually had two active mobile units and a third reserve unit "roving the city at all hours to report news events direct from the scene" (McLendon, 1956, p. 80). Mobile unit reporters were allowed to break into KLIF programming as often as necessary with on-the-spot news coverage (McLendon, 1956, p. 80). So extensive were mobile unit reports that there were times when reporters in one unit would interrupt reporters in another unit who already were on the air (McLendon, 1957b, p. 5).

Edd Routt recalled that any mobile unit news report was considered something special. On-air announcements to alert listeners of an upcoming mobile unit report were produced accordingly. "The most famous," said Routt, "was 'First news first,' and then a siren, 'KLIF now takes you to the scene of a *major* news story.' Sometimes it was a shooting, sometimes it was a fatality, and sometimes it was just a fender bender that we probably emphasized a little too much" (Routt, 1989).

Besides the siren used in the on-air announcement, Gordon also tried to persuade Dallas city officials to allow him to equip KLIF mobile news units with sirens and flashing red lights. City officials balked at going that far, but Gordon nonetheless required that his mobile news crews make every effort to cover any breaking story and to get to the scene of a story as quickly as possible. According to Les Vaughn, whenever Gordon said, " 'Go get it.' We did it." As a result, KLIF was constantly having to pay traffic citations for speeding or other violations that occurred as a result of mobile news unit personnel doing what Gordon had ordered them to do (Vaughn, 1989).

There was a lighter side to the KLIF mobile news unit story that has to do with radio's ability sometimes to play small deceptions on the public, even though the public probably would not have been at all bothered by the truth. As it happened, KLIF never had more than three mobile news units, all of which were designated by different sets of numbers. These numbers were not simply 1, 2 and 3, but rather mobile unit #4, mobile unit #7, mobile unit #9, etc. And the designations changed daily. Mobile unit #4 on one day might become mobile unit #8 the next. Or perhaps the number would change at different times on the same day. All the changing numbers made it seem that KLIF "had vast numbers of cars running around the streets" ("The Top-40" n.d., p. 24). Whatever the public's perception, the KLIF mobile news units did their job in spectacular fashion.

Gordon scored another news first of a very unique nature in February 1962, when he replaced the local hourly newscasts of all McLendon Stations with newscasts directly from Radio Moscow. Shortwave English language versions of Radio Moscow newscasts—112 in all—were aired without commentary (McLendon Corporation, 1962). "Most listeners will be hearing for the first time the unrelenting stream of lies and invective which Moscow spreads like a red stain over all the English-speaking world," said Gordon in announcing the broadcasts (McLendon, 1962a).

Gordon and his staff had been planning the Radio Moscow experiment for several months. Cloaked under a veil of secrecy and code-named 'Operation Matthew,' the experiment's progress was relayed to McLendon Station managers by numerous confidential memos (Keyes, 1961b, 1961c, 1961d, 1962). Gordon purposely did not notify the FCC of his Radio Moscow intentions, but he did notify the White House. When the FCC learned of the plan and began raising questions about it, Gordon simply referred the commission to members of the presidential staff who already had given Operation Matthew their wholehearted endorsement (McDougal, 1984, p. 19). Any restrictions the FCC might have considered placing on the Radio Moscow broadcasts thus were stopped in their tracks by a higher authority.

Gordon said that his stations had received "thousands of letters [expressing] gratitude and incredulity at what they had heard" (McLendon, 1962b, p. 2). What's more, said Gordon, "Foreign press reaction was astonishing. Newspapers, such as the Paris edition of the *Herald Tribune*, Stockholm's *Aftonbladet*, the Rome *Daily American*, the *Berliner Zeitung*, Paris's *Ce Soir*, and more than 150 U.S. dailies gave it extensive and mostly first-page attention" (McLendon, 1962b, p. 2).

The one area in which McLendon Stations might have been expected to excel, if only by tradition, was in sports coverage. But, Gordon had determined that his radio stations would be limited to providing sports news and very little play-by-play coverage of anything. He was quite serious about his stations being the sports news authority in their communities, and issued elaborate policies on how disc jockeys and news personnel were to handle sports information. Play-by-play coverage, however, would be allowed only in cases of major events that were generating plenty of public interest (Harper, 1986, pp. 49–50).

Gordon made at least two exceptions to his play-by-play rule. He did carry the Saturday night football games of Louisiana State University on KLIF, perhaps in deference to his father-in-law, former Louisiana Governor James Noe (Strickland, 1959). The second exception came at the urging of Gordon's good friend Clint Murchison. When Murchison organized the Dallas Cowboys professional football team in 1960, he asked Gordon to carry the Cowboys' games on KLIF for the wide exposure they would receive. Gordon complied (Miller, 1987). The Dallas Cowboys remained a regular fixture on KLIF until the end of the 1971 football season (Bart McLendon, 1991).

6 *McLendon Station Group: Acquisition and Management*

Gordon's genius for promotional wizardry put KLIF on the map, but his attention could not be confined exclusively to the one station, for he and B. R. already were at work in the mid-1950s building one of the premier independent radio station groups in the United States. The nucleus for the group was in place with McLendon ownership of stations in Houston (KLBS) and El Paso (KELP) to add to the KLIF flagship station. Subsequent station acquisitions would soon stretch the group from coast to coast, with outlets in most of the major U.S. broadcasting markets.

The corporate title under which this formidable array of stations first came into existence was Trinity Broadcasting. However, by 1956 that title gave way to the McLendon Investment Corporation shortened later to McLendon Corporation ("Trinity," 1956), and stations that were part of the corporation's group were known far and wide simply as the McLendon Stations (Group Ownership, 1961/62–1973).

Just how many stations the McLendons owned is a matter of some debate. The FCC, whose records on such matters should be accurate, said in a 1969 report that the McLendons had acquired a total of twenty-five radio and television stations "during the span of their existence as broadcasters" (*City of Camden*, 1969b, p. 429). Since records show no more station acquisitions after 1969, the FCC's twenty-five facility count should stand. Reports showing different totals, such as one in 1979 that placed only sixteen stations (radio and television) in the McLendon's possession (McInnis, 1979, p. 5), may have failed to account for the combination AM/FM stations that existed in several markets.

Adding somewhat to the confusion, too, were the station call letter changes that Gordon made, particularly when putting a newly acquired station on the air or when changing the format of an existing McLendon Station. And then there were the many associations that Gordon had with stations either only partly owned by the McLendon Corporation or that had a special sales or consulting arrangement with the McLendons. Finally, there were those stations that Gordon and B. R. had made arrangements to purchase but whose final acquisition for one reason or another fell through (*City of Camden*, 1969b, p. 435).

Regardless of the total number of stations owned by the McLendons or the total number of stations with which Gordon had a business association, the role that many of these radio stations played in the industry's history is unique. Through these stations, Gordon exhibited format innovations that went far beyond just Top 40. He was not always successful with the formats he invented, but he succeeded more often than he failed in injecting excitement and interest wherever a McLendon Station appeared.

Several of the more notable McLendon format experiments will be examined in detail in the following chapter. This chapter will concentrate on the organizational and management foundation of the McLendon Station group.

STATION ACQUISITION POLICY

With the exception of KLIF and KELP-TV, all of the radio and television stations acquired by Gordon and B. R. were operating prior to their purchase. KLIF, of course, was built from the ground up. The decision to purchase a particular station came only after the McLendons' decision to move into a market. And choice of market was conditioned on the predicted impact that a McLendon Station would have there. The basic acquisition procedure, explained Gordon, was first to investigate the radio programming already available in the market. If listeners were being served adequately by existing stations, there generally would be no reason to establish a McLendon Station in that market. "But," said Gordon, "where we find an opening—a void—that enables us to offer a substantial number of people a new programming service or a better programming service than that then existent in the community, we go in" (McLendon, 1969a).

Gordon asserted that he could "never be anything else but a program man" (McLendon, 1969d, p 2), and it was in this one element that he obviously keyed his every move in buying a new station. "I have never bought a radio station for other than one reason: because I believed I could improve its programming and make it a success," Gordon once said. Moreover, he continued, "I have never bought a successful station. I have always bought sick stations, stations sick because of their sick programming, and because of their sick programming, sick in sales" (McLendon, 1969d, p. 2). And what did he do time after time with these ailing stations once they were in the McLendon fold? He "phenomenally [built] them to top status" (Barker, 1957, p. 52).

Gordon also was not married to his most successful format, Top 40. Whenever he and B. R. moved into a market to develop a new radio station, Gordon was willing and ready to install whatever format he felt might win an audience. That could involve changing a format completely, radically altering an existing format, or inventing a new format from scratch. Gordon was up to doing any of the three. Common sense and something he called "the economic law of utility" guided Gordon's format decisions as he entered a new market. "You must discover what has the maximum utility for that market, whether it is good music or Chinese soap opera," he said ("Zany," 1961, p. 131).

Bill Stubblefield, a longtime associate of Gordon's who was instrumental in selecting many of the McLendon Stations, said that "Gordon had a preconceived idea every time we bought a station as to what we would do, but if it didn't start working on the profit-and-loss statement pretty quickly, we'd change it" (MacFarland, 1973, pp. 269–270). Generally, Gordon was correct in his assessment of programming needs that would spell success—and usually quick success—for a new radio station. But, he was guilty occasionally of exporting formats that had proved popular in one market into a market where there was little chance of survival. One striking example of Gordon's miscalculation in this respect was his effort to install the beautiful music format that had been developed for KABL in Oakland/San Francisco to WYSL in Buffalo, New York. The format flopped in its new home (MacFarland, 1973, p. 273). Gordon quickly dropped the unsuccessful format and replaced it with a more successful one.

Once Gordon had assessed the shortcomings of his competitors in a new market and had determined what direction his own format would take, he lost no time whatsoever in constructing and introducing that format. His method was not to phase in his new format subtly but rather to hit the market like a blitzkrieg. Don Keyes emphasized the point in the context of his role in implementing a format change at the newly acquired McLendon Station, WAKY, in Louisville:

> We were there to come in and invade Louisville, Kentucky. And that was . . . probably the biggest success story of the whole chain. We went from zero to a 60 percent Hooper Rating in two months. Absolutely destroyed people. When we went in, there was an old-timer called WINN. They were the music station for Louisville, Kentucky. They were playing fifteen minute segments of a given artist. That was the state of Louisville radio 1957 or 1958. Fifteen minutes of Kaye Starr, fifteen minutes of Frank Sinatra, fifteen minutes of Montovani. That was it. . . . And we went on the air with the usual flying circus. It was devastating, just devastating. (Keyes, 1989)

Edd Routt described the impact that a "McLendon invasion" style of format change had on employees, both old and new, at a McLendon Station. Gordon would gather "six guys in a motel room and get them hired and signed up and briefed and the next day the station would go from one format to the Top 40 format. And when you came to work your [final] check was waiting for you if you were a jock, and they didn't happen to think you'd fit into it" (Routt, 1989).

What about competitors in markets where the McLendons acquired a new station? How did they regard the arrival of a new McLendon Station? According to Routt,

> Whenever a market heard that McLendon was coming, everybody got shaky because they knew what was going to happen. He'd come in there with mobile news units; he'd come in with promotions that they could only dream about; he'd spend money; and he'd capture the market. And he did it time, after time, after time. (Routt, 1989)

Routt told of how news that the McLendons had purchased a radio station in one particular city affected the owner of the city's only Top 40 station. Before Gordon even got to town, Routt said, "the Top 40 [owner] had changed to country, 'cause he knew McLendon would destroy him" (Routt, 1989).

Doctoring the programming and changing the staff of a newly acquired station were major ingredients in the success of McLendon Stations, but there were other factors equally as important to that success. Most important of these, perhaps, was the station facility itself. The station had to be capable of transmitting a clean signal to the audience, and it had to have the necessary production gear to create the sound that Gordon wanted.

"He always wanted the best technical facility in the market," Edd Routt said. "If there was a 50,000 watter, he really wanted that one. If he couldn't have that one, then he'd take the next best, realizing that if you don't have the technical facility, if you can't reach your market, it doesn't matter what you do" (Routt, 1989). Station broker Joe Sitrick added that Gordon did not care about the revenue, cash flow or programming of a station he was buying. He simply looked for a "competitive" signal and "was willing to overpay to get it" (Sitrick, 1990). Oftentimes when the McLendons purchased a station whose signal strength was less than desirable, the first order of business was to upgrade the signal to make it as powerful as the FCC would allow (Callison, 1989).

Don Keyes said that Gordon "bought a strong physical plant just to get the license—didn't give a damn about property. If real estate was included, that's fine, but that wasn't why we were there" (Keyes, 1989). In fact, Bill Meeks recalled that many of the McLendon Stations physically were located in some very undesirable parts of town. One station was even located near a city dump. Each station, said Meeks, "looked almost like a restroom in a bus station. But, they sounded great over the air" (Meeks, 1990).

Evaluation of a station facility for purchase consideration by the McLendons was generally a four-stage process. First came the initial contact from a station broker. McLendon Station acquisitions were arranged by the Blackburn-Hamilton Company's Joseph Sitrick, whom Edd Routt jokingly said became rich because of his role in McLendon Station transactions (Routt, 1989). Sitrick, who had met Gordon through Marcus Cohn, was instrumental through the years in buying and selling all the McLendon Stations (Sitrick, 1990).

Once the broker had decided that the facility met with Gordon's and B. R.'s expectations, Don Keyes would be dispatched to evaluate the station's potential from a programming point of view, and Glenn Callison would be dispatched for an evaluation of the station from an engineering angle (Callison, 1989). Sometimes Gordon would accompany one or the other. Glenn Callison recalled traveling with Gordon while "he was researching the station to give him some idea of the field strength, the coverage of the station, and so forth. So I made quite a few field measurements on the stations we were looking at," Callison said. "And as a result he would make his decision as to whether he wanted a signal there" (Callison, 1989).

The final stage in the station acquisition process involved negotiating the selling price. Gordon sometimes negotiated directly with a station owner or asked Marcus Cohn to negotiate with the owner's attorney. Gordon and Cohn together occasionally would negotiate a deal (Cohn, 1989).

Once the McLendons had purchased a station, Don Keyes would be off once more to install the format prescribed by Gordon and to make ready the big promotion package to introduce the station's new or improved format. Essentially, Keyes's job in the latter regard was to make certain that listeners in the market understood that a McLendon Station was now on the air (Keyes, 1989).

While Keyes tended to programming and promotion matters, Glenn Callison and Les Vaughn tended to engineering and production matters. Their jobs were important, because in practically every station "control rooms and studio facilities had to be rebuilt to accommodate the disc jockeys" (Callison, 1989). A special console and a four-turntable operation were installed in all McLendon Stations. Most control rooms at that time were operating with only two turntables, but the addition of two more provided greater programming options for the disc jockeys (Callison, 1989). Installation of a remote control unit, and in many instances a new transmitter, also improved overall signal and sound quality (Keyes, 1989).

Gordon was insistent that production facilities at all McLendon Stations be compatible with one another so that the quality of recordings produced at one station, particularly at KLIF, would not be diminished when played back at another station. This was vital to Gordon, who recorded many promotional spots and editorials at KLIF for distribution to other McLendon Stations for broadcast, and who required that his voice quality on the radio remain consistent wherever he might be heard. Les Vaughn said that Gordon was meticulous to a fault about how he sounded. In fact whenever Gordon was displeased with a recording of his voice, he oftentimes would send the recording to Vaughn with a demand that it somehow be improved. Vaughn said that Gordon became "picayunish" on this point. Even when he explained to Gordon that the quality of recording was fine and that Gordon's voice was at fault, Vaughn said that he was required to fix the recording so that Gordon's voice sounded the way he wanted it to sound (Vaughn, 1989).

There was a second reason for production compatibility among the McLendon Stations that did not become apparent immediately. But as the McLendons moved into more and more markets, especially in the major cities, Gordon found that engineers', musician's and performers' unions were making demands on his stations that impeded commercial and program production. For example, Gordon was required at one station to hire several persons—a musician, an engineer and a producer—to record a commercial that could have been recorded by only one or two persons. So, said Les Vaughn, "Gordon just got sick and tired of this," and decided to do practically all McLendon Station production work at KLIF (Vaughn, 1989).

One peculiarity of McLendon Station control rooms that originated with Les Vaughn was placement of all control boards or consoles at such a level that disc jockeys were required to stand throughout their board shifts. There were facilities for resting while not on the air, but disc jockeys never were allowed to sit while on microphone. The reason, according to Vaughn, was that while standing, the disc jockeys could "breathe better, particularly on the long shifts, the night shifts" (Vaughn, 1989). Moreover, disc jockeys who were required to undergo what might seem a tiresome experience insisted that they worked better while standing (Vaughn, 1989).

Once programming was in place and engineering and production problems were resolved, an ordinary station now transformed into a McLendon Station was ready for a rousing public unveiling. That usually meant changing station call letters, not only to separate the station from its past, but to provide one more promotional hook for the audience. Gordon had a fondness for mnemonic call letters. In his view, call letters that were pronounceable and that perhaps made reference to something indigenous to a station's service area added to the station's personality ("The Top-40," n.d., p. 26). Marcus Cohn saw a different side to call letter choice. He said it had "creative significance" and showed Gordon's "love of the word" (Cohn, 1989).

McLendon employees took great delight in trying their hand at four-letter combinations whose pronunciation as single words added a spark to the station identification. Probably no call letters for a Top 40 station were as descriptive as those given the McLendon Station in Louisville. The station's original call letters were WGRC—the GRC in honor of Revolutionary War hero George Rogers Clark. When WGRC became a McLendon Station, though, an effort was made to create a "ziggy call sign that people remember and that kids relate to," said Don Keyes (1989). Gordon's secretary, Billie Odom, suggested WAKY (pronounced "wacky"), call letters that Don Keyes declared were "a natural" (Keyes, 1989).

To draw maximum attention to the initial broadcast of a new McLendon Station called for a maximum promotional effort. When asked how the promotional process worked in the case of WAKY, Don Keyes explained: "We had a schedule of events: What was going to happen on day one. On day two we did this. On day three we did the balloon drop. On day four we did the treasure hunt. . . . Everything all laid out. It was a killer plan . . . when we went on" (Keyes, 1989).

The point that Keyes stressed was how well-orchestrated the promotion campaign introducing a McLendon Station had become. With few variations, most components of the campaign plan could be used regardless of market. There might have been some necessary alterations whenever formats other than Top 40 were being implemented, but for the most part the plan remained intact from market to market (Keyes, 1989).

Gordon was expert at delegating responsibility to those persons in whose abilities he had great faith. And so it was that he would depend on the expertise of a Glenn Callison, a Les Vaughn and a Don Keyes to get a new McLendon Station off the ground. Gordon remained away from the station throughout most of its transformation, but then, as Don Keyes recalled,

> He was always there when putting a new station on the air. I did 90 percent of the detail work—the writing of promos, the recording of them, the recording of jingles, the hiring of disc jockeys (with his approval), set salaries. . . . I did all that work, but he was always there the first day on the air, fine tuning, listening. (Keyes, 1989)

McLENDON STATION MARKET LOCATIONS

The decision as to where McLendon Stations would be located was a combination of preplanning and chance. Gordon and B. R. preferred to locate in major markets, certainly those in the top fifty. Stations in these markets were more likely to generate substantial revenue from national advertisers. If the McLendons were unable to buy in the top fifty markets, they would try at least to buy within the top 100 markets (Keyes, 1989), always conditioning the final decision to locate in a new market on the probability of success by filling a void there.

Sometimes if a station could not be found in the city proper where the McLendons wanted to locate, they would search for a station in a nearby market. If available, the station would be upgraded and its signal aimed into the neighboring major market. This method of indirectly entering a major market met with resistance on one or two occasions, which will be documented more fully in a later chapter.

The McLendons purchased eleven radio stations and constructed one television station during the 1950s. In addition to KELP (El Paso), purchased in 1951, and KLBS (Houston), purchased in 1952, other stations joining the McLendon group during the decade included WRIT (Milwaukee), purchased in 1955; WGLS, which later became WTAM (Decatur, Georgia—near Atlanta), purchased in 1956; KTSA (San Antonio), also purchased in 1956; KEEL-AM/FM (Shreveport), purchased in 1957; WAKY (Louisville), purchased in 1958; and KZAP-FM (Houston) and KABL (Oakland), both purchased in 1959. The McLendons sold KLBS in 1954 and repurchased the station in 1957, changing its call letters to KILT. KELP-TV (El Paso) was built by the McLendons in 1956. The station call letters were first KOKE-TV and then KILT-TV (*City of Camden*, 1969b, pp. 428–438).

The remainder of the McLendons' station acquisitions came between 1960 and 1966. WYSL-AM/FM (Amherst, New York—near Buffalo) was purchased in 1960. The McLendons purchased a Buffalo facility one year later and moved the Amherst stations, along with their WYSL-AM/FM call letters, to Buffalo. The McLendons next purchased WNUS (Chicago) in 1962, KABL-FM (San Francisco) in 1965, and WNUS-FM (Chicago) in 1966. WWWW-FM (Detroit) and KCND-TV (Pembina, North Dakota—near Winnipeg, Canada) also were purchased by the McLendons in 1966. The FCC granted a permit in 1967 for construction of KLIF-TV in Dallas, but the station was never built (*City of Camden*, 1969b, pp. 428–438). KADS (Los Angeles) was purchased in 1966, and in 1968 the station's call letters were changed to KOST-FM (Kushner, 1972, pp. 270–274). And although the McLendons had a license to construct an FM radio facility in Dallas alongside KLIF, that station, KNUS-FM, was not built until 1961 (*City of Camden*, 1969b, p. 430). From 1965 through 1969, the McLendons also had given serious acquisition consideration—to the point of drawing up purchase contracts—for four other stations, but none of the four ever came into their possession. The stations were KBVU (Bellevue, Washington—near Seattle), KYXI (Oregon City, Oregon—near Portland), WIFI-FM (Philadelphia) and WCAM (Camden, New Jersey—near Philadelphia) (*City of Camden*, 1969b, pp. 435–439).

The effort to purchase WCAM was a particularly sore point with Gordon and B. R. Ownership of the station would have given them entree into a major northeastern market. Stations in the area that included Washington, D.C., Philadelphia, New York City and Boston had remained beyond the McLendons' grasp, either because the most desirable market stations were never for sale or because stations that were for sale there were never at an acceptable price (Keyes, 1989). The McLendons had made one unsuccessful stab at entering the Philadelphia market in 1967 with the proposed purchase of WIFI-FM. That effort had fallen short, however, when the station's owner exercised his option to terminate the WIFI-FM purchase contract (*City of Camden*, 1969b, p. 435). WCAM then became available, and the McLendons made a strong pitch to buy that station. The effort fell short in 1969 when the FCC refused to allow the purchase (*City of Camden*, 1969a, p. 413).

The WCAM experience was said to have so affected Gordon that he lost interest in any further expansion of the McLendon Station group. It may have been the single most important factor, too, in persuading Gordon very shortly to begin moving out of broadcasting altogether (Routt, 1989). A closer examination of the WCAM matter appears in a subsequent chapter.

McLENDON STATIONS

Stories abound on the subject of McLendon Stations. While most stations were similar in many respects, there were particular characteristics that set each one of the stations apart from the pack. Most, however, did share a common trait: market dominance. By 1961, five of the seven McLendon Stations led their respective markets in ratings and one other was tied for first place ("Zany," 1961, p. 126).

As noted earlier, several McLendon Stations have a unique place in radio history, and will be examined more closely in the following chapter. A quick glance at some of the other stations, though, will show that for one reason or another, they, too, played important roles in making the colorful and successful McLendon Station group a powerful leader in the broadcasting industry.

KELP holds a special place in McLendon Station lore for two reasons. First, it was Gordon's and B. R.'s initial purchase as they made their foray outside the Dallas radio market. The station, purchased in 1951 for only about $3,000, was run nearly single-handedly for several years by Joe Roddy (Meeks, a 1990). KELP's low purchase price and relatively inexpensive operation may have been a major factor in convincing the McLendons to search for other good station buys that eventually would catapult them into the elite of group ownership (Meeks, 1991).

The second reason for KELP's importance is that the station's format served as a model for the beautiful music format that Gordon later would install at KABL in San Francisco. Much of KELP's musical programming was of the soft, easy-listening kind that itself had been copied from one of Gordon's Dallas competitors, KIXL (Meeks, 1990). But Gordon gradually added some of the more low-keyed promotional components of Top 40 to pep up the KELP sound in order that the station might stand out in the El Paso market.

By 1954, Gordon was contemplating a move that would remake KELP into the KLIF Top 40 image (McLendon, 1954). The move appeared complete by August 1955 when Hooper Ratings showed the station pummeling its El Paso competition. The station's 8 A.M.-to 6 P.M. Sunday through Saturday audience share of 59.8 and its 12 noon-to-6 P.M. Monday through Saturday audience share of 63.2 led Gordon to ponder in a trade magazine ad whether KELP might be the "highest rated station in radio history" (Advertisement, 1955a).

The origins of Houston's KILT stretch back to 1952, when Gordon and B. R.'s business enterprise was still the Trinity Broadcasting Corporation. The McLendons purchased Houston radio station KLEE, changed its call letters to KLBS and prepared to transfer the flagship operations of the Liberty Broadcasting System from KLIF to KLBS ("Radio Station," 1952). The demise of the Liberty network ended any transfer plans and shortly thereafter the station was sold. Its one brief claim to fame was that Bill Stewart, soon to become a Top 40 legend at KLIF, first broke into the McLendon organization at KLBS (Hall and Hall, 1977, p. 162).

The McLendons repurchased KLBS in 1957 and changed its call letters to KILT. The letters, forming the word for the plaid garment worn by male Scots, were perfect as a direct tie to the Old Scotchman, Gordon McLendon. KILT even used plaid designs in all of its station promotion announcements (Macias, 1981).

Along with the new call letters came the famous McLendon Station promotion package to announce KILT's arrival. Within one month (from May 14 to June 15, 1957), all three radio audience ratings companies—Hooper, Trendex and Pulse—showed that KILT had moved from last to first place in the Houston market (Advertisement, 1957). The KLIF Top 40 format had been installed at KILT and was working to perfection. The station equaled and in some respects maybe even surpassed KLIF with its entourage of personality disc jockeys and outlandish promotion campaigns (Newport, 1981, pp. 41–42).

Two years before KILT began operating, Gordon and his father-in-law, James Noe, who owned two radio stations and one television station in Louisiana, decided to join their stations in an advertising alliance called NOEMAC. McLendon Stations KLIF, WRIT, KELP and KOKE-TV and Noe stations WNOE in New Orleans and KNOE and KNOE-TV in Monroe ("McLendon, Noe," 1955) were put "under one umbrella for selling purposes," according to Don Keyes. Thus, a national advertiser buying the entire NOEMAC lineup could place advertising on all stations represented in the group at a package price that was less than what it would have cost to buy advertising on individual NOEMAC stations. "There was never any ownership or legal ties" in the NOEMAC alliance, said Keyes. "It was Gordon trying to help out his father-in-law" (Keyes, 1989). Gordon also dispatched Keyes periodically to consult with Noe station managers and program directors on programming matters (Keyes, 1989), and at one point sent Bill Stewart to WNOE to help improve its ratings. He succeeded in spectacular fashion, pulling the station from twentieth place in the New Orleans market to second place in only two weeks (Hall and Hall, 1977, p. 162). Gary Owens was part of that success story, having been recruited by Don Keyes to move from Denver to work at WNOE before moving on to McLendon Stations in Texas (Owens, 1990).

The NOEMAC alliance was at the core of a controversy that threatened the McLendons' move into the San Antonio market. The McLendons had agreed to purchase San Antonio's KTSA, pending FCC approval, in March 1956 ("KTSA," 1956). The FCC did approve KTSA's license transfer in May, but one month later, owners of rival San Antonio station KITE asked that the commission reconsider its approval. KITE owners charged that KTSA, as a member of NOEMAC, would give the station an unfair economic advantage in the San Antonio radio market. What's more, KITE owners also protested McLendon programming practices that would be used by KTSA, claiming that such practices were "designed to destroy competition" ("KITE Protests," 1956). The matter was resolved amicably between the McLendons and the KITE owners before the FCC had to intervene in the fray ("KITE Agrees," 1956).

The way now was clear for the McLendons to add yet one more radio station to their group. A newspaper account of the first days of KTSA noted that Gordon's arrival in San Antonio was "one of the most important influences on local radio, other than television. . . . When the 'Old Scotchman' bought KTSA . . . he brought in his 'shock troops' and the fast-talking DJs turned the station into one of the top-rated stations in the nation" (Elliott, 1978). Sure enough, even before Gordon's disagreement with the KITE owners had been settled, he already had propelled KTSA into a first-place market position, according to Hooper and Trendex ratings (Advertisement, 1956).

On its way to the top, though, KTSA was the site of one of Gordon's biggest and most humorous blunders. The misstep centered on what Gordon later would say was "one of the least important ideas I've had in my life, and I've had some *real* bad ones" (McLendon, 1978). The idea was to give KTSA a new image when its ratings started to sag by beefing up its format and changing its call letters. Gordon chose KAKI (pronounced "khaki") for the station's new call letters. The letters were meant to more closely identify the station with San Antonio's sizable military population ("Tribute," 1986). Gordon had succeeded in creating call letters that were pronounceable as a word, but he did not yet realize just what that particular word meant to many of his listeners.

The FCC approved the new KAKI call letters, and they were unveiled to the San Antonio market with the usual McLendon flourish. But, instead of KAKI's ratings going up, they continued to slide downward. Gordon's secretary, Yolanda Salas, who understood Spanish, was the first to alert him to what the problem might be. It so happened that the pronounceable word formed by the KAKI call letters was the Spanish slang expression for human feces. And it happened that the sizable Spanish American population of San Antonio, not taking kindly to such a blunder, was ignoring Gordon's station. The station's original KTSA call letters were back in place within twenty-four hours ("Tribute," 1986).

The additions of KTSA and KILT to a McLendon Station group that already held the powerful KLIF for the first time placed radio stations from the three major Texas markets into the hands of a single owner. Since the 1930s broadcasters had been hoping to complete the elusive "Texas Triangle." Now, with stations in Dallas, Houston and San Antonio, Gordon and B. R. had formed that triangle. McLendon Stations now would have access to more than 90 percent of the entire Texas population, a fact that made Gordon an "indispensable man" to recording artists and advertisers alike, said *Variety* (Barker, 1957, pp. 37, 52).

Gordon had accomplished the feat of building the "Texas Triangle" with speed and skill. He had moved key personnel from one triangle station to another in order to bolster ratings. Popular disc jockeys at one McLendon Station were "loaned" to a sister station to help boost listenership. Gordon dispatched Don Keyes from KLIF to apply his expertise as program director first at KTSA and then at KILT. Bill Weaver followed the same route, moving from KLIF to manage both KTSA and KILT. Gordon also "unloaded lotsa dough in contest gimmicks" in order to give KTSA and KILT a quick ratings boost. In fact it was rumored that KILT alone had a $100,000 promotion budget (Barker, 1957, pp. 37, 52).

While the hoopla and money giveaways surrounding the appearance of these new McLendon Stations might have accounted for their rapid ratings climb to first place (MacFarland, 1973, pp. 420–421), the fact remains that for nearly a decade following the formation of the "Texas Triangle," KLIF, KTSA and KILT generated "unprecedented ratings" and "huge advertising revenues" while "forming the cornerstone of modern radio's greatest independent empire" (Patoski, 1980, pp. 101–102).

The McLendons made several ventures into television, but never equaled the success in that medium that they had achieved in radio. For a time the McLendon Corporation operated KELP-TV in El Paso. Plans were originally to program the station primarily in the Spanish language to serve the predominantly Spanish-speaking market (Advertisement, 1955b). Another McLendon-owned television station, KCND-TV, was located in Pembina, North Dakota. Why a small market like Pembina? The map shows that just up the road and across the border sat big-market Winnipeg, Canada, where thousands of viewers were well within reach of KCND-TV's signal.

The FCC had granted the McLendon Corporation a permit to construct Dallas station KLIF-TV in 1953, but the McLendons asked that the permit be cancelled in 1956 ("Trinity," 1956). As indicated earlier, the McLendons revived plans to build a Dallas television station in the 1960s, but nothing ever came of the venture.

Gordon had financial interests of a sort in at least two radio stations that were outside the United States. One was station XETRA (or XTRA, as it was more commonly known), in Tijuana, Mexico. Although a foreign station, XTRA was targeted to serve a primarily Los Angeles audience. The full story of the station's development and of its pioneering all-news format is told in greater detail in the following chapter.

The second foreign station in which Gordon held financial interest was Radio Nord. This was not an ordinary radio station, but rather was one of an unusual and even exotic breed of operation known as a "pirate" radio station. These were radio stations that beamed programming to various European cities from ships located outside the three-mile international boundary. The pirate stations had no license to broadcast in the countries where their programming was targeted. Their chief purpose was to provide commercial outlets for advertisers in countries where broadcasting systems were essentially noncommercial and government-controlled (Kebbon, 1964, pp. 52–53). More important to listeners, though, was something else the pirate stations provided that most domestic stations were not providing—popular contemporary music (Gordon, 1965, p. 5).

Just what business interest Gordon had in Radio Nord, how he became interested in it and why he became interested in it are unclear. By his own account, Gordon was intimately involved in putting the station on the air and running it ("Pioneer," 1984), but ownership of Radio Nord and the ship *Bonjour* where the station was based was claimed by Robert F. Thompson of Dallas. Thompson was an officer in a company owned by Gordon's close friend Clint Murchison ("Texan," 1961). The *Bonjour* was officially listed as the property of Nord Establishments, based in Liechtenstein but owned by Americans (Wiskari, 1961, p. 1). Glenn Callison's recollection of the Radio Nord story was that Clint Murchison actually financed the whole operation after Gordon's suggestion that a pirate station might work. Gordon's interest in the project grew from a 1960 visit to Sweden where he listened to the rather boring programs aired on Swedish radio and decided that Swedes would be attracted to American radio programming.

Gordon oversaw putting the station on the air by acquiring an old German trawler that had served at one time as a herring boat and turning it into the *Bonjour* (Callison, 1989). The transition from herring boat to radio station was not easy. The first chore was to remove all the dead fish that were still in the ship's hold when purchased. That job fell to Glenn Callison (McKinsey, 1990). Next, a 180-foot vertical antenna had to be constructed amidships for transmission purposes. The structure made the *Bonjour* such an extremely unstable vessel in the choppy North Sea that Callison was certain the ship would not stay afloat. Besides that problem there was the great expense of just keeping Radio Nord on the air once it did become operational. An unreliable generator, for instance, required that a second one be brought aboard ship so that there would be enough power to keep Radio Nord's transmitter on the air (Vaughn, 1989).

Plans were for Radio Nord to broadcast for twelve hours a day using twenty kilowatts for daytime and ten for nighttime transmissions. At that power level, the station easily reached Stockholm and vicinity from the *Bonjour's* anchorage some fifteen miles off the Swedish coast ("Radio Vessel," 1961). Stockholm's nearly 2.5 million inhabitants made it a prime target very much worth reaching ("Texan," 1961).

Radio Nord's format was designed by Gordon, but once that was done, he stepped out of the picture. Jack Kotschack, a Swede, was in charge of actually producing Radio Nord programming in his Stockholm recording studios (Callison, 1989). A week's worth of programming, commercials included, was recorded in the Stockholm studios, placed on fourteen-inch reels and transported to the *Bonjour* by boat. The automated tape playback system aboard ship was capable of operating for nine hours unattended ("Radio Vessel," 1961).

Radio Nord began its pirate broadcasting service on March 8, 1961, transmitting a blend of popular music and commercials where the former had been scarce and the latter had been prohibited (Wiskari, 1961, p. 1). "Within 90 days we were the number one station in Sweden, running a listener rating like 95 percent to 5 percent for the government station," Gordon said with great satisfaction (Porter, 1972, p. 1E). *Time* magazine reported that within one month of its debut, Radio Nord was receiving over a thousand fan letters a day. Moreover, such companies as Westinghouse, Max Factor and B.M.W. were eagerly lining up to buy commercial time on the station ("Sweden: Piracy," 1961, p. 35). The demand for advertising time actually was more than Radio Nord could accommodate, even with commercials airing about every five minutes. Some seventy advertisers in all—about half of them American companies—had bought time on Radio Nord by its second month of operation ("Radio Vessel," 1961).

Radio Nord's popularity among Swedish listeners became apparent almost immediately. On May 4, 1961, the Swedish Radio Corporation began a commercial-free, all-music program schedule to recapture the audience lost to the pirate station ("Sweden in Radio," 1961). Heretofore, both funding and time had been unavailable for such programming. But when forced to compete with Radio Nord, the Swedish government approved funds for a new program service called "Melody Radio" to operate from 6 A.M. to 6 P.M. initially and then, later, throughout the entire evening hours (Rydbeck, 1963, p. 246).

At the same time that the Swedish government acknowledged the impact Radio Nord had made on its own radio service, it also launched efforts to put the pirate station out of business. The government first tried to get the

Bonjour's country of registry to revoke the ship's flag. That failed because the ship was registered in Nicaragua and sailed under the Nicaraguan flag. It so happened that the head of Nicaragua's government, Anastasio Somoza, was a very close friend of Clint Murchison and, therefore, ignored Swedish requests regarding the *Bonjour* (Callison, 1989).

When the tactic failed, the Swedish Ministry of Communications, declaring that Radio Nord's "broadcasts are a violation of international law and therefore of Swedish law," attempted to invoke an international convention that would bar the ship's broadcasts. The convention became effective on April 1, 1961, and ordered that Swedish ports henceforth would be closed to the *Bonjour*. Docking at any of the ports would subject the ship to a fine and confiscation of its broadcast transmitter. A legal expert for the Communications Ministry even said that the Swedish government had the legal right to block transport of tapes and supplies from Swedish ports to the *Bonjour*. Jack Kotschack would not be intimidated, though, citing a license he had obtained from the government for transporting supplies to the *Bonjour* by sea or air, and noting that the ship could dock easily at German or Polish ports if barred from Swedish ports (Wiskari, 1961, pp. 1, 21).

For more than a year the Swedish government pressured Radio Nord to cease broadcasting. The pirate station finally gave in to the pressure and signed off for good on July 1, 1962 ("Floating," 1962). The end to Radio Nord and to other pirate radio stations that had come into existence in Scandinavia resulted from passage of a Swedish law that prohibited Swedes from associating in any way with pirate stations. The law stipulated that anyone who contributed to the operation of a pirate radio station by maintaining or supplying the station, by taking part in its broadcasts or by carrying out "other activities aimed at furthering the broadcasting" could be tried for conducting illegal activity (Hunnings, 1965, pp. 417–419). The last portion of the law was aimed specifically and effectively at advertisers.

Robert F. Thompson's comments when shutting off the switch of his, Gordon McLendon's and Clint Murchison's successful and adventurous but short-lived pirate radio station were a fitting conclusion. "For the sake of international relations," said Thompson, "we will stoke up *Bonjour* and putt off into the night" ("Sweden: *Bon Soir*," 1962, p. 74).

BUYING THE AFRN

Gordon's taste for the exotic in radio stations led him on a quest in 1973 that was even more unusual than his pirate radio venture ("Miss Stafford," 1973). Ken Dowe remembered the moment quite vividly when Gordon turned to him while sitting beside the swimming pool at the Las Brisas Hotel in Acapulco, Mexico and asked when he would be returning to the United States. Ken indicated that he would be leaving for the States the next day. Gordon then proceeded to instruct Dowe that as soon as he reached his office after returning to Dallas, he was to call the Pentagon, find the appropriate person to arrange the transaction, and buy the Armed Forces Radio Network (AFRN). Dowe, not certain he had heard correctly, asked Gordon to repeat the instructions, whereupon Gordon said once more that he wanted to buy the AFRN. "Why?" asked Dowe, and Gordon replied, "Because the government's really got no use for it, and they don't know what to do with it and, besides that, we could broadcast all over the world." Dowe said, "Broadcast what?" "We'll figure it out," Gordon said. "But, let's get it first!" (Dowe, 1989).

Dowe was uncertain just how to approach the project, not knowing exactly whom to speak with or what to say. Gordon told him not to worry. No one at the Pentagon would know quite what to do, Gordon insisted, since they were all bureaucrats. Dowe found that Gordon's assessment was exactly right. He could not find anyone at the Pentagon who knew precisely how to react to an offer to buy the AFRN. When persons who appeared capable of dealing with Dowe finally stepped forward, he made them an offer of $1 million for the network. He assured them that the offer was a serious one, and for the next nine months Dowe devoted considerable time to pursuing this most unusual purchase offer. And for that length of time, said Dowe, he kept the powers that be at the Pentagon busy because they did not know what to do or how to say no to Gordon's offer (Dowe, 1989).

Gordon laughed at the improbable quandary he had caused the government. "The worst that will come out of it," Gordon told Dowe, "is you and your ol' buddy Gordon will have to travel all over the world to inspect the locations." If the Pentagon did the improbable and sold Gordon some useless AFRN facilities, Gordon still figured the equipment that he would acquire would be worth at least the million dollar price he was willing to pay for the entire network (Dowe, 1989).

Needless to say, the Pentagon passed on Gordon's offer, and his vision of owning the AFRN remained just a vision.

McLENDON STATION ORGANIZATION

Gordon McLendon was the McLendon Corporation's visible guide and company spokesperson. Always less visible, though, was B. R. McLendon, who played an equally important role in the company's success. B. R., also known to McLendon Station employees as Mr. Mac (" 'Mr. Mac,' " 1969), actually held greater formal control of the McLendon Corporation than Gordon, since the latter always carried the title of president, while B. R. was chairman of the board ("Group ownership, 1961/62–1973). B. R.'s "public low-profile," it was once said, "cloaks the business acumen of a Rothschild and the tenacity of a pit-bulldog" (Hitt, 1979).

Much has been said already about B. R.'s mastery of the McLendon Corporation's business side while Gordon held rein over the company's creative side. The demarcation was a perfect arrangement, according to those who knew both McLendons and who had observed their working relationship. Edd Routt remarked on the Gordon-B. R. McLendon relationship:

> He and his father made a great team because his father was a hard-nosed conservative businessman. Everything had to add up to him on the profit-and-loss sheets. He loved his son very much. But I think he would be the business brain and Gordon would be the creative brain and together they made a great team (Routt, 1989).

Routt went on to say that Gordon and B. R. "were very close" and that B. R. "was terribly, terribly proud of Gordon, and Gordon had an awful lot of respect for his father's business acumen" (Routt, 1989).

Les Vaughn characterized B. R. as "an older Gordon McLendon." The two "clashed in their thoughts oftentimes," said Vaughn, "because Gordon had the modern way of thinking and Mr. B. R. wanted to stick with the older ways." B. R.'s objection to some of the things that Gordon did would sometimes lead to "some knock-down-drag-outs," Vaughn observed, but "whatever Gordon wanted, Gordon got" (Vaughn, 1989). And getting some things for Gordon did not always come with B. R.'s consent, nor even his knowledge. "There are some things we don't tell Dad," Gordon sometimes would say (Callison, 1989).

B. R.'s fiery temper was well known throughout the McLendon organization, and it was by no means confined just to clashes with Gordon. Ken Dowe recalled Gordon's admonition to him about B. R.: "I'd stay out of the old man's way if I were you. Do whatever he says, if he says it" (Dowe, 1989). B. R. was a man who wanted his way and would put the fear of God into those around him, who knew to go out of their way to please him. He made the point abundantly clear to everyone. "I don't pay you to tell me what I can't do," B. R. once said to a McLendon Corporation attorney, "I pay you to tell me how to do what I want to do" (Dowe, 1989).

B. R. "was always first and foremost dedicated to the motion picture business," noted Ken Dowe (1989). After all, that is where the McLendon family fortune began, and that is where much of the company revenue still originated. But B. R. still gave plenty of attention to the broadcasting side of the McLendon Corporation. He was even more keenly aware than Gordon of some industry trends. For example, at a time when few persons, including Gordon, saw much value in FM radio, B. R. had determined that FM had such a bright future that the McLendon Station group would be among the first to have FM radio stations within its fold (Meeks, 1990).

The division of responsibility for overseeing the McLendon Corporation gave B. R. control of the company's finances. He was always in on the buying and selling of a McLendon Station, and made purchasing decisions on new property or facilities needed for the stations. "It's not the kind of thing that Gordon would really get into, because who wants to buy a building? There's not any fun in that. There's no creativity in that" (Routt, 1989). B. R. liked "to get in on the bottom line of things" as far as corporate financial matters went, but he was content to remain in Dallas while Gordon moved around the country tending to station and other McLendon Corporation business (Routt, 1989). But when decisions were made affecting key matters of the McLendon Corporation, Gordon and B. R., usually accompanied by Dorothy Manning, made them together. Tom Merriman came to call the trio the "McLendon Clan" (Merriman, 1990).

In many respects the working arrangement that Gordon and B. R. had was a perfect partnership. Each contributed to the McLendon Corporation his own capabilities, and each understood and respected the capabilities of the other. This mutual respect played no small role in the enormous success enjoyed by the McLendon Corporation through the nearly three decades that Gordon and B. R. were at the company's helm.

The success of the broadcasting side of the McLendon Corporation was not entirely due to Gordon and B. R. The company prospered also from the well-chosen staff that Gordon selected through the years. Many of the persons on the staff had been with Gordon from his earliest years in radio. Glenn Callison, Edd Routt, Les Vaughn and Mitch Lewis had helped build KLIF and the Liberty Broadcasting System, and then had contributed in the development of the McLendon Station group. Others, such as Don Keyes and Billie Odom, had come along later but were no less instrumental in their contributions to the McLendon Corporation.

The company consisted of two management staff levels. One was based in Dallas and was responsible for overseeing various facets of operation for the entire McLendon Station group. Some of the persons working at this level, besides those already mentioned, included Bill Morgan, Jack Fiedler, Jim Foster, Art Holt, Homer Odom, Jack Lee, Cy Ostrup, Charles Payne, Bill Weaver, Richard Wilcox, Nathan Reeder, James Mackin, Leigh Robertson and Ken Dowe. There were apparently seven titled positions that one or more of the above occupied at some point during his or her career with the McLendon Corporation. The positions included national program director, national sales director, national music director, national production director, national engineering director, national advertising and public relations director and national director of operations. Glenn Callison appears to have been the sole occupant of the national engineering director's position, Mitch Lewis appears to have been the McLendon Corporation's only national advertising and public relations director ("Group Ownership," 1961/62–1973), and Ken Dowe was the company's only national director of operations (Dowe, 1989).

Two very important persons who played key roles at the McLendon Corporation for many years were Dorothy Manning and Billie Odom. As noted earlier, Dorothy Manning had started as B. R.'s secretary while he was still only in the theater business in East Texas. She moved with B. R. to Dallas and eventually assumed a position as secretary-treasurer in the McLendon Corporation. "She was," according to Don Keyes, "the queen mother of the organization" (Keyes, 1989). And in fact, Dorothy Manning was instrumental in decisions and arrangements for many of the McLendon Corporation business deals, especially those involving real estate (Manning, 1990). Edd Routt recalled Dorothy Manning as being extremely knowledgeable about the broadcasting business. One of her duties was to serve as a liaison between Gordon and B. R., to whom she remained fiercely loyal (Routt, 1989).

Also fiercely loyal and trusted was Dorothy Manning's counterpart in the Company, Billie Odom. Ms. Odom was Gordon's executive secretary (Keyes, 1989). She had started as a secretary with the McLendon Corporation, working under Dorothy Manning and learning the business side of the company's operation. When Gordon's secretary, Ursala Schweitzer, left, Billie Odom took over that position. She was described by Edd Routt as "an extremely competent, very bright woman" and the only person in whom "Gordon confided everything." In return, Routt said,

> Billie was totally dedicated to Gordon and his needs and interests. And if she ever gave you an opinion on something or gave you a little counsel or advice, you knew that it was coming straight from Gordon. She would never presume to speak for Gordon, because he could change his ideas overnight, but when Billie gave you some guidance or direction, it was like Gordon speaking. (Routt, 1989)

Billie, Routt concluded, "would be typical of the kind of bright people [Gordon] surrounded himself with. He simply could not tolerate a dullard" (Routt, 1989).

The second tier of the McLendon Corporation management staff consisted of the station managers and key personnel at all McLendon Stations. Gordon was primarily responsible for the over-the-air operation of these stations, but tended to delegate authority in business matters to individual managers. David MacFarland has said, in fact, that among other radio station group owners of the time, the McLendons were the "most democratic, in the sense that individual managers had considerable autonomy in running their stations" (MacFarland, 1973, p. 285). Gordon often made suggestions to his managers, but he seldom issued directives or "orders."

Programming was different, though. Gordon was willing to allow his station managers to choose their own music and for local station program directors to create their own playlists, but his interest in the total sound that came from his stations led him to dictate key programming policies that were to be followed without question. "Gordon would walk into town and say, 'This is what we're going to do . . . boom,' " regarding McLendon

Station programming ("Radio—The Industry," 1988, p. 9). And more than his fellow group owners, Gordon kept his hand in station programming by both writing and voicing commercials, promotional announcements and editorials (MacFarland, 1973, pp. 519–520).

Whenever contact did occur between Gordon and his local station managers, the subject most often addressed was programming. Part of this, said MacFarland, "was a reflection of the typical Top 40 management pattern which separated sales from programming in order to concentrate first on the programming" (MacFarland, 1973, p. 523). A bigger part, however, was Gordon's distaste for the business side of broadcasting. His position on such matters was well known throughout the McLendon organization. Edd Routt told of attending a McLendon Station managers' meeting in Dallas at a time when advertising "billing was not what it was projected to be":

> And [Gordon's] warning was, "Don't let me get into the business end of this thing. Let me stay in programming where I can use my creative talents to make us a great operation. You keep the sales where they are supposed to be. Don't let me get into the business end." And we all worked hard to keep him out of the business end. (Routt 1989).

While managers of McLendon Stations carried the title of general manager, they really were that in name only. "We had strong office managers who were to look after all the paperwork dealing with FCC attorneys, dealing with license renewal—all the non-revenue-producing things," Edd Routt recalled. The general managers "were effectively sales managers" (Routt, 1989). Don Keyes agreed that McLendon Station general managers were "hired for their managerial/sales ability. Through exposure to Gordon at managers' meetings . . . they became more familiar than most general managers with the programming concepts of the company. But . . . most of them were sales people" (Keyes, 1989) .

Gordon was never one to be complacent about what his stations were doing. The very idea was offensive to him. "The pattern of our radio stations calls for *constant change* of the little things. . . . Keep something new and fresh in front of the people all the time," Gordon would say (McLendon, n.d., "On Continuing Change").

In order to ensure change, Gordon admonished his station managers to be on the lookout for new ideas that might be incorporated into their stations' programming and to monitor their competitors' stations to see what programming ideas they were using. If a McLendon Station was to outperform the competition, then the station manager obviously had to know what he was up against. Likewise, Gordon felt that his station managers should monitor their own stations' programming as a method of quality control (MacFarland, 1973, pp. 318–324).

The national program director (or national PD, as the title was better known) provided a vital link between Gordon and McLendon Station personnel. The person occupying the position was regarded as a kind of resident consultant who traveled periodically to each city where a McLendon Station was located, monitored the station's programming to detect problems, and recommended changes that might improve programming and therefore increase the station's ratings (MacFarland, 1973, p. 285).

Gordon chose Bill Stewart as his first national PD in late 1953. Stewart served in that capacity through 1956 (MacFarland, 1973, p. 298). This was the same Bill Stewart who had been a KLIF disc jockey and was credited with developing the McLendon brand of Top 40. His tenure as national PD saw the McLendon Station group grow from three to five stations.

The most significant growth period for the McLendon Station group, however, occurred during Don Keyes's tenure as national PD. Keyes held the position from 1957 to 1966 (MacFarland, 1973, p. 285). Keyes came well equipped for the job, since his and Gordon's minds seemed "on the same wavelength all the time. . . . I was his alter ego," said Keyes. "We talked the same language" (Keyes, 1989). Don Keyes had worked initially for Gordon as a part-time disc jockey at KLIF in 1954. From there Gordon had moved him to KTSA in San Antonio as program director, and then to KILT in Houston, also as program director. Finally, Gordon moved Keyes back to Dallas and into the national PD position—a position for which Keyes seemed perfectly suited and in which he was perfectly happy.

The nature of what the national PD did was always fluid. Along with being a consultant, he was expected to be a troubleshooter and to carry the message from home office about how things were to be done. "This is what's coming down. This is what we're going to do" were essential ingredients of that message (Routt, 1989). The method of troubleshooting and message delivery eventually developed into a routine that Keyes said began when Gordon called him into his office:

> I'd go in with my little yellow pad. We'd sit there and do great and wondrous things. And he'd say, "Well, I think it's time for you to drop down to Houston and visit KILT for a few days, monitor and see how they're doing. The Hooper came out. They're not doing as well as I hoped. Go down there and put an ear on and see what you think." So, I would sneak into Houston. I say "sneak" because I didn't want the staff to find out that I was coming in and listening. I'd get a hotel room and my little transoceanic Zenith portable and I'd monitor. And I'd make copious notes. And then—surprise! Next day, I'd call the station: "It's me, I'm in town. I've got to have a meeting with the manager and PD." Struck fear into their hearts, which was not my intent, but it happened. I was there to try to help. (Keyes, 1989)

Ken Dowe followed Don Keyes a while later with an equally impressive title of national director of operations. The position really was only that of a "glorified national program director," according to Dowe, who served in the position from about 1969 to 1974 (Dowe, 1989). The title was enhanced somewhat when Gordon changed it to McLendon Corporation executive vice-president and made Dowe responsible for all management liaison activity between home base and what was by then a decreasing number of McLendon Stations (Dowe, 1989).

For a time the business and sales counterpart to the programming function that the national PD performed was left to Gordon's administrative assistant. Edd Routt held that position for three years, and called it the "most interesting job I guess I ever had.":

> As his administrative assistant, the duties ranged from being a valet to lighting his cigarettes to running the corporation. You never knew what the next move would be. I was kinda the corporate SOB. I made the rounds of every station every month. And we'd sit down with operating statements and pound out the problems: "What is this expense? Why did you spend that? Was that authorized? Can't you get a copywriter for less than $1,200 a month?" Just hammering on expenses and making sure that sales procedures were being followed. I had a lot of experience in management at that point. And I was close to Gordon at that point. And really when I would hit these stations I was there more or less with his authority and about the same authority that he would have himself rarely, rarely ever used, but the managers did pay attention because we were there to talk serious business. (Routt, 1989)

THE McLENDON STATION EMPLOYEE

Gordon was asked once what it was that he looked for when hiring people. His reply: "Educational background first. And then I'd like to be sure that they're legitimately crazy" ("The Top-40," n.d., p. 25). Gordon was willing to admit that a little bit of zaniness certainly would not hinder an employee's effectiveness with the McLendon Corporation.

The measure of anyone's worthiness to becoming a McLendon Corporation employee was, above all else, intelligence. Gordon even required for a time that all prospective McLendon Station on-air talent take and pass a rigorous aptitude test and that once hired, they keep up-to-date on current events (Bart McLendon, 1990). He wanted his disc jockeys to have a broad base of knowledge, noted Gary Owens (1990). Gordon also detested mispronounced names or misused terms. He was a perfectionist in this respect (Bart McLendon, 1990).

This concern about an employee's education was not at all a matter that Gordon took lightly. He himself was intelligent—many would say brilliant—and would not countenance employees who themselves did not possess a reasonable degree of intelligence. It was not unusual for Gordon to follow up a conversation with an employee by asking what book that person had read lately. Gordon had a keen intellectual curiosity that, maybe by osmosis, oftentimes was passed along to McLendon Corporation employees ("Tribute," 1986).

Edd Routt recalled some of the other qualities Gordon looked for and received from his personnel:

> Experience, basically smart, productive. Really, the cream of the cream. . . . He expected, though I don't think he ever demanded it, but he got . . . almost total loyalty. He wanted everything up front. He hated to fire people and would avoid it whenever he could. He couldn't stand people who were stupid. He couldn't stand people who would let drinking or anything else get in the way of doing the job. . . . He was a leader by example, though, except maybe in sales. (Routt, 1989)

Don Keyes also noted the manner in which Gordon led by example: "He possessed tremendous executive charisma to get his people to do things a lesser executive could not. He set a rapid pace, and we had to run alongside him to keep up" (Blackwell, 1986, p. 6C).

McLendon Corporation employees were expected to do whatever had to be done and when it had to be done. "Just do it!" was Gordon's response whenever questioned about the chances that a task would be difficult and perhaps even impossible to undertake (Vaughn, 1989). As a result of Gordon's demands, most McLendon Station employees "wore several hats. If something needed to be done, whoever's available, go do it. And do it the very best you can, because that's what we're here for," Les Vaughn recalled (1989). Resulting from all this, of course, was the simple fact that "after you worked for McLendon, you could work for anybody" (Dowe, 1989).

One person wearing several hats appealed to Gordon's Scottish instincts for thriftiness. Fewer persons doing more things resulted in money saved for the company. And those employees who were filling several roles at once in the McLendon Stations were less apt to show wealth for their efforts than to carry an impressive title. In a carryover from the Liberty Broadcasting days, Gordon was more than liberal in bestowing lofty sounding titles on his staff. "Yeah, there was a lot of that, and in Gordon's defense he knew what he was doing," Don Keyes remarked. "He was dealing with young men, and those titles at the time were really neat. We ate that . . . up. I was a vice president of the McLendon Stations. Well . . . that's pretty good stuff. But I was having so much damn fun that I didn't care about money" (Keyes, 1989).

Gordon was not much for inviting input from his staff. He preferred generating ideas from his own imagination rather than brainstorming for ideas with others. Thus Gordon did not care much for meetings (Routt, 1989). Frequent staff meetings were necessary, though, and when they occurred Gordon took center stage. The agenda usually consisted of programming matters. "He brought the ideas and we listened," Don Keyes said.

> You were free to speak up. You didn't feel at all intimidated. If you felt intimidated, it wasn't intimidation, you felt somewhat in awe: "Here's the great man with the ideas. Surely I have nothing important to say." But . . . as you got to know him . . . and if you wanted to raise your hand and contribute something, that was fine. We'd kick it around a little bit. It was quite open. (Keyes, 1989)

Gordon was the idea man for certain, but it took his employees to consummate those ideas. Gordon surrounded himself with persons he knew would carry out projects the way he wanted. He was not foolish enough to proceed with an unworkable idea, and certainly he heeded the warnings of McLendon Station staff about ideas that obviously could not work (Callison, 1989). But Gordon was apt to try anything—to develop any idea that seemed the least bit doable—and practicality was irrelevant (Dowe, 1989). Gordon would not allow any barriers or boundaries to inhibit the ideas that he wanted to accomplish ("Tribute," 1986). And given his drive and aversion to quitting (Vaughn, 1989), Gordon saw most of his ideas become reality.

Creativity was always the catalyst for whatever kind of meeting Gordon conducted. His imagination was always projecting itself onto the agenda. And if anyone chose to contribute to the agenda, Gordon required that the contribution be of the imagination as well. If a McLendon Corporation employee seemed not to have a creative mind by nature, Gordon made certain that the employee had at least enough of an appreciation for the creative process to fit securely into the McLendon organization. Don Keyes said that Gordon

> chose his people carefully. I never could get into his head to find out what he looked for in an individual, but a lot of us . . . stayed with him all these years when others drifted away . . . or didn't work out. But if there was a common denominator among those who stayed, it was a sensitivity and an appreciation of the way his mind worked. And we absorbed a lot of it ourselves, so we could go and do likewise. (Keyes, 1989)

By and large, Keyes concluded, Gordon "trained us by example to think as he did, to develop the feel for the bizarre. . . . You never had classes in it" (Keyes, 1989).

McLENDON STATION POLICY BOOKS

Whatever there was about meetings that was unappealing to Gordon, there was none of that to be found in the mode of management-staff communication he seemed to prefer—the memo. He was a prolific memo writer and by all accounts had developed the McLendon memo style into a literary form. Dallas newspaper columnist Dick Hitt referred to Gordon's memos as "gems of brevity and profundity" (Hitt, 1986a, pp. A-1, A-8).

Gordon would not tolerate a memo from any employee that was more than one page, and it had to be double-spaced. He said that any idea should be expressed in one page or less (Routt, 1989). Gordon may have believed that for his own memos, and may have even attempted to practice it with respect to memos of a more personal nature. But many of his memos stretched on for several pages and had as their purpose statements of policy on a variety of McLendon Station operational matters.

These memos, along with memos written by other McLendon Corporation management personnel, were filed under different operations categories at first, but they eventually were placed in black, loose-leaf ring binders that became collectively known as the McLendon Policy Books. As new policy statements and accompanying documents frequently were placed into an ever-expanding array of binders, they eventually took up nearly an entire wall of shelf space in Gordon's office (Keyes, 1989). *Business Week* gave the bookshelf measurement as six feet, and said it was full of ingredients that would create the "right sound" for the McLendon Stations ("Zany," 1961, p. 131). Chuck Blore said that the McLendon Policy Books contained the ingredients for running the "ideal radio station under ideal conditions" (Blore, 1990).

"Policy book was really a misnomer," Don Keyes said. "They were more like operations manuals—'thou shalt do this; thou shalt not do that.' And every damn memo that concerned anything of programming was in the policy book" (Keyes, 1989). The fact that Gordon apparently never purged anything from his policy books accounts for the size and bulk to which the collection grew.

The policy books "were pretty well secured" in Gordon's office, Don Keyes said, but not because of any great fear Gordon had of their contents leaking to competitors. Keyes said the policy books "weren't so much confidential as they were precious. [Gordon] didn't want them taken out of the building lest they be lost, destroyed in a fire" (Keyes, 1989).

Besides Gordon and his management staff, Keyes said, "any manager who came to town could thumb through them. If a PD [program director] came to town to visit he was welcome to sit down and thumb through them." The policy books were not required reading, said Keyes (1989), but it would seem that the prudent McLendon Corporation employee would have been familiar with their content.

The McLendon Policy Books now are housed in the Southwest Collection at Texas Tech University. A perusal of the rather substantial contents of the books shows that few matters related to McLendon Station programming were omitted. Most revealing perhaps are the memos, which show Gordon's attention to detail. He wanted to know everything that was happening at his stations. His concern with criticism of program content at McLendon Stations is also apparent, as are his efforts to solicit and to praise criticism that proved beneficial to his stations' programming success.

The McLendon Policy Books are so comprehensive, in scope of subject matter as well as in the chronological progression of station operation, that they constitute an invaluable record of radio station format development during the 1950s and 1960s. In fact, David MacFarland, whose masterful study of top 40 radio has been cited frequently in this book, credits Gordon with having left the only record of its kind that allows broadcast historians to view a unique period in radio management history (MacFarland, 1973, pp. 2–3).

7 *McLendon Station Format Innovations*

The group of radio stations built by Gordon and B. R. McLendon eventually stretched across America, from New York to California and from Michigan to Texas. And while Gordon's talent was applied first to perfecting Top 40 and implementing that format at several McLendon Stations, he also pushed format innovation in other directions. Radio programming that appears commonplace today was not so until Gordon McLendon created it. Not all of his format experiments were successful, of course, but miscalculations as to what listeners would accept hardly deterred the brash experimenter from trying ever more intriguing program ideas. To Gordon, much of radio's allure during the 1950s and 1960s seemed to be in the way a talented person could mold the medium with only the imagination as a guide and create fascinating aural sculptures in the process.

KABL'S BEAUTIFUL MUSIC FORMAT

When Gordon and B. R. decided to expand the McLendon Station group to the West Coast, Gordon was forced by marketplace circumstances to depart from the Top 40 format that had made such a success of KLIF, KTSA and KILT. Just what the new format would be was not apparent at first, according to Don Keyes. " 'I'm gonna buy KROW, Oakland,' " Keyes recalled Gordon telling him one day, " 'So, let's go out to San Francisco and figure out what the hell we're going to do with it' " (Keyes, 1989). At that point—presumably in late 1958 or early 1959—Gordon, accompanied by Keyes, went to San Francisco, checked into a hotel room for two days, swept the radio dial back and forth, and took notes on what stations in the market were programming. They discovered that at least five stations were airing a Top 40 format and that "they all had jingles, they all had disc jockeys, they all had mobile news units" (Keyes, 1989). In a word, the stations were all carbon copies of one another and, ironically, all had been modeled after the McLendon Station brand of Top 40 sound.

How was Gordon to compete? There was no doubt in his mind that a McLendon Station could "outprogram" the other Top 40 stations in the market. "We can take this 5,000 watts at 960, which is a fine signal," remarked Don Keyes, "and we can put a great Top 40 station on the air, but will the listening public differentiate? Will we be able to garner enough audience to make it worthwhile?" (Keyes, 1989). In other words, said Keyes, would the expense and the uphill struggle required of going head-to-head with five other Top 40s be worth the splintered and somewhat meager audience likely to result? The answer, of course, was no. However, what had caught Gordon's attention while meandering around the radio dial was the absence of any good music or beautiful music—something that Gordon called "schmaltz" (Keyes, 1989).

As a result of that session in a San Francisco hotel, a decision was made to create what would become known as the "KABL format." The name derived from the station call letters that eventually would replace the KROW call letters. The essence of the KABL format "was simply beautiful music" ("The Top 40," n.d., p. 25). By itself, a beautiful music format was nothing new. One of the oldest and best stations airing such a format—KIXL in Dallas—no doubt had inspired Gordon to some degree. The station, owned and programmed by Lee Segall, traced its heritage "back to the 1940s, when several independent local stations programmed nothing but music, lush and tasteful, as an alternative to the news-drama-features-and-music mix on the networks" (Fornatale and Mills, 1980, p. 78). Segall's own brand of beautiful music programming "emphasized charm and grace," and KIXL commercials were purposely nonintrusive (Fornatale and Mills, 1980, p. 78). Gordon, it will be recalled, already had experimented with a format similar to KIXL's at KELP in El Paso.

Here, then, was Gordon's starting point, but there would have to be some major alterations in the KIXL brand of beautiful music format if such a station was to succeed, especially in San Francisco. "After all," Gordon would say later, "good music stations have arrived in San Francisco before and been received with all the cordiality of Eisenhower at a Khruschev [sic] family reunion" (McLendon, 1960b, p. 1). So there would have to be an evolution from the KIXL sound to a "modern" beautiful music sound (Fornatale and Mills, 1980, p. 78) or the KABL format.

Gordon's theory centered on running his beautiful music KABL in much the same fashion as he ran his Top 40 stations (McKinsey, 1990). As he explained it:

> Until we proved this new theory at KABL, it was thought that good music stations must be replete with dignity and deficits, better music and boredom,

> symphony and suffering, melody but monotony, arpeggios with anodyne, and generally have all the personality of a dental drill. It was even considered almost socially improper for a good music station to mention occasionally that it was going quietly broke. It was the damndest psychology I ever saw.
>
> We believed there could be a good music station with *color*, with flamboyance and excitement and delicious anticipation. The macabre concept of a good music station fitted the old theory about like socks on a rooster. (McLendon, 1960b, pp. 2–3)

One very important market factor element would have to be considered before Gordon could fashion the particular format that would succeed in San Francisco. That factor was listener expectation. San Francisco was, after all, "a city that's very much in love with itself":

> It just looks at itself in the reflection of the bay, and says, "Ain't I beautiful; ain't I cultured." . . . The cultural element there with the symphony and the ballet was so strong. And this was the audience we were appealing to—the upscale, affluent, well-educated adult in San Francisco; a very cosmopolitan bunch of people. (Keyes, 1989)

Recognizing the special character of his audience, Gordon set about to design a musical sound best suited for that character.

A common programming practice at beautiful music stations had been to place a long-play album of the Montovani or Percy Faith variety onto a turntable, position the tone arm at the first album cut, and then allow the stylus to track through all the remaining cuts on first one side and then the other side of the album. "That was beautiful music. No thought; no nothing. It was somnolent; it was dull; it was just a drag," said Don Keyes (1989).

> So we designed a music policy that repeated every 15 minutes. We opened up with category one—big, full, lush instrumentals, *ala* the Boston Pops' *I Could Have Danced All Night*. . . rollicking, merry, full. We'd come out of the news with that. Then for a change of pace into the Art Von Damme Quintet for a lighter sound without the intensity of a pop orchestra, with *Stardust*. Then into a vocal which in most cases was a chorale—Norman Luboff Chorale, Roger Wagner Chorale . . . with a choral version of *Summertime and the Livin' Is Easy*. The fourth selection [was] usually Latin, maybe Xavier Cugat. . . . That was the format. It repeated every 15 minutes. (Keyes, 1989)

The idea was to create a sound that made listeners comfortable: favorites from years past, heavy on the lush strings and light on the brassy big band sound. It "was simply beautiful music following the same programming philosophy as the Top 40 stations in that we played . . . familiar music," recalled Don Keyes (1989).

Once the "familiarity" ingredient of the KABL format had been fashioned to Gordon's standards, the format's second ingredient—promotion—was added. Promotion obviously was the one element that gave the KABL format a distinct place in radio history. And like the musical design, the KABL format also borrowed heavily from the Top 40 promotion concept in that the promotion had "to excite, to interest, to titillate" the audience. However, "you don't excite the beautiful music audience by giving away Beatles tickets," said Don Keyes. "But you do come at them with a terribly sophisticated, puckish sense of humor" (Keyes, 1989). Gordon added that the station's promotion would have to depend "upon an offbeat *New Yorker Magazine* approach, upon subtlety itself" (McLendon, 1960b, p. 4).

Once the music and promotion policies were set, the KABL format was nearly ready for unveiling. Only one more hurdle had to be cleared: securing the KABL call letters. Gordon had wanted to change the KROW call letters to something that would more closely identify the newest McLendon Station with San Francisco. Billie Odom, whose husband Homer would manage the station, suggested KABL—pronounced "cable" (Odom, 1990). The link between the call letters and San Francisco's famous cable cars was a perfect match.

There would be a slight problem, though, with the KABL call letters assignment. When Gordon asked attorney Marcus Cohn to arrange the change from KROW to KABL, Cohn discovered that the KABL call letters already had been assigned to a U.S. Navy vessel. Gordon was not content to give up, however. He asked that Cohn find the ship. Cohn pursued the matter and finally located records of the ship's whereabouts. It happened to be resting at the bottom of the ocean. The KABL call letters obviously were no longer of any value to the original user, so the FCC approved transferring them to Gordon (Cohn, 1989).

Promoting the new station to its potential audience came with a typically McLendon touch. A forty-five-day promotion campaign consisting of billboards, newspaper ads and skywriting and costing nearly $35,000 preceded the day in May 1959 when KROW would cease to exist and KABL with its tailor-made format would take to the airwaves. A full-page San Francisco newspaper ad appearing on the day of the switchover told the public to prepare for a big surprise at KROW. Gordon then aired a recording of a 1951 Brooklyn Dodgers-New York Giants baseball game—a broadcast that no doubt delighted San Franciscans with their newly franchised San Francisco Giants. Between innings Gordon announced that a big change would happen at KROW at the end of the game ("Zany," 1961, p. 126). Sure enough, at game's end Gordon announced to his listeners what kind of programming they might expect to hear on KABL (McKinsey, 1990). The KABL format was born.

Gordon had no idea how well or how quickly KABL would grab hold of an audience. He therefore was taking not only an aesthetic risk but a financial risk as well. "When you do this," Gordon would say later, "you have to have the guts of a cast-iron monkey" ("Zany," 1961, p. 126). One of the more risky financial moves was KABL's rejection of several advertising clients who formerly had bought time on KROW. They were deemed unsuitable for the new KABL image. "We had to kick off a lot of business not in keeping with the new format—you just don't advertise laxatives on a good music station," Gordon remarked ("Zany," 1961, p. 126).

KABL suffered through a brief period of red ink before turning the corner to profitability. By the end of December 1959, KABL had taken in $360,000 in revenue, and by the end of the following year the station's income figure had zoomed to $1,275,000. The station was on its way to becoming one of the McLendon Station's "biggest money makers" ("Zany," 1961, p. 126).

Financial success was equaled by ratings success. KROW had been in last place in the San Francisco market when Gordon bought the station. Within six months of implementing the KABL format, the station had overtaken the previous market leader, KSFO, to move into first place (McKinsey, 1990). In fact, Gordon asserted that KABL became the first beautiful music station "in the history of broadcasting" to attain a number one in the Hooper Ratings (McLendon, 1981b).

Gordon took full advantage of KABL's extraordinary climb in ratings by promoting his station in the business community as an advertiser's dream. During a 1960 speech to the San Francisco Advertising Club, Gordon boasted:

> We believe that our 17 to 25% of the San Francisco audience is, at the *minimum*, the equivalent of a 50% share for any pop music station, because we deliver predominantly an adult, moneyed, *buying* audience. Even the teenagers we have are the more thoughtful, better educated and perhaps upper-income level group. (McLendon, 1960b, p. 6)

Much of the appeal of KABL came from the wry sense of humor—the sophisticated, puckish sense of humor that became a KABL trademark. To the degree that he could, Gordon rewrote the Top 40 promotion policy to fit comfortably with the KABL sound. There were giveaways and contests in the same spirit as those at McLendon Stations airing Top 40 formats, but at KABL these promotional devices took a decidedly different spin that carried with them "the unmistakable McLendon flair" (Keyes, 1989).

One of KABL's more notable contests was arranged in conjunction with the San Francisco Symphony. The contest winner, whose entry card had only to be selected by a simple drawing, did not win tickets to a symphony concert, as likely would have been the case had the contest been run by an ordinary radio station. No, the winner of KABL's contest won the entire San Francisco Symphony. The symphony had seen a wonderful chance to promote itself by agreeing to perform an evening concert on the front lawn of the KABL contest winner (Keyes, 1989).

Other KABL contests caused listeners to talk and the station's reputation to grow. Some of the contests had legitimate albeit rather outlandish objectives, such as the one that offered "ten cents in cash" for "the best letter theorizing an explanation of the Joliot-Curie craters on the backside of the moon" (McLendon, 1960b, p. 3). Some of the contests simply were outlandish. Take for example the one that offered the contest winner a one-week vacation in Death Valley. The second-place prize winner received a two-week Death Valley vacation, and the third-place winner received a three-week Death Valley vacation (McLendon, 1960b, p. 5).

Gordon also loved to play practical jokes on his KABL listeners. He ran a newspaper advertisement in April 1960 announcing that KABL soon would change its format to Top 40. Unseen by many KABL listeners who called the station to protest the format change were the words "Late April Fool," printed in small type in the corner of the ad ("Radio's Merry," 1961, p. 129). Commercials and station breaks on KABL were often voiced by Gordon himself in Chinese and Japanese ("Radio's Merry," 1961, p. 130). Even serious commentary on KABL was not off-limits to an injection of humor, as in the time that newscaster John K. Chapel paused during a news analysis to announce regrets "that the traditional lion-washing ceremony to have been sponsored by KABL at San Francisco's Civic Center at 3 P.M. has been called off because of lack of experienced lion washers" ("Radio's Merry," 1961, p. 132).

Gordon's whimsical touches complemented KABL's serious programming by means of another device that he and Don Keyes called exotics. Exotics, said Don Keyes, were "make-believe commercials for a product or service that you would not normally find offered to the general public." Keyes said that he "looked up Webster's definition of 'exotic' and it does tie in, and that's why we called them that" (Keyes, 1989). Bob Stevens, KABL program director, conceived the idea for exotics and produced the first one. Stevens played the exotic for Gordon and other McLendon Station staff members, who loved the idea (McKinsey, 1990).

From then on, Gordon and Don Keyes took on the task of writing exotics. The two, either individually or in collaboration, would write more than a hundred of them over the years. Then, with music and sound effects added by Les Vaughn, Gordon and Keyes voiced each exotic in the KLIF studios in Dallas and shipped them to KABL for airing (Keyes, 1989).

One of the earliest KABL exotics was purportedly sponsored by the Tanganyika Tourist Commission and encouraged listeners to plan their next vacation for the "incomparable Tanganyika Territory." Buried with the glowing description of this jungle paradise amidst the sound of African drums and wild animals was the line, "Rumors of Tse Tse flies and sleeping sickness in the area have been vastly exaggerated." It was the kind of line that caused the unsuspecting listener who otherwise might have thought the exotic was a legitimate commercial to sit up and say, "Huh? What was that?"

(Keyes, 1989). These were lines that grabbed the listener, that caught him or her entirely off-guard.

Don Keyes noted that some KABL exotics "crossed the bounds of believability" and were "obviously a joke. But the fun ones were the ones right down the middle. You couldn't really be sure from listening if it's legitimate or not" (Keyes, 1989).

What Gordon attempted to achieve with the KABL exotics was what he tried to achieve with any other programming component. He wanted people to talk about them. That would spread the word about KABL faster than any other method of promotion. And it worked. Fortunately, it worked in the very circles that Gordon wanted to attract as KABL listeners. The "adult sophisticated element" began tuning to KABL to see what the exotics were all about (Keyes, 1989). Once they made the initial effort, they usually remained loyal listeners.

Listener loyalty was rewarded by KABL programming that stretched beyond offbeat promotions. The structure of the KABL format by itself appealed to listeners. KABL was said to be the first radio station to cluster both its records and its commercials. Four or five records were played in a row, often with no interruption. Spot announcements were played at fifteen-minute intervals and were held to about twelve announcements per hour. Eventually, all KABL music was transferred from records to audio tape, giving the station a lead in creating an automated programming system (McKinsey, 1990).

All of the music that KABL played eventually caused a dilemma. As the 1960s wore on, fewer and fewer U.S. record companies were producing records of the type that KABL programmed. Gordon's solution was to send Ken Dowe to Europe with orders to search the record stores of several major cities and to buy as many easy listening record albums as he could find. Dowe said that he was viewed as a "crazy American" as he went about buying hundreds and hundreds of albums from Denmark to France and shipping them back to the United States.

Ken Dowe's job of securing music for KABL did not stop there. He decided that rather than Gordon scouring the world for record albums, why not create his own? Gordon liked the idea and put Dowe in charge of producing such an album. A group of vocalists, who were to be called the McLendon Singers, were recruited to travel to Los Angeles, where arrangements were made with MGM Records to record the first McLendon Singers album. Gordon was delighted with the finished product (Dowe, 1989). Needless to say, the McLendon Singers were heard frequently on KABL.

Besides the musical appeal, KABL identified itself with listeners by airing "mood introductions, vignettes, or programettes which describe landmarks, historical events, and other facts relating to area tradition and legend" (*McLendon Pacific Corporation*, 1966b, p. 865). Each of these was about thirty seconds in length and was broadcast twice each hour. All were produced in

Dallas (*McLendon Pacific Corporation*, 1966b, p. 865). Gordon voiced each one at first, but later, Don Keyes also began voicing them. Neither of the two would trust anyone at KABL itself to do the job as they felt it should be done (McKinsey, 1990).

The serious tones of KABL mood pieces were juxtaposed by Gordon's efforts to poke fun at the station. Listeners were surprised by frequent comments from a female "Girl Friday Afternoon" who would break into programming at various times to say, "That last guy I heard on KABL had a real bad case of announcer's mouth," or "You know what . . . ? I once had a trained seal that read commercials better than you do," or "I've been listening to your station all week. Tell me something, what have you got against Elvis Presley?" (McLendon, 1960b, p. 5). And in response to the KABL station ID, "This is Cable, K-A-B-L Oakland—960 on your dial, in the air everywhere—in San Francisco" (*McLendon Pacific Corporation*, 1966b, p. 865), Girl Friday Afternoon often would respond sarcastically: "In the air everywhere in San Francisco. What's the matter with the air over Oakland?" (McLendon, 1960b, p. 5).

In a way unintended by Gordon, there were others asking the same question about the air over Oakland, and they were not asking in a humorous tone. Gordon was having great success with KABL, probably because it suited his demeanor so well. The kind of music KABL aired—schmaltz as Gordon called it—was his kind of music (McLendon, 1981b). The humor employed so effectively by the station was his kind of humor. Gordon so much as admitted at one point that among the McLendon Stations, KABL was his "pride and joy of all of them" ("The Top-40," n.d., p. 25). The fact that the San Francisco audience for his station could appreciate all of these things right along with Gordon made owning and programming KABL just that much more a delight.

Unbeknownst to most listeners, though, was the fact that KABL had not been licensed to serve San Francisco at all. The station had been assigned by license to serve Oakland, San Francisco's neighbor across the bay. Gordon had been able to deftly conceal that fact in the manner by which he identified KABL to listeners during station breaks. In fact, when several disgruntled Oaklanders finally complained about KABL's ignoring that city, the FCC found that the station had not at all ignored Oakland in actual service. But in terms of targeting KABL programming and verbally citing the station's service area during on-air station IDs, there was no doubt as to which city Gordon wanted KABL to serve (*McLendon Pacific Corporation*, 1966b, pp. 863–879). KABL was in his mind a San Francisco radio station.

Gordon's notions about linking KABL with San Francisco came almost entirely from his romantic image of the city. Being the creative type, Don Keyes said, Gordon

> was very sensitive to art and beauty in any of its forms, not the least of which was the City of San Francisco with its beautiful vistas of the Bay and the ocean

> and the bridges and the fog creeping in in the afternoon, and the little hide-away restaurants and lounges and terrible sophistication of the people who lived there. (Keyes 1989).

It was this image of the city and its inhabitants that had formed in Gordon's mind prior to the westward expansion of the McLendon Stations. "Consequently," said Keyes,

> when we had the opportunity to purchase a facility that would cover San Francisco, he wanted to have it regarded as a San Francisco station. He wanted to make love to San Francisco on the air. It's hard to do when the station's licensed to Oakland. Oakland just doesn't have the glamor of San Francisco with its cable car bells and all its rich history and Jack London and the waterfront and Barbary Coast and all these things. Oakland sort of sat over there like a giant frog on the other side of the bay. So, you can't romance Oakland. There's nothing to it. It's industrial, it's dirty, it's grimy. (Keyes, 1989)

There was, of course, the more practical matter of San Francisco being a more lucrative financial market than Oakland for tapping potential advertisers. San Francisco, with a population nearly twice that of Oakland, "is where the money is," noted one former KABL station manager (*McLendon Pacific Corporation*, 1966b, pp. 864, 877). The creative angle still was the most important draw to Gordon, though. Creative programming simply was easier to produce for listeners who appreciated it and for a city, in Gordon's opinion, that deserved it.

But to several citizens of Oakland, Gordon's low regard for that city's cultural, scenic and financial attributes did not matter so much as what they regarded as poor service from a radio station licensed to serve Oakland. The circumstances of this complaint that eventually drew the FCC into the matter are interesting. First, the complaints about KABL were filed with the FCC in February 1965, some six years after the station had been in operation. Second, the complaints came from only three persons: the Oakland mayor, city manager and city attorney (*McLendon Pacific Corporation*, 1965, p. 132).

Subsequent FCC hearings showed that a motive behind these complaints may not have had so much to do with KABL's service to Oakland as with the several occasions when the KABL news director opposed mayoral decisions on certain policy matters (*McLendon Pacific Corporation*, 1966b, p. 874). Gordon went so far as to suggest, off the record, that relations between Mayor John C. Houlihan and KABL newsman John C. Chapel were "strained" and that they were "political antagonists" ("Bureau," 1966, p. 48). Houlihan's ire over Chapel's on-air opposition to a mayoral pay increase evidently was the specific provocation that had led to the mayor and his associates filing their FCC complaint (McKinsey, 1990).

Formal proceedings to resolve complaints against KABL were conducted by the FCC on November 16 through 19, 1965, in Oakland and on January 20, 1966, in Washington, D.C. (*McLendon Pacific Corporation*, 1966b, p. 863). What the record from these proceedings showed was not a station that ignored its requirements to serve the Oakland market but rather a station that served Oakland exceedingly well. Testimony from numerous prominent citizens of Oakland and leaders of Oakland civic organizations built a strong case for KABL's involvement in and assistance to the community. The FCC rejected claims filed by the Oakland city officials that KABL was negligent in fulfilling the "needs, tastes, and desires of the city of Oakland," as required by commission rules (*McLendon Pacific Corporation*, 1966b, pp. 869–877).

Also in KABL's favor was the coverage area over which its 5,000 watts of power spread the station's signal. That FCC-assigned area included San Francisco as well as Oakland. Somewhat complicating matters was a new FM station, KABL-FM, that the McLendons had acquired in April 1965. The station was firmly located in San Francisco and was licensed to serve San Francisco, but its programming duplicated entirely the programming of its AM sister station (*McLendon Pacific Corporation*, 1966b, p. 864).

Certainly not in KABL's favor, though, was the location of the station's commercial offices and some of its key personnel in San Francisco, although main and auxiliary studios were located in Oakland (*McLendon Pacific Corporation*, 1966b, p. 864). Standard KABL advertising contracts gave a San Francisco address for the station, as did the Oakland telephone directory. What's more, station letterhead stationery carried a logo that showed "the picture of the front of a cable car, with KABL to the left, MUSIC to the right, SAN FRANCISCO above, and DIAL 960 below" (*McLendon Pacific Corporation*, 1966b, pp. 866–867).

The most serious offense committed by KABL in the FCC hearing examiner's view pertained to its station ID policy. In the end it would be the examiner's considered opinion that KABL willfully had violated the FCC rule that required broadcast licensees to identify their stations by call letters and location at appropriate times throughout the day (*McLendon Pacific Corporation*, 1966b, p. 877).

The hearing examiner concluded that KABL station IDs "obviously [were] designed to create only one impression in the minds of listeners, viz., that San Francisco, and not Oakland, [was] the station's central point, as well as its principal area of interest and activity" (*McLendon Pacific Corporation*, 1966b, p. 877).

Based on this conclusion, FCC Chief Hearing Examiner James D. Cunningham ordered in May 1966 that the McLendons be fined $10,000 (*McLendon Pacific Corporation*, 1966b, p. 879). At the time, this was the maximum that the FCC could impose ("McLendon Faces," 1966).

Gordon was not willing to acquiesce to the hearing examiner's judgment. His attorney, Marcus Cohn, appealed the examiner's decision to the full panel of seven FCC commissioners. Once the commissioners agreed to hear the appeal, they paid close attention to the one KABL station ID that seemed to draw the most interest: "This is Cable, K-A-B-L Oakland—960 on your dial, in the air everywhere—in San Francisco." After carefully considering the ID's content, the commissioners concluded that undoubtedly KABL "was attempting to create the impression that [it] is a San Francisco rather than an Oakland station," but "the fact remains that by announcing the station's call letters and the city in which it is licensed, KABL complied with the literal provisions of the rule and nothing more was required." Accordingly, the hearing examiner's decision was reversed, and no fine was ordered on the station ID matter (*McLendon Pacific Corporation*, 1966a, pp. 856–857).

Marcus Cohn had engineered a major win for Gordon in his skirmish with the FCC. This was not the first time nor would it be the last time that Gordon would go head to head with the regulatory agency. The two frequently were at odds with one another, simply because the FCC staff had far different visions than Gordon of what the broadcasting industry should be and how broadcasters should serve the public. Only two years before, as a matter of fact, the FCC had concluded a protracted case involving McLendon Station WYNR (later WNUS) in Chicago, which will be examined later. Gordon often spoke out, angrily in many instances, about his low regard for the FCC. What he said, along with a more extensive account of his relationship with the commission, also follows in a later chapter.

Gordon's close call with the FCC over the KABL station ID matter actually may have been closer than the printed record suggests. Don Keyes recalled with a smile many years later how the infamous "This is Cable, K-A-B-L Oakland—960 on your dial, in the air everywhere—in San Francisco" station ID was produced, and how it was meant to sound when aired.

Although the FCC had dropped its fine against KABL based on the fact that Oakland was mentioned in the station ID, Gordon had tried his best to make the city's name as indistinguishable as possible without completely omitting it (Keyes, 1989). The ID had been copied from and, in fact, was nearly identical to a Paterson, New Jersey radio station ID that read: "This is WPAT, Paterson—in the air everywhere over New York City." Since the FCC had never charged WPAT with violating its station ID rule, Gordon decided that KABL could safely use the WPAT ID as a model (*McLendon Pacific Corporation*, 1966b, p. 865).

So, Gordon went to work creating the ID. Two voices, Gordon's and Don Keyes's, actually were used in the ID, which was produced at KLIF. Keyes was first to speak, saying "This is cable." Gordon then said, "K-A-B-L, Oakland." And Keyes added the rest. Les Vaughn attached music and a "clang, clang" sound effect at the end of the ID to represent a cable car bell. It was a simple production—one that ordinarily would have allowed Gordon to use his announcing voice most effectively. But in this case it was not Gordon's intention so much to sound good as it was not to sound at all. Keyes said that Gordon made every effort to throw away or to swallow the word "Oakland" so that it was barely audible to the listener. "It really got funny after awhile," Keyes said, "because it got to the point we had a contest who could swallow 'Oakland' the most and still have it discernable. . . . We were throwing away 'Oakland' something fierce" (Keyes, 1989).

Gordon had such success with the KABL format in San Francisco that he eventually implemented it at other McLendon Stations. KOST in Los Angeles, following the station's ill-fated all-want-ad experiment, became a beautiful music station, as did WWWW in Detroit and WNUS and WNUS-FM in Chicago (McLendon, 1969a). In fact, Gordon eventually decided that he wanted all the FM stations that had been brought into the McLendon Station group to carry at least some version of the KABL format. Dave McKinsey, who had worked at KABL, was appointed as national FM program director and given the task of installing the programming components of the format, while Glenn Callison took care of necessary automation and other technical installations (McKinsey, 1990).

Imitation being rampant in the radio industry, station owners throughout America followed close on the heels of Gordon's success with the KABL format and created similar formats at their own stations. Without Gordon's creative instincts to guide them, though, most of the imitators quickly failed (Hall and Hall, 1977, p. 189).

WYSL-AM/FM

Even Gordon himself failed in transferring the KABL format to WYSL-AM/FM. The combination AM/FM station in the Buffalo, New York suburb of Amherst had been added to the McLendon Station group in 1960. One year after purchasing the station, Gordon purchased WBNY in Buffalo and moved the Amherst station there, complete with the WYSL (Pronounced "whistle") call letters (*City of Camden*, 1969b, pp. 432–433).

WYSL's programming complexion actually had been undergoing a major change prior to its move from the Amherst location. The station was, in fact, becoming an eastern version of KABL, even to the extent that WYSL music was the same music carried by KABL. This experiment in moving the KABL format to a very different kind of city with different kinds of listeners and expectations was Gordon's way of showing that a beautiful music station could work anywhere. Moreover, he was anxious to prove to critics who said that the experiment would not work that it would work very well indeed (McLendon, 1960b, p. 1).

Gordon recounted during a 1960 speech how advisors had warned him that Buffalo was not San Francisco, that Buffalo was "an industrial city—second largest steel city in the nation," that Buffalo was "the home of the awesome, endless ovens of Bethlehem Steel," and that Buffalo had "a highly immigrant population, a polyglot of Polish and Slovak descent" (Mc-

Lendon, 1960b, p. 1). But Gordon was not buying any of this. As he told his audience: "Our decision was to assume . . . that people are fundamentally alike and, in musical taste, peculiarly alike" (McLendon, 1960b, p. 2).

The gamble that Gordon took with beautiful music at WYSL seemed to be paying off in the early going. Within six weeks of operation, WYSL was attracting 12 percent of the Buffalo audience—*"almost exactly the same as KABL at a similar stage,"* Gordon boasted (McLendon, 1960b, p. 2). Unfortunately, the trend did not last. Buffalo was, after all, a city with different radio tastes from San Francisco.

Gordon was never one to admit defeat easily. To him, the WYSL miscalculation was a temporary lapse in finding just the right format for Buffalo listeners. A retrenchment of sorts occurred, and by 1966 Gordon had introduced yet another format concept at WYSL-FM. This one he called a "telephone discussion format—*programmed entirely by listeners*" (McLendon, 1966a, p. 3). WYSL-AM, in the meantime, had been airing a popular music format, once the KABL format was removed (McLendon, 1969a).

Gordon described the experimental WYSL-FM format as "a startling new variation in the old 'open line' telephone listener discussion format." Its basic ingredients were these:

> Each day between 11 in the morning and 2 in the afternoon, three hours each day, in-so-far as our responsibilities as a licensee will permit, we allow the citizens of Buffalo to program WYSL-FM. During those three hours, WYSL-FM listeners do all of the station's announcing. They do the station breaks and they select the subjects which they wish to discuss on the air with other WYSL listeners who call them on the telephone. (McLendon, 1966a, pp. 9–10)

Listening to this kind of programming, according to Gordon, was the equivalent to sitting "around our electronic cracker barrel" (McLendon, 1966a, p. 11). This "telephone listener discussion format," an early cross between modern talk radio and public-access cable television, would not last either. WYSL-FM eventually would go the same format route as its popular music WYSL-AM sister station (McLendon, 1969a).

XTRA: ALL-NEWS RADIO

There is no chronological sequence of Gordon's format successes and failures. They happened concurrently—success with success, failure with failure, or success with failure. Gordon's mind did not work in sequential fashion whereby one idea was born, nurtured and sent on its way in order to make way for another. Gordon's ideas were the product of multiple births. They happened in rapid-fire succession. Such was the case in the early 1960s, when Gordon's mind was particularly fertile in terms of producing ideas for new radio formats. And so, a little less than two years after the KABL format was firmly in place, Gordon conceived the idea for his own version of an all-news format.

Gordon did not give birth to all-news radio, as is commonly suggested. That distinction belonged to San Francisco's KFAX Newsradio, which launched what was billed as "America's first all-news station" in 1960 (Salzman, 1961, p. 65)—fully one year before Gordon's efforts got underway. The KFAX schedule cycled every hour throughout its broadcast day with "twenty-five minutes of 'hard' news on the hour and fifteen minutes on the half-hour. The intermissions were filled with features, discussions, special events, and reports covering specialized subjects such as religion, education, Social Security, science, books, and even cooking" (Salzman, 1961, p. 65).

KFAX was popular among listeners and gained respectable ratings, although the ratings failed to place the station among the top five in the San Francisco market. As a result, national advertisers were reluctant to place advertising on what they regarded as an experimental radio station. Thus, much-needed revenue never materialized to keep the KFAX all-news format alive. After the station had lost some $250,000 in its first seven months, the KFAX board of directors decided to drop the all-news format in favor of one that incorporated music programming (Salzman, 1961, p. 65).

Gordon no doubt was aware of the KFAX all-news experiment. His very popular KABL may even have led to the lower-rated all-news station's demise. Watching the competition struggle in a losing effort while experimenting with a new format, however, was never a reason for Gordon to doubt that he could succeed with his own version of that same format. And so it was that he prepared to create an all-news format for installation at a McLendon Station. Gordon was fortunate that his first chance to try out his all-news format would be in Los Angeles. There was a problem, though, in that the station that would originate the programming was located in Mexico.

Gordon had set sight in particular on the northern Baja California region, near Tijuana. From here broadcasters had realized that a radio station with enough transmitting power "would carry into Los Angeles with a signal as clear as moonlight over the Pacific Ocean" (Fowler and Crawford, 1987, p. 205). Legendary station XERB had been broadcasting programs meant for Los Angeles listeners since the late 1930s. The hundred-thousand-watt, clear-channel "border blaster" originated its signal from a resort beach near Tijuana called Rosarita (Fowler and Crawford, 1987, p. 209).

Another Tijuana station with less popular programming and much less signal strength than XERB (only 50,000 watts) was XEAK. It was here that Gordon would stake his claim in 1961 as an all-news radio pioneer (Fowler and Crawford, 1987, p. 213).

Gordon was prohibited by Mexican law from owning a radio station in that country. But he managed to obtain enough financial interest in XEAK to allow total control over the station's programming (Fowler and Crawford, 1987, p. 216). The extent of Gordon's interest in XEAK was publicly said to be limited to ownership of U.S. "sales rights" for the station, while his input regarding XEAK's day-to-day operation was said to be that of a "program consultant" (Routt, McGrath, and Weiss, 1978, p. 169). Luis Carrillo, whose family was XEAK's owner of record, served as the station's general manager (McKinsey, 1990).

Once XEAK was firmly in his grasp, Gordon's first task was to improve its signal strength into the Los Angeles market. Glenn Callison took over at this point and moved XEAK's transmitter from its inland location, "where its signal had to traverse very rugged terrain, mountainous terrain to get into the U.S.," to a site on the beach near Rosarita. The water path that the XEAK signal would now travel provided a conductivity that carried the station into Los Angeles with absolutely no impediments (Callison, 1989).

Don Keyes later described just how clear the XEAK signal was in Los Angeles. On the day that he and Gordon flew to the West Coast to determine how to format the station, the two were riding to the Beverly Hills Hotel in the hotel's limousine at about seven o'clock in the evening. Gordon reached over the front seat and tuned in XEAK. Recalled Keyes:

> *It comes booming in* at 690, 500,000 watts, 125 miles away. KMPC, Gene Autry's station, is at 710, right up from [XEAK] a couple of clicks, and we're as loud as KMPC on the dial. . . . This is really incredible. This is a unique opportunity here. We can invade Los Angeles from Mexico with this signal. Never mind San Diego which is sitting right there under the tower. We're both like a couple of kids. We're so excited. (Keyes, 1989)

That particular day was an eventful one, since Gordon only earlier had decided to install the all-news format at XEAK. He evidently had not broached the idea to anyone until the flight to Los Angeles when he mentioned it to Don Keyes. "What about all-news?" Keyes remembered Gordon saying as the two considered format possibilities for XEAK. Keyes said that it "was an electric moment. I don't recall when my mind has been so charged, grasping this . . . mulling it over, fine-tuning in my head. How can it work?" (Keyes, 1989)

Making the all-news format work was the key to its success, of course. Most broadcasters said that it could not work, because why would people stay tuned in all day to an all-news station? The answer to that question, said Don Keyes, was:

> They won't. This is the first format ever designed not for sustained tune-in but for spasmodic tune-in. . . . It took broadcasters a while to get a hold of that, 'cause heretofore we've been doing whatever you can to hold that audience all day long. . . . We knew there was no way to do that, so you put that aside. (Keyes, 1989)

With the basic idea in place, the components that would make the all-news format fly eventually would fall into place as well. That would have to wait, though, until Gordon could start the promotional wheels rolling to sell the all-news format to listeners.

The first item on the promotion agenda was a change of call letters. Inspiration for the new letters belonged to Don Keyes. In what remains as one of the most perfect matches of call letters to station format, Keyes suggested XTRA, as in "the newsboy standing on the corner, yelling, 'Extra, extra, read all about it.' " Gordon "almost fell out of the chair," recalled Keyes (1989). Needless to say, he loved the kind of identification that XTRA would provide his new format. Legally, the Mexican government required that the call letters be XETRA, but the "E" was never inserted by the station, so that all of its print promotion carried the logo, "X-TRA, 690. All the news, all the time. The world at your fingertips" (Keyes, 1989).

The XEAK call letter and format change occurred on May 6, 1961, with a promotional announcement that was one of hundreds of similar announcements that would bombard Southern California in the following weeks. "Most stations have just one word in their names," the announcement said. "X-TRA NEWS has two words. The reason is that we wish to make the name X-TRA NEWS descriptive of the service we offer—news and nothing but news" ("News and Nothing But," 1961, p. 108).

Actually, XTRA had to overcome a minor disaster its first day on the air. The station, an unair-conditioned two-room adobe building (McKinsey, 1990), was located in an open field where the station manager's collection of turkeys, chickens and goats were allowed to roam free. Because the spring day was rather warm, the outside door that led into the XTRA newsroom had been left standing open. The paper feeding through one of the station's teletype machines presented an enticing morsel for one of the manager's goats, which had wandered into the station and before being chased outside had begun chewing through XTRA's only source of programming (Keyes, 1989).

Russ Barnett was XTRA's managing editor. He supervised all facets of the station's twenty-four hour, seven-days-a-week program schedule. XTRA programming itself was described as "hard news and nothing but hard news" that most resembled a broadcast version of a metropolitan newspaper's front page. Gossip items, book reviews, editorial, society and fashion pieces were not to be heard on the station, at least during its first few years ("News and Nothing But," 1961, p. 108). Later, XTRA added "local Los Angeles news, international news, national items, sports reports, financial summaries, weather bulletins, [and] Hollywood blurbs" (McLendon, 1965, p. 11).

The station "was essentially a rip-and-read operation" (Routt, McGrath, and Weiss, 1978, p. 169). News items were gathered from an assortment of wire services, which eventually numbered more than a dozen (McLendon, 1965, p. 11). At first the station relied almost entirely on the wire services of the Associated Press and United Press International. Very quickly, though, a clipping service was added as a news source with material it supplied from major newspapers from around the United States and major cities around the world. Very important to the success that XTRA hoped to achieve was the Los Angeles City News Service, which provided news from the station's primary target area ("News and Nothing But," 1961, p. 108).

Newscasts were delivered at first in seven-minute cycles during each hour. Three persons in all would work a one-hour shift. One news person would deliver two back-to-back newscasts every seven and one-half minutes and then gather, edit and update his news package while another newsperson did his fifteen-minute airshift. Then a third person would take over. This gave each newsperson about thirty minutes to prepare fresh material ("News and Nothing But," 1961, p. 108). Individual news blocks were extended to twenty minutes each (McLendon, 1965, p. 11) after a 1962 survey found that listeners tuned in to XTRA an average of eighteen minutes ("Pulse," 1962, p. 98). News blocks eventually went to thirty minutes each to accommodate the many Los Angeles commuters who were spending thirty minutes or more driving to and from work (Fowler and Crawford, 1987, p. 216).

The station promoted itself as offering listeners the same advantage as a telephone time service with programming that it alone, out of the 147 or so stations with their marginal news operations in the Southern California radio market, could provide ("All-News," 1966, p. 103). Whenever there was a need to tune in on the events of the day, boasted the station, one need only turn to "X-TRA NEWS, the world's first and only all-news radio station. In the air everywhere over Los Angeles" ("News and Nothing But," 1961, p. 109).

The "in the air everywhere over Los Angeles" slogan was loaded with double meaning, of course. Gordon wanted XTRA to be identified with Los Angeles as closely as possible. Suggesting that the station's newscasts were "in the air" as well as "everywhere over Los Angeles" was to suggest a ubiquitous kind of operation. The wording also was cleverly phrased so as neither to reveal XTRA's true location nor to suggest that the station indeed was located in Los Angeles. What Gordon had done to disguise subtly the location of KABL in Oakland, he now was attempting to do with XTRA in Tijuana.

The problem of disguising XTRA's origination point became most acute during station identification time. How could the station deliver an on-air ID, as required by Mexican law, without actually mentioning its location? Yolanda Salas, then working for Don Keyes, provided the solution. She suggested that the XTRA (or XETRA) call letters be pronounced in Spanish. And so it was that come station ID time at the top of the hour, XTRA listeners would hear "a soft female voice . . . over a bed of Mexican music" say: " 'Equis a tay erray ah,' Tijuana, Mexico" (Fowler and Crawford, 1987,

p. 217). Most Los Angeles listeners were oblivious to what they were hearing during XTRA's station ID, and were never aware that they were listening to a Mexican radio station (Keyes, 1989).

Gordon later told of an idea that one of the Mexican nationals connected with XTRA's ownership concocted that—had it worked—would have relieved the station of having to camouflage its location. The idea was to have the small area of land on which the XTRA studio stood renamed "Los Angeles." That way, the station really could have identified itself, and quite legitimately, too, as "XTRA, Los Angeles" (McLendon, 1978).

Actually, XTRA did have a legitimate tie to Los Angeles, since its executive and sales offices were located in the city. Also, station logs, commercial tapes and other program material were transported to XTRA everyday from the Los Angeles offices (Routt, McGrath and Weiss, 1978, p. 169). But the fact that XTRA was nonetheless a Mexican station making every effort to nudge its way into the Los Angeles market did not sit well with area broadcasters, who saw the station's operation as deceptive, but more importantly as an economic threat. Robert M. Light, president of the Southern California Broadcasters Association, remarked that XTRA's effort "to camouflage itself as a Los Angeles operation strikes us as unethical, if not actually illegal" ("News and Nothing But," 1961, p. 109). Light worried that XTRA's success would invite other Mexican broadcasters to follow a similar route of attracting U.S. advertising dollars across the border ("News and Nothing But," 1961, p. 109).

There is no record showing that the FCC ever made an issue of Gordon's involvement with XTRA; the matter of deception seemed of concern only to radio station competitors in Los Angeles. Economics more than deception was really the main issue among Gordon's competitors, and for good reason. XTRA already had snared some major national advertisers during its first month of operation. And audience reaction to the all-news format was enthusiastic from the very beginning. Phone calls and letters to the station voiced support and made suggestions, but in no instance were there any complaints ("News and Nothing But," 1961, pp. 108–109). The audience stayed, too, as Gordon noted during a 1965 speech. "X-TRA News," he said, "is tuned by more listeners in one three hour period in one morning than rival KNX, a CBS owned-and-operated, 50,000 watt station, beaming a diversified format, reaches in an entire broadcasting week" (McLendon, 1965, p. 12).

XTRA had proven itself financially, turning a profit during its second year, but that was with a staff of twelve announcers who only read wire copy over the air and then rewrote it to be read again. None of the announcers really were reporters in the sense that they gathered raw news from its source (Fornatale and Mills, 1980, p. 102). That would change only a few years later. By 1966 the XTRA staff had grown to fifty, including twenty full-time, on-the-air news announcers and a supporting staff of sixteen. Many of these were actual reporters. Two of them even manned mobile news units in Los Angeles ("All-News," 1966, p. 103).

A minor catastrophe struck XTRA in 1966, when Tijuana police deported the station's announcers to San Diego following accusations that none of them had valid Mexican work permits. Until the situation was resolved some weeks later, XTRA newscasts were taped by the staff in San Diego and carried across the border to Tijuana (Fowler and Crawford, 1987, p. 217).

The all-news format at XTRA finally was doomed when Los Angeles radio station KFWB converted from a Top 40 format to all-news in March 1968. Not only was the station physically in Los Angeles, but with its mobile units and field correspondents, KFWB covered the city in a way that XTRA could not ("Dry Run," 1968).

The competition was too much for Gordon to overcome. He replaced XTRA's all-news format in 1967 with an automated all-music, no-talk format. Dave McKinsey had to smuggle equipment and tapes across the border, after which Glenn Callison secretly readied XTRA for its new programming (McKinsey, 1990). Gordon relinquished his business interest in the station to its Mexican owners shortly after the format conversion was completed.

WNUS, ALL-NEWS IN CHICAGO

Gordon was shortly to follow his initial success with XTRA by installing the all-news format at his Chicago station, WNUS, on September 3, 1964. WNUS financially surpassed the break-even point in March 1966 to make it the first successful all-news domestic U.S. radio station ("All-News," 1966, p. 100).

The decision to create WNUS (pronounced "W-News") may have been inspired by Gordon's creative drive, but there was also a more practical reason, which will be examined in much greater detail in a later chapter.

The WNUS version of all-news followed very closely the format model established at XTRA. Fifteen-minute rotating newscasts eventually gave way to thirty-minute newscasts. Wire service readers rather than station reporters provided the bulk of newscast material, although WNUS did employ three "news vans" to cover "on-the-scene" events in Chicago. Each van carried a "telesign" on its roof that not only displayed up-to-the-minute news items, but also helped promote WNUS to Chicagoans.

WNUS was never able to break into the ranks of the dominant market stations in Chicago. Gordon dropped the station's all-news format in 1968, just as he recently had done at XTRA, and replaced it with a music format (Fornatale and Mills, 1980, p. 103). By then, the idea for all-news radio had been planted firmly in major markets elsewhere. New York City's WINS and WCBS had converted to an all-news format in 1965 and 1967, respectively. Philadelphia's KYW converted to all-news in 1965, and the previously mentioned KFWB in Los Angeles adopted the format in 1968 (Fornatale and Mills, 1980, pp. 104–105). Gordon's plans to create a Seattle all-news equivalent to WNUS in 1965 by purchasing KBVU and changing its call letters to KNUS never materialized ("McLendon's New," 1965, p. 29). His purchase of the station fell through, but he eventually did use the KNUS call letters in Dallas.

The all-news format, like the KABL beautiful music format and the Top 40 format, were not original with Gordon. What he did with them, though—enhancing them with McLendon style—made the formats workable and profitable. Radio station owners who later would copy these formats usually copied the McLendon version because of its high potential for success.

KADS, ALL-WANT ADS IN LOS ANGELES

One of Gordon's radio format creations that no one yet has copied was all-want ads. Unfortunately, the only success that this format ever had was locked away in Gordon's optimistic mind. Even he had doubts at the outset about the all-want ad format's potential. To his credit, though, he was willing to give it a try. He was the captain of this all-want ad ship, and he was determined to sail the course.

The idea for the all-want ad format arose only a few weeks after Gordon's 1966 purchase of radio station KGLA-FM in Los Angeles, where the new and revolutionary format would be installed ("McLendon's New," 1965, p. 28). Gordon's original intention was to change the station's format from popular music to all-news. With that format the station would have provided an all-news format for FM listeners that complemented the all-news format already available on XTRA for AM listeners. But after determining that the cost of operating an all-news FM station would be prohibitive ("McLendon's New," 1965, p. 28), Gordon decided to change KGLA's format to beautiful music.

Don Keyes had been given the go-ahead to assemble all the necessary components to implement the new format when Gordon announced a change of mind. "Instead he wants to do something that's never been done before," Keyes recalled:

> He's always said over the years that there's one area of newspaper advertising revenue that radio has never been able to touch: classified ads. There's got to be a way to do it. And he proposes that we put together the first all commercial station—no entertainment, no news, no nothing. (Keyes, 1989)

Keyes, ordinarily an enthusiastic supporter, was not intrigued by Gordon's idea. He tried to dissuade him from going ahead by suggesting that FCC regulations would never allow such an idea to proceed. But Gordon was determined to take those regulations, according to Keyes, "twist them around and get that license" (Keyes, 1989).

The FCC, at the time, required that radio station licensees conduct what were termed community ascertainment surveys as a means by which licensees could determine community needs and how best to program their stations to meet those needs (*In the Matter of Primer*, 1971). Three such surveys of the Los Angeles market were conducted for KGLA, but not until the final one, conducted in November 1965, did the idea that listeners would be receptive to a want ad station emerge.

Armed with the survey results, Gordon went to the FCC with an application to change KGLA's programming to a want ad format on a one-year experimental basis. The station's's goal, said Gordon, would not be just to fill "a need" but rather a "unique need" ("All-Ad," 1966). He said that one of the values of his proposal would be the elimination of long deadlines that newspaper want ad customers ordinarily had to face. Gordon also pointed to the decreased cost of classified advertising on radio vis-à-vis the newspaper as a second value that an all-want ad station could offer. Gordon's plans called for running classified ads on the station for 112 hours a week, from 6 A.M. to 10 P.M. And he wanted to change KGLA's call letters to KADS, pronounced "K-Ads" ("McLendon's New," 1965, p. 28).

A few days after publicizing his proposal, Gordon told a *New York Times* reporter: "We have made surveys and talked to a lot of people in Los Angeles, and they say a classified-advertising station would be a good thing." So, said Gordon, "If the F.C.C. turns down our application . . , it will have to go to some important citizens in Los Angeles and say they don't know what is good for them, but the commission does" (Adams, 1965).

Gordon made much to-do over the survey, which he said had convinced him to create the want ad format. Actually, the survey had yielded exactly what Gordon had designed it to yield. An academic research term for the kind of information provided by Gordon's survey respondents is "cooked data," meaning that the survey was manipulated in some way to yield desired results. Gordon's survey had not been cooked so much as it had been simmered. And the chef in charge was Don Keyes, who later told how the survey was conducted:

> I was detailed to go to L.A., delay beautiful music . . . do an ascertainment that would support our filing for a 100% commercial station. I don't know how long it took me. . . . I called on everybody and his dog. . . . I got them to tell me that this [all-want ad format] would be a desirable thing. Because they'd never heard of it, I had to set it up in their minds first. "Here's how it would work, Mr. President of Rockwell Aviation. You suddenly have a need for 30 machinists—big job comes in. Radio can respond quickly. Pick up the phone, we're on the air advertising for machinists. You don't have to wait to go to press." He said that would be good. . . . I must have been out there

> ten days, maybe more, interviewing community leaders, getting them to say this would be a desirable thing. (Keyes, 1989).

Gordon officially filed his application asking that the FCC approve his proposal for an all-want ad station on December 23, 1965 ("McLendon Station," 1965). The application proposal presented the FCC with what *Broadcasting* magazine playfully termed a "Gordian knot." The magazine went on to say that "McLendon is proving to be one reason the members of the FCC feel in need of a one-month vacation once a year." His all-want ad radio station proposal "may not pose the most profound problem the commission will face in 1966," declared *Broadcasting*, "but its probably one of the thorniest" ("A Gordian Knot," 1965, p. 34).

Ironically, Gordon's proposal came at a time when the FCC had just launched a policy to "curb excessive overcommercialization." How would the commission enforce such a policy when a station's only programming happened to be commercials? Also, the FCC had a policy that radio stations were "to contribute to the overall diversity of programming" within their service area. With Los Angeles the home of twenty FM and twelve AM stations with numerous signals coming into the city from distant stations, "what kind of service would represent more diversity than a want ad station?" *Broadcasting* magazine asked ("A Gordon Knot," 1965, p. 34).

Newspaper classified-advertising executives in Southern California did not appear overly concerned about Gordon's contemplated station. The matter was discussed, but the general feeling seemed to be that the FCC never would approve Gordon's application. And even if the application were approved, an all-want ad station was seen as providing greater competition for other radio stations in the market than for newspapers ("Papers View," 1966).

The FCC gave Gordon the chance to see just how competitive a want ad station could be when it approved his application on July 1, 1966 (McLendon, 1967b, p. 1). The license grant was unique—for the first time in this country, and probably in the world, a radio station airing predominantly commercials would be allowed on the air. There were some rigid stipulations for the station's operation, though. Since KADS would broadcast on an experimental basis, the FCC allowed only a one-year trial period for the experiment, at the end of which Gordon could apply for a full three-year license renewal. Also, periodic reports on the station's operation were to be filed with the FCC. A final report to be filed at the end of the one-year experiment also was stipulated. Included in the report would be listener and community leader reaction to KADS, a statistical summary of the types of ads aired on the station and whatever financial information the FCC thought it might need regarding the KADS operation (*The McLendon Pacific Corporation*, 1966, pp. 722–723).

Soon after the FCC's action, Gordon went to work promoting his soon-to-be all-want ad radio station. One of his first steps was to write a letter to Frank Lester, president of the Association of Newspaper Classified Advertising Managers, asking for membership in the organization. Gordon's letter, among other things, addressed the matter of the competition that KADS and any future radio stations patterned after KADS posed for newspapers. All-want ad radio, said Gordon, would "never have more than a small fraction of the classified advertising dollar which newspapers enjoy. Yet," he said, "because of radio's far lower operating costs, that small fraction will be *enough* to support radio want ad stations in markets throughout the country" (McLendon, 1966b, p. 2).

Gordon recognized the obvious, as his above comments suggest. In sheer numbers, radio could not compete with newspapers in the classified advertising arena. As an example, the number of ads that one estimate showed KADS capable of airing came to about 2,000 daily. The *Los Angeles Times*, on the other hand, carried about 10,000 classified ads in each daily issue ("Ad Station," 1966).

What also seems obvious from Gordon's comments to Lester is Gordon's subdued enthusiasm. He appeared more optimistic for the eventual success of his format idea than for the more immediate success of his new station. Given what lay in waiting for KADS, this less than ringing endorsement would prove Gordon once more prophetic, although in a curiously self-defeating way.

However muted his optimism might have been in July, it had been nearly boundless only four months earlier. Speaking before the Chicago Federated Advertising Club, Gordon explained the "almost unlimited advantages" that his yet-to-be-approved all-want-ad station would offer Los Angeles residents:

> It will be the first free circulation of want ads since it costs nothing to turn on your radio—whereas the newspaper charges you for each copy. You do not need to subscribe to or buy a copy of the radio. For those who need results urgently and cannot wait two or three days for the next edition of a newspaper, the immediacy of radio want ads will be a blessing. (McLendon, 1966a, p. 6)

Gordon noted in that same speech that one of radio's greatest advantages over newspapers in terms of the selling power of classified advertising rested in the ability of radio to utilize the human voice:

> Imagine the effectiveness of the little boy who has lost his dog asking for the return of his puppy on the radio in his own voice. What about the worker who badly needs work yet cannot present his case satisfactorily in the sterility of print? How much more effective to hear this man in his own voice speak his abilities and capabilities? There is nothing cold, impersonal or antiseptic

about radio—the warmth and emotion of the human voice are legend. (McLendon, 1966a, pp. 6–7)

Gordon and his staff spent long hours pulling together all the ingredients for converting KGLA to KADS. To Glenn Callison fell the task of improving the station's signal, installing new control room equipment and perfecting the automation system so that announcements for different categories of classified ads could be accommodated by a series of tape machines (Callison, 1989). To Gordon and a planning staff that included Don Keyes, Bill Stewart, Mitch Lewis and Andre Dunstetter fell the task of devising the specific components of the all-want ad format. Together these five prepared a policy manual that stretched for more than 300 pages, containing the very essence of how the new format would operate (McLendon, 1967b, p. 7).

Three very important matters of policy that were addressed by the group were acceptable and unacceptable categories of advertising; pricing; and method of announcement production and presentation. The five basic advertising categories selected for the KADS format included "help wanted, automobiles, general announcements, real estate and merchandise for sale." Ads in each of these categories were to air in thirty-minute blocks and be repeated from five to seven times throughout the sixteen-hour broadcast day. KADS would refuse ads from "so-called social clubs, introductory organizations and date bureaus" ("Ads Are Broadcast," 1967, p. 20).

Ads would cost five cents a word, with a fifty-word minimum. Advertisers who voiced their own ads, a practice that would be encouraged by KADS, would pay ten cents a second. Rates also would be available for local retail advertisers who chose to buy station time. Ads would run for either twenty, thirty or sixty seconds and would be separated from one another by a "sound divider" or "curtain," which was the equivalent of the newspaper "hairline rule" used to separate one ad from another. These sound dividers would be musical cues to listeners that one ad had ended and another was beginning.

Many of the ads that KADS would air would be heavily produced with, in some instances, multiple voices, musical background and sound effects. Children, celebrities and public figures would sometimes be used to voice the ads. And sometimes a dramatized or "man-in-the-street interview-type" production approach would be employed ("Ads Are Broadcast," 1967, p. 14).

Two final programming decisions remaining to be made were what to do during the non-want ad period of KADS's broadcast day, and how to promote the station. The hours between 10 P.M. and 6 A.M. were to be filled primarily with classical music and public service announcements. Heavy promotional advertising announcing KADS's arrival would be purchased in local Los Angeles newspapers, and XTRA would carry a heavy schedule of advertising to promote its sister station. At a later time, contests and other promotional gimmicks were planned for airing on KADS itself.

The last bit of business that Gordon needed to transact was hiring of staff personnel. Jack Danahy, then working at WNUS, was picked to manage a KADS staff of fifteen that would include four telephone solicitors and five announcers. All would work from the KADS studio and sales office located near downtown Los Angeles ("Ads Are Broadcast," 1967, p. 14).

Once all plans had been made, KADS was readied for its debut on November 4, 1966. Several days before, though, on October 24, Gordon and his staff went on the air at 6:00 A.M. to begin a "final, preliminary on-the-air survey of [KADS] listeners—a round-the-clock, 24-hour, live, call-in interview program—as to what their ideas were for the broadcast presentation of classified ads" (McLendon, 1967b, p. 3). The survey concluded on November 4, after nonstop on-air interviewing that Gordon later referred to as "by far the longest and most comprehensive such examination of public reaction ever attempted" (McLendon, 1967b, p. 3). After that, KADS was on its own to sink or swim.

Gordon had put an enormous amount of time and effort into perfecting the KADS format. But after all the energy expended to make KADS work, Gordon seemed more convinced in November 1966 than at any time before that the format would fail. Glenn Callison recalled an unforgettable remark that Gordon made to him and Don Keyes as all three were leaving Los Angeles after putting KADS on the air. "What do you think? Is it going to go?" Callison asked Gordon. "It hasn't got a chance, Cal, but don't tell Dad," was Gordon's reply (Callison, 1989).

Nearly three months after KADS had been on the air, station manager Danahy conceded during an interview that advertising volume had been small, but said that he was confident of the station's eventual success once more listeners learned of its existence. After all, nearly three million radio households of potential buyers and sellers lived in KADS's 200-mile radius coverage area ("Ads Are Broadcast," 1967, p. 14).

Gordon continued the process of soliciting listener reaction to KADS that had begun during his marathon on-air survey prior to KADS's sign-on date. For the next five months after the debut of KADS, fifteen minutes—3:00 to 3:15 P.M.—were set aside daily in the station's schedule to allow callers to air complaints and to make suggestions about the KADS service (McLendon, 1967b, p. 7).

By April 1967, Gordon was ready to file his first major written progress report on KADS "to acquaint the Commission with the scope of pre-debut preparations and with some of the problems so far encountered, as well as efforts being made to solve them" (McLendon, 1967b, p. 1). One of the major discoveries regarding KADS's operation, according to Gordon, had come during the station's pre-sign-on survey, when persons calling in ads were invited to deliver the ads over the air at that moment. Gordon contended that these "call-in" or "interview-type" classified ads were the most listenable and, thus, the most effective type of ad that KADS had aired.

With such ads, though, there was a risk that pranksters might take advantage of being on the air live to say things that were prohibited on the airwaves or otherwise not worthy of broadcast. For this possibility, Gordon indicated that KADS had installed a mechanism whereby "call-in" ads were taped and delayed several seconds before actual broadcast. This delay allowed announcers or engineers to judge a caller's real intent and to cut off the phone call if necessary (McLendon, 1967b, pp. 4–5).

Gordon concluded his written report on a somewhat ominous note: "Following the corporation's initial projection, KADS has operated at a loss since the inception of its all-classified format last November. Our initial projections called for an accounting break-even either during the months of August or September, 1967. We hope to stay with our projections both in programming and revenue" (McLendon, 1967b, p. 9).

Unfortunately, events that were soon to follow would prevent Gordon from knowing whether financial projections actually would be reached in August. Also to be made clear very soon were specific figures on just how much of a financial loss KADS had sustained.

There were problems with the KADS format from the very beginning. Many of them had been anticipated, since KADS was, after all, an experiment. One such problem was an especially tricky one to deal with, because it had to do with the very basic way an individual processes want ad information. Don Keyes argued that it was this processing factor that had "doomed from day one" any chance that the station had of succeeding. He explained his misgivings about the all-want ad format this way:

> This will not work in radio because unlike a newspaper, the ear cannot rehear the commercial where the eye can re-read it. . . . If you're looking to buy a used Mustang convertible, most major metropolitan newspapers list them alphabetically. . . . Maybe there are 10 in L.A. on any given day for sale. And I can look at those and consider what's on them, the mileage, the color, whatever I can glean from the ad that might pique my interest and compare this one to that one. And finally, pick up the phone and make some calls to see the car. You can't do that in radio. Once your commercial is broadcast, it's gone. And here comes the next commercial for a used Mustang. Here comes the next one. You're not going to sit there and make notes. (Keyes, 1989)

Coping with the problems was a matter of improvising—making adjustments here and there, tinkering with and fine-tuning the want ad format as its operation progressed.

One major revamp of the format occurred in May 1967. Keith Trantow had succeeded Jack Danahy as station manager in April. Trantow's first move was to drop the two-and-one-half hour want ad cycle, which consisted of thirty-minute blocks for different service and merchandise categories, to a much shorter one-hour cycle. Within each hour would be a fifteen-minute "instant want ad" feature whereby persons could phone KADS and be put on the air immediately to voice their own ad. This revised format was implemented on May 1.

Trantow had decided originally to charge a dollar for each instant want ad, but soon he was charging nothing. One reason for the free ads was the interest being generated by the instant want ad idea. Another reason was the difficulty in collecting the one-dollar fee.

The free instant want ads idea seemed successful enough that Trantow decided to revise the KADS format once more, starting June 1, to air free ads during most of the broadcast day. Paid ads were scheduled at the rate of thirteen per hour. As a result, more and more people began to take notice of KADS and to use its service. From 17 want-ad related calls received by the station between April 1 and April 11, the number zoomed to 2,043 between June 1 and June 11.

More phone calls meant that more staff was needed to handle the calls. More staff meant more expenses to KADS. For most companies, when business increases, greater operating expenses usually can be justified. But when the main product of the company is time, and most of that time is being given away, there is no income to cover increased expenses. This was the situation with KADS when Gordon decided to call a halt to his bold experiment. At the August 1967 completion date for the FCC's one-year all-want ad format experiment, Gordon filed an application to renew the KADS license, but indicated a desire to replace the station's current format with another one yet to be determined.

Gordon's final report filed with the FCC detailed the effort put into developing the all-want ad format. None of the various methods tried at KADS, said Gordon, had been effective enough in drawing an audience of sufficient size. As such, there was no remaining justification for continuing the all-want ad format ("Classified-Ad," 1967). The financial section of Gordon's report told the real story of the format's demise. During the first six months of 1967, KADS income had totaled only $22,807. Expenses during the same period had been approximately $109,000. That meant a whopping six-month loss of more than $86,000. The station's best month had been March, when its losses amounted to "only" about $10,000. February had been the worst month, with losses totaling nearly $18,000 ("Classified-Ad," 1967).

Gordon decided to forego any dramatic new programming experiments at KADS and instead to replace the all-want ad format with a music format. One twist would be that the new format would contain no news ("McLendon Gets," 1968, pp. 66–67). This would be a slight innovation—and as it turned out, Gordon's last radio format innovation—since at the time the FCC required that all broadcasters provide some news and public affairs programming on their stations (*Report and Statement of Policy Res: Commission en banc Programming Inquiry*, 1960). However, Gordon argued that the news and public affairs needs of Los Angeles were being adequately served by the many other stations in the market. The FCC agreed with him, and voted in March 1968 to approve both the KADS license renewal application and Gordon's request to change the station's call letters to KOST-FM ("McLendon Gets," 1968, p. 67).

Gordon's KADS experiment had failed, but it had caught the attention of broadcasters across the nation. The station's successes were measured in small doses, to be sure, but the precedent set by the FCC—a major McLendon nemesis—in approving Gordon's application for a one-year trial run with an all-want ad format was indeed significant. For the first time, the commission had "allowed virtually unlimited advertising . . . and it assigned a one-year license for experimental rather than probationary purposes" (Kushner, 1972, p. 267).

Despite Gordon's early doubts about KADS's success, he nonetheless held fast to a belief that an all-want ad format could succeed in time, under the proper circumstances and given the proper supervision. Gordon underscored these points during a 1981 interview, saying that all-want ad

> was a format that, in order to succeed, required my own or at least any owner's presence right on the spot. And with the full complement of radio stations that we had . . . it was impossible for me to be in all places at once, and thus due to my own inability to be physically present in Los Angeles for the length of time necessary to make that station a success, the all-want ad format fell by the wayside. And it has never been tried again. Were it tried again under the proper circumstances—at least, if I were to try it again—I'm convinced it would be one of the great successes in broadcasting. (McLendon, 1981b).

Broadcasting magazine concluded an article about the KADS failure by reviewing the McLendon radio format success stories. The closing sentence of the article was a terse two words: "What's next?" ("Classified-Ad," 1967). The question was a fitting one to ask, because his fellow broadcasters always knew that Gordon had a new format trick or two up his sleeve. But not this time. Gordon and B. R. already had begun dismantling their radio empire, reducing the size of the McLendon Station group to a manageable number of stations, which they would hold onto for a few more years until these stations, too, were sold.

The urge to put his format ideas into practice had ebbed, but Gordon's creative mind continued to generate format ideas that, if not he himself, then perhaps some future entrepreneur might try. Even as late as 1981, when Gordon had moved away from the radio business entirely, his mind instinctively kept in touch with possibilities for the medium. Gordon responded to a 1981 interview question about his format successes by contending that of all the specialized radio formats that had come into existence there was yet "one simple radio format" that remained untried and undiscovered. When asked to divulge the format, Gordon refused. "I have no reason to tell anybody what it is," he said ("Tribute," 1981). There is no evidence that he ever revealed the exact nature of his idea to anyone.

8 McLendon Station Editorials

Gordon McLendon's role in radio programming and promotion was well known to his colleagues in broadcasting, but few in the general public were aware of Gordon's many behind-the-scenes activities that so often affected what they heard. Nonetheless, Gordon indeed was well known to the public. He had entertained listeners across America with his baseball announcing, and in 1964, Gordon's campaign for the U.S. Senate (discussed in a later chapter) once again brought his name before the public. But, Gordon probably was best known for the many editorials that for nearly three decades carried his voice to millions of McLendon Station listeners.

McLENDON EDITORIALS: THE PROCESS

Radio editorials had been a part of programming at a number of stations during the earliest days of radio. However, the FCC in 1941 rendered a decision in the infamous Mayflower case, so named for one of the principals in the case, that effectively prohibited editorializing by broadcasters (*Mayflower Broadcasting Corp.*, 1941).

The *Mayflower* decision was controversial from the very beginning. Broadcasters opposed the imposition of such an all-inclusive prohibition on what they regarded as a right to express their views on public matters. They collectively petitioned the FCC to reverse its 1941 decision (Griffith, 1950, pp. 574–591). And in 1949, after a series of hearings on the subject during the previous year, the FCC complied (*Editorializing By Broadcast Licensees*, 1949).

Gordon claimed to have been the first to editorialize as soon as the FCC had lifted its prohibition on the practice (McLendon, 1981b). That very well may have been, but there is no record to verify the date when Gordon actually did air his first editorial at KLIF. One other broadcaster, Daniel W. Kops, general manager of WAVZ in New Haven, Connecticut, claimed that he had begun voicing editorials on his station in 1949 as well ("Radio Needs," 1955, pp. 140–151). And several unidentified broadcasters who responded to a survey on the subject said that they had editorialized throughout the 1940s, despite the FCC's ban on the practice (Carter, 1951, pp. 471–472).

If Gordon was not the first to editorialize following the FCC's 1949 decision, he definitely was among the first. And there would be few if any broadcasters during the coming years who would be as prolific as Gordon regarding the sheer number of editorials aired and the number of subjects covered. One count credited him with writing and airing more than 5,000 editorials during his broadcasting career (Patoski, 1980, p. 168). An alphabetized listing of Gordon's editorials, now housed at Texas Tech University's Southwest Collection, runs for more than thirty-two pages and carries over 1,500 editorial titles, ranging literally from A to Z ("Inventory," n.d.). A perusal of the editorial files at the Southwest Collection, however, shows that general titles were often attached to more than one editorial. Also, many of the editorials on file date from the latter half of Gordon's editorial career. Not present, and perhaps lost forever, are many of the editorials that he wrote and aired during the 1950s.

Gordon's philosophy of editorializing was summed up in a speech he delivered to the Georgia Association of Broadcasters in 1957 (McLendon, 1957c). By then he had become well known nationwide for his KLIF editorials and for the seriousness with which he approached his editorial subjects. "We believe that KLIF editorials are potentially the most powerful single weapon in Dallas for molding opinion in matters of public interest," Gordon told the Georgia broadcasters. Moreover, he said, "Our only policy in running editorials is to be sure that we are *right.* We feel that when you take an editorial position that is in any way selfish or prejudiced, the public knows it and your position is as dangerous as a Neiman-Marcus charge account" (McLendon, 1957c, pp. 9–10).

Gordon's policy was to limit his editorials to only one minute because, as he had determined, "That's about how long it takes you to read a newspaper editorial" (McLendon, 1958a, p. 11). His editorials sometimes exceeded that length if the subject matter warranted, but usually a one-minute editorial was the rule. Also a policy was the number of times an editorial would run. At first, Gordon required that it air "eight times a day—AFTER the seven, eight and nine a.m., twelve noon, 5PM, 6PM, 10PM and 11PM newscasts." That schedule included "two or three differently-worded versions of the same editorial to keep from boring the listener" (McLendon, 1958a, p. 11).

Gordon later revised his editorial schedule upwards to thirteen times a day. One 1968 schedule, for instance, shows that Gordon's editorials were to air at forty-five minutes past the hour for thirteen selected hours during the day on Wednesdays and Sundays. The schedule for editorials aired by local McLendon Station managers and for editorial rebuttals followed the same hourly schedule, but were aired on Monday, Thursday and Saturday. Hourly editorial slots were clumped during morning and late afternoon hours to take advantage of motorists listening to McLendon Station programming while commuting to and from work (Routt, 1968). The Wednesday and Sunday dates for Gordon's editorials were chosen because, according to Mitch Lewis, experience showed that the editorials gained "maximum attention" when aired on those dates (Lewis, 1968b).

Gordon seldom delivered editorials on more than two subjects per month during his first few years of editorializing. He "didn't believe . . . in a routine of editorials," Edd Routt said. "If he was moved, or if someone gave him a good idea that would move him, then fine, he'd do an editorial. But, he might go a month or two months without one" (Routt, 1989). This time lapse between editorials decreased dramatically in later years as Gordon gave more attention to his editorials. By the late 1960s, for example, he was airing editorials "every other day" (McLendon, 1969a). And by the 1970s, Gordon appeared to have accelerated his schedule to one new editorial every day (Editorial File, n.d.).

Gordon seemed not the least bit bothered by whose toes his editorial comments might step on, whether advertiser, listener or (least of all) public official. He was not reluctant to tackle controversial issues and to take strong positions on those issues. Gordon even criticized fellow broadcasters who either were too timid to address tough issues or were reluctant to commit themselves one way or the other on the issues (McLendon, 1969a).

Gordon was sincere in wanting his editorials to be heard and to count for something. Thus, at one point he decreed that his editorials, which heretofore had run outside the McLendon Stations' newscasts, now would "be placed *within* newscasts." His reasoning:

> We believe that we will be hitting an audience listening to, and thus presumably concerned with, news. We believe the editorials will spice our newscasts. Further, it should overcome the frequently heard objections from teenagers that we editorialize too much, interrupting the music. This group in the main mentally tunes off during newscasts so we haven't lost a thing. (McLendon, 1962g)

A general policy statement on editorials in 1963 required that Gordon be the primary voice for McLendon Station editorials, although other individuals in management positions might occasionally deliver an editorial if necessary (Keyes, 1963). Actually, a standing policy always had been that managers of McLendon Stations were to deliver editorials on local matters

(McLendon, 1969a). All editorials on matters of national or international interest, though, were to be voiced by Gordon only (Keyes, 1963).

Gordon recorded all of his editorials at the KLIF studios, either in person or over the phone from wherever he might be at the moment. That often meant some farflung corner of the world (Dowe, 1989). Once the original recording was done, Gordon's editorials were copied at KLIF and sent to McLendon Stations across the country, where they were aired with localized "intros" and "outros" (Keyes, 1989).

Gordon wrote most of his editorials himself, although he did employ editorial writers periodically to assist him. Even when handed an editorial written by another person, though, Gordon would usually add his own touches to it. "He would read it, and he would do something with the last line or two and turn it into a 'hooker.' And he'd take a good editorial and make a brilliant editorial out of it," Edd Routt said (1989).

A "hooker" in editorial parlance was defined by Routt as "a sting, a rebuke, sarcasm, and sometimes humor" (Routt, 1974, p. 105) that Gordon employed to conclude his editorials. They were often short but pointed, wrapping up the entire thought of his editorial in a memorable phrase that listeners easily could recall. Gordon did not use a hooker to close all of his editorials, but he used them often enough that listeners could anticipate the punch that became somewhat a trademark.

Examples of Gordon's hookers are numerous. Here are two: regarding the byzantine ways of a bureaucracy, Gordon commented: "But ask the bureaucrats to show us how to simplify anything? That's like asking George Armstrong Custer to show us how to fight Indians." About fellow Texan Lyndon Johnson, Gordon said, "Mr. Johnson seems, as always, to speak in terms of high idealism. It is just that, as usual, we cannot understand what he is talking about. We is a simple country boy" (Routt, 1974, p. 106).

Ideas for editorials, especially in later years, came to Gordon at any time and any place. He was a "voracious reader," Don Keyes remembered. "And the inevitable yellow pad was always there—always making a note about something" (Keyes, 1989). As already mentioned, ideas would pop up sometimes while Gordon was traveling. Recalled Edd Routt: "He would do them [editorials] by phone from Switzerland, from Paris, wherever he was. If he had an editorial idea he'd get it down on typewriter and phone it in" (Routt, 1989).

The editorials that Gordon decided to write and deliver allowed him an undisturbed channel to express his particular views on a myriad of topics, both serious and not-so-serious. The McLendon editorial became a natural extension of Gordon's personality and, as Don Keyes concluded, a perfect device to accommodate Gordon's "ego drive" (Keyes, 1989). What better outlet for someone who had views—strong ones at that—on practically every subject.

Most often at the top of Gordon's agenda were matters of politics. His keen interest in that subject led him eventually to an unsuccessful quest for a U.S. Senate seat in 1964 and the Texas governorship in 1968. Quite likely, Gordon's campaigning whetted his appetite for speaking out on public issues. The number of editorials that Gordon delivered following his run for office increased noticeably, as did the urgency with which he addressed various editorial matters. His radio stations provided him a perfect forum.

If the Texas electorate prevented him from speaking his mind in one public forum, then Gordon would turn to the multiple forums of his own radio stations to have his say, unfettered by the constraints of political exigencies. Gordon even admitted during a 1969 interview that he was better off not winning a U.S. Senate seat because doing so "meant that I would have given up my editorial prerogative" (McLendon, 1969a).

Gordon was an unabashed conservative. If listeners to his editorials were uncertain of that fact, then his political campaigns would make the point loud and clear. Gordon took conservative positions on most issues in his editorials. Many times he made specific reference to the conservative versus the liberal point of view. And he usually spoke with some derision of the liberal position (Editorial File, n.d.). But while Gordon was by nature a conservative, he was not hardened enough in that particular ideology to prevent him from recognizing that the conservative position was not always the most meritorious. Gordon, in fact, took stands on certain issues that clearly were liberal and that clearly were antithetical to conservative thinking. Some of the editorial examples that follow later will illustrate that Gordon attempted to approach his editorial subjects more as a pragmatist than an ideologue. He said as much when describing his editorial philosophy to former KLIF news director Dave Muhlstein:

> The main rule I have for editorials is that they be right and fair. We must never editorialize on any issue in which there is any motive of self gain, other than our normal self gain as part of the community, and I do not think that we can or should be either conservative or liberal in approach. Each editorial must stand on its own merit, upon the facts of the case, and without regard for where the chips may fall. (McLendon, 1959b, p. 2)

Subjects that Gordon chose for his editorials were, as previously mentioned, more international or national than local in scope. Activities in Washington, D.C. were particularly ripe for Gordon's comments. He sometimes seemed on a rampage when it came to editorializing on congressional expenditures, government boondoggles, judicial decisions and the economy. Government bureaucracy and regulation were squarely placed on Gordon's editorial punching bag, no doubt in response to his many bouts with the FCC. He editorialized not once but numerous times on some aspect of these subjects (Editorial File, n.d.). Ironically, Gordon withheld making editorial endorsements for candidates running for public office until near the very end of his editorial career. He announced in a 1979 editorial that he was breaking his thirty-two-year policy by endorsing the Dallas City Council candidacy of Susan Meade (McLendon, 1979b).

McLENDON EDITORIAL EXAMPLES

Gordon's editorials ranged from the frivolous to the serious, from the witty to the sentimental, and from the self-promotional to the self-critical. For example, a 1963 editorial had him calling for more excitement from modern-day baseball announcers (McLendon, 1963b). A while later, Gordon was addressing the problem of stray dogs in Fink, Texas. He ended the editorial by imploring listeners to let KLIF "know what you fink" (McLendon, 1963c).

An indirect KLIF promotion and a direct slam at Gordon's nemesis, the local Dallas newspapers, came in a 1958 editorial in which Gordon chided his print media competitors for not carrying news of the effort by two KLIF-sponsored pilots to break the world endurance flying record (McLendon, 1958c). In a 1975 editorial, though, Gordon criticized a movie that was then playing at one of the McLendons' own Dallas theaters. The movie, *Mandingo*, portrayed the story of a slave-breeding farm in the pre-Civil War South and contained vivid torture scenes. Gordon said that the McLendons had acquired the rights to the film because it had done well in other markets and that once a contract had been signed to exhibit the film there was no way that the McLendons could back out of the deal. That did not keep Gordon from warning his listeners to avoid *Mandingo* (Safran, 1975).

Gordon's verbal jabs just as easily could turn to poetry when he used his editorials to pay tribute to those persons he admired. One of his most moving tributes came as he memorialized the passing of baseball great Jackie Robinson. Robinson "played his game with the proud ferocity of an ebony lion," said Gordon. "We may never see his likes again. The lion sleeps tonight, but from the gathering mists of memory that have begun slowly to obscure those summers of youth at Ebbets Field, there are still the memories of Robby moving at second, like a dark bird in flight" (McLendon, 1972).

Gordon most often was taking positions on subjects both serious and controversial. For example, he made a foursquare stand against capital punishment in a 1963 editorial in which he called for support of a pending bill in the Texas legislature that would abolish the practice. Said Gordon: "It is high time this barbaric method of exacting official cold blooded vengeance belongs to the age of tar and feathering, bear-baitings, shanghaiing and duelling" (McLendon, 1963a).

Gordon's attention turned to civil rights in 1963, and on the eve of the Great March on Washington he remarked editorially that the march "asks for civil rights exactly one hundred years overdue." What's more, he said,

"The March should not have been necessary. The Declaration of Independence did not intend that any man should have to demonstrate so or plead for his rights. The Fourteenth Amendment clearly guarantees equality" (McLendon, 1963d).

Gordon subsequently published the "Great March" editorial in a full-page advertisement purchased in the *Washington Post* (Advertisement, 1963). Among several letters sent to Gordon expressing appreciation for the piece was one from Bill Moyers, at that time deputy director of the Peace Corps. Moyers commented: "That was a magnificent editorial which you ran in the *Washington Post* last week! It made me prouder to be a Texan to know that a man of your influence is using that influence so boldly and courageously. My hat's off to you!" (Moyers, 1963).

Gordon's civil rights advocacy for blacks later extended to homosexuals. But the route to his defense of homosexual rights required a total shift in his original views.

In a 1977 editorial, Gordon criticized a decision by the Minneapolis Civil Rights Commission (referred to by Gordon as the "Civil *Wrongs* Commission") that required the Big Brothers organization in Minneapolis to accept homosexual men as volunteers (McLendon, 1977a). Two months later, Gordon returned to the homosexual issue and, recalling his earlier editorial on the Minneapolis Big Brother case, said he was wrong: "Sexual attitudes and preferences not only should be, but must be, a matter of individual choice and preference. To hold otherwise would be the most dangerous tampering with fundamental freedoms guaranteed Americans by the Constitution," noted Gordon. "We were wrong in our Big Brother editorial, and let us hasten to admit we were wrong" (McLendon, 1977b).

Gordon moved into even more controversial waters when he editorialized in favor of abortion rights. He made his opinions known on the subject not once but several times (McLendon, 1969c; 1970a; 1970b). His pro-choice message in previous editorials was similar to the one carried in a 1971 editorial in which Gordon emphasized that abortion is a personal right. "The decision of whether or not to bear a child *must* rest with the woman involved, not with the government," he contended (McLendon, 1973a).

The conflict in Southeast Asia was central to many of Gordon's editorials. Perhaps owing to isolationist views that he had held since childhood, Gordon had long favored America's departure from Vietnam. That position was partially responsible for his decision to oppose the reelection of President Lyndon Johnson in 1968 (McLendon, 1968e). The decision to part company with the president was no doubt a difficult one. Gordon and the president had been friends since Johnson's days in the U.S. Senate. Gordon had aired Johnson's taped radio programs on his "Texas Triangle" stations (Johnson, 1958), and had even coached Johnson on how to produce more effective programs (McLendon, 1958b). Johnson had responded with personal notes of appreciation for Gordon's help and for editorials that Gordon occasionally had aired in support of the then senator (Johnson, 1960a; 1960b; 1960c).

But, by early 1968, something had drastically changed Gordon's feelings toward the president. It was during this same time span that Gordon had decided to enter the Texas gubernatorial campaign. His campaign ended abruptly on February 27, 1968, when he made a statewide television address bowing out of the governor's race. Gordon cited as his main reason for ending the campaign his inability any longer to support President Johnson. Gordon remarked that he could "no longer avoid the conclusion that our nation is without leadership. It drifts without plan or program, flailing helter-skelter, floating rudderless day by day" (McLendon, 1968d, p. 3).

When President Johnson announced that he indeed would not seek reelection, Gordon responded with an April 7, 1968 editorial that must hold the record for brevity. In a nine-word editorial Gordon simply said, "Lyndon Johnson is to be commended on not running" (McLendon, 1968f).

Gordon's editorials, especially his more controversial ones, evoked plenty of response from listeners. The letters that Gordon received ran the range in tone and intent. Some were complimentary of his remarks and expressed agreement with his views, while others were anything but complimentary.

One particular editorial—actually a series of them—that Gordon aired on successive dates, beginning in November 1967 and stretching through January 1968, sparked perhaps the highest volume of listener mail ever for a McLendon editorial (Editorial File, n.d.). The editorials' subject was French President Charles de Gaulle, not one of Gordon's favorite persons, and the response to the editorials was international in scope. In fact, the publicity that the de Gaulle editorial squabble brought to the McLendon Stations was tremendous. And Gordon loved every bit of it. Had there not been so much publicity, the squabble probably would not have been nearly so protracted (Routt, 1989).

Gordon's initial foray into what later would become somewhat an international cause célèbre came in his November 28, 1967 editorial, which began: "About Charles De Gaulle, we have even ceased being amused by 'De Gaulle' of the man." Gordon proceeded to question the integrity of de Gaulle's and France's friendship with the United States and other allies (McLendon, 1967c).

Gordon returned to his anti-de Gaulle theme less than a week later with another editorial that suggested French government approval for the anti-American activities of the French president. One of those activities, Gordon noted, had been a "recent move to force devaluation of the American Dollar by causing a run on the gold supply of the free world" (McLendon, 1967d). Copies of both of Gordon's de Gaulle editorials were sent along with a letter to the French ambassador to the United States, notifying him that the McLendon Stations were prepared to offer equal time to respond to the editorials' comments (Boyles, 1967).

Mitch Lewis also sent a memo to all McLendon Station managers and news directors notifying them that Gordon planned to air more de Gaulle editorials. Since the first two had stirred up so much controversy and comment, Lewis wanted all stations to give heavy promotion to the next ones. Suggestions also were included for interviews that would help promote the editorials from owners of local businesses whose products or services somehow were connected with France. "In conclusion," said Lewis, "let's milk the most out of these editorials. It is a rare instance of universal interest—and one with which we can reap a great deal of adult comment around the market" (Lewis, 1967).

Gordon's third de Gaulle editorial aired on December 6, 1967. He spoke primarily of the failure of France to repay its long overdue war debt to the United States, and charged that the French president was "an ungrateful fourflusher whose hands should have been called long ago" (McLendon, 1967e).

Gordon's criticism of Charles de Gaulle grew even more caustic in two more mid-December editorials aired on the subject (McLendon, 1967f; 1967g). Nearly a month passed before number six of Gordon's de Gaulle editorials aired. This one, delivered on January 14, was less editorial comment than an important announcement that the French government would accept Gordon's offer of response time to his recent unkind remarks about President de Gaulle. Gordon said that Gerard de la Villesbrunne, Counselor at the French Embassy in Washington, would arrive at the KLIF studios in Dallas on January 22 to record his government's rebuttal to Gordon's editorials (McLendon, 1968a).

In anticipation of the French official's arrival, Gordon urged his listeners during a January 16 editorial that they not travel to France, that they avoid any mode of French-owned transportation, and that they abstain from buying such French products as wine, perfume and automobiles (McLendon, 1968b). As a follow-up gesture, B. R. McLendon cancelled plans for an extended run of the French movie, *A Man and a Woman*, at the McLendons' Park Forest theater in Dallas (McLendon Corporation, 1968b).

A McLendon Corporation press release announcing France's decision to dispatch an embassy official to Dallas noted that "for the first time in broadcast history, a foreign government will answer directly charges made by an individual over U.S. radio stations concerning the policies of the particular foreign government" (McLendon Corporation, 1968a). Later, when a reporter for the *Dallas News* asked Gerard de la Villesbrunne why his government chose to reply to Gordon's editorials instead of others of similar vein then being published and broadcast, the French diplomat replied that it was because Gordon's editorials "were particularly brutal in their attacks" ("McLendon Jabs," 1968).

De la Villesbrunne underscored how surprised and saddened he was with the tone and language of Gordon's editorials as he began the first of six editorial rebuttals in late January (de la Villesbrunne, 1968a). The diplomat proceeded to refute various contentions made by Gordon regarding manipulation of the gold market, devaluation of U.S. currency, the French war debt and the balance of trade between France and the United States (de la Villesbrunne, 1968b; 1968c; 1968d; 1968e).

The rebuttals were full of factual errors that Gordon claimed begged to be answered (McLendon, 1969a). Gordon also saw his own set of rebuttals as a chance to keep the de Gaulle controversy alive and to keep the many listeners who closely followed what now had become a debate entertained for a while longer. The national news media also had tuned in on the McLendon-de Gaulle feud. *Newsweek* magazine cleverly headlined a story on Gordon and his editorial bouts "The Gall of Gordon," and then quoted him on his reaction to Villesbrunne's remarks: "I won't rebut everything he said, just 95 per cent of it. I won't rebut the part where he said hello" ("The Gall," 1968).

Gordon's rebuttals formed a series of seven individual editorials aired on January 29 and 30. The rebuttals included excerpts from Villesbrunne's statements interspersed with Gordon's comments on the statements (McLendon, 1968c). The format allowed Gordon to cite specific errors made by Villesbrunne and then to provide his corrections to those errors. The seven rebuttals brought the marathon round of de Gaulle editorials to a fitting end.

Gordon oftentimes editorialized on a subject more than once, but seldom did he choose to air a series of editorials on the same subject in such close proximity as the de Gaulle editorials. And seldom if ever did a subject provoke such a pointed series of editorial rebuttals and responses.

Gordon's editorials assumed a more national and international scope in general during the 1970s, because by then he had begun syndicating them to Texas radio stations other than his own. The McLendon editorial service began in late July 1968, with stations in seventeen Texas cities enlisted to carry the editorials. The service would be in business for more than a decade, until discontinued in September 1978 (McLendon Corporation, 1978).

Gordon retired from the editorial scene in 1980, at a time when his broadcast career in general was coming to an end. The loss of such a vibrant conservative voice did not go unnoticed among broadcasters, who urged Gordon to continue his editorials and to syndicate them once more. He said he felt guilty about that during a 1980 interview, but "I frankly just don't have the time to do it" (" 'Old Scotsman,' " 1980).

9 *Departure from Radio*

Gordon and B. R. had purchased and sold radio stations throughout their joint careers in the broadcast business. There was little surprise, then, when the McLendon Corporation sold KEEL-AM/FM (Shreveport) and WAKY (Louisville), both in 1962. The sale of KTSA (San Antonio) in 1965 (*City of Camden*, 1969b, p. 429) came as a mild surprise because of the station's key role as part of the McLendons' Texas Triangle. The broadcast community's biggest surprise came when Gordon announced plans in 1967 to sell KLIF in Dallas, along with KILT and KZAP-FM, both in Houston. The three stations were being sold to LIN Broadcasting Corporation for a combined $15 million, "the highest price ever paid in a single transaction involving only radio" ("Biggest," 1967). A separate transaction also was underway to sell KLIF's sister station, KNUS-FM ("Biggest," 1967)

Speaking of the pending sale of radio stations that would have removed the McLendons not only from Dallas but from the entire Texas radio broadcast scene, Gordon said that it "should be taken only as a desire on the part of my family to begin an even greater participation in the affairs of Dallas" ("McLendon Sells," 1967). He noted as well that, although leaving Dallas radio, the McLendon Corporation would be moving into Dallas television as soon as the FCC approved the company's application for a UHF television station to operate there ("McLendon Sells," 1967).

As it happened, the two McLendon Stations in Houston were sold in 1968, for a combined $6.5 million (*City of Camden*, 1969b, p. 432), but KLIF and KNUS-FM were withheld from the deal. The McLendons placed KLIF back on the market after a short time and in 1971, Fairchild Industries agreed to purchase the station for $10.5 million. When KLIF changed ownership in January 1972 (Reed, 1971), Gordon and B. R. still would be in possession of KNUS-FM, but the station that they had built from ground up physically and the station that had been the model for what much of U.S. radio had become throughout the 1950s and 1960s would, after a quarter of a century, no longer be a McLendon Station.

Gordon's announcement to his station staff that KLIF had been sold came not in person but rather by a recording sent to Les Vaughn and played for the assembled personnel in the main KLIF studio. Gordon's words were brief. As best as Vaughn could recollect, Gordon said:

> Through the years we've all worked to build this station to what it is today, and we're very proud. But my father and I have decided we are . . . coming to the end of the autumn years. . . . We have decided to dispose of the station and go on living our waning years as we see fit. . . . Each and every one of your jobs will remain status quo. Good luck. Goodbye. God bless you. (Vaughn 1989)

REASONS FOR THE DEPARTURE

Why did the McLendons decide to initiate what appeared by the early 1970s to be a major divestiture of their broadcast properties? Gordon's son Bart said the move was B. R.'s idea. "Granddad wanted to get out," according to young McLendon (Blackwell, 1986, p. 6C). At the time of KLIF's sale, Gordon explained the transaction as "just an inheritance tax matter" (Reed, 1971). Given B. R.'s age (he was seventy-one at the time), Gordon said that he and his father felt that it would be wise to have plenty of money on hand to pay inheritance tax just in case B. R. or Gordon himself suddenly passed away (Reed, 1971).

The McLendons' station divestiture was certainly well timed from a business perspective. The growing popularity of FM radio during the late 1960s and 1970s and the appearance of so many new FM stations meant that market listening shares would be spread among more and more competitors. No longer would a KLIF, KTSA or KILT be able to dominate the market as before. The value of these once-giant AM stations would drop as their audience began to erode. Knowing that this would happen, the McLendons made a calculated economic decision that eventually proved to be a very wise move (Patoski, 1980, p. 170).

There were other reasons for the departure from radio that had little to do with money, though. By the early 1970s, Gordon had achieved all that he could in the medium. "What other horizons were there for him? I mean he had done virtually everything that he could," remarked Bart McLendon (1990). Billie Odom said that Gordon decided to leave radio because "running the stations was getting to be too much a burden" (Odom, 1990).

All the time and attention that Gordon had devoted to the McLendon Corporation's frequent wrangling with the FCC during the 1960s had been especially burdensome. The 1960s had been a decade of "maximum government regulation" (Sitrick, 1990), and Gordon, according to Marcus Cohn, had grown tired of all the hassle (Cohn, 1989). The broadcasting industry, said Gordon, had become "stifled" by Washington bureaucrats (Porter, 1972, p. 13E).

Gordon "just didn't like bureaucracies. He didn't like anything that interfered with laissez-faire capitalism," Don Keyes noted (1989). Gordon objected to the influence and pressure the FCC placed on broadcasters through its regulations. Such regulations, in Gordon's view, were an affront to the principles of free enterprise. Don Keyes said that Gordon hated

> to have to kowtow to the FCC and politicians . . . to get something finessed in Washington that shouldn't have to have been finessed at all. Lesser lights up there getting in the way of the free enterprise system. His philosophy was get the regulations out of the way, and let me serve more people and make good money while I'm doing it. I'm not asking for anything free. I'm just asking you to loosen these shackles so I can do things that will serve more people, that will serve more advertisers, that will make money for all concerned. Everyone's a winner. (Keyes, 1989)

Gordon used similar words while campaigning for the U.S. Senate in 1964. "I am an intractable believer in the free enterprise system," he told a statewide Texas television audience during one of his campaign speeches.

> To me, the two most perfect organisms in the world are [the] human body and the free enterprise system. Both can withstand incredible abuse, but, like the body, the free enterprise mechanism will finally rebel. The free enterprise system, absolutely unfettered, absolutely functions. But like the body, if you bind and throttle this marvelous free enterprise system with enough shackles, and restraints, you slowly strangle its circulation until one day it chokes, gasps and dies. This most perfect of all political organisms, the free enterprise system, must be loosed from these thousands of garroting tourniquets which finally will suffocate this great and precious bodily mechanism called free enterprise. (McLendon, 1964b, p. 4)

Gordon could find little logic in how the FCC viewed the broadcaster's responsibility to his audience. Referring to the commission's edict that radio broadcasters were "to serve the *broadest* possible community need," Gordon contended in a 1962 speech to the World's Fair of Music and Sound in Chicago that "such a requirement is *diametrically* opposed to better radio, defies all laws of the free market place and, in so doing, throttles radio. A radio station today should serve not the broadest need but rather the *narrowest*" (McLendon, 1962f, p. 2).

Gordon quite correctly foresaw radio stations in multistation markets, if unimpeded by "artificial program restraints," specializing in agriculture, religion, classical music, news and all-talk. "In the free market place, where talent and imagination have freedom from fear," said Gordon, "the good operators will drive out the bad. Any law forcing a *sameness* of radio, forcing a programming common denominator, acts as a protection to the talentless, a shield for the lazy, a haven for the idea thief, a *legal shelter and sanction* for the mediocre" (McLendon, 1962f, pp. 4–5).

Gordon saw the FCC's overzealous effort to burden broadcasters with numerous, unclear regulations as particularly troubling. Even more troubling were the "non-objective" or "retroactive" laws, as Gordon termed them, that the FCC had begun enforcing (McLendon, 1969a). These were regulatory edicts that applied not just to future programming or operational practices, but also to similar practices that might have occurred in the past.

Gordon did not soften his view toward the FCC and its "non-objective law" with the passage of time. During a 1981 interview, after he had almost totally removed himself from broadcasting, Gordon once more remarked on the commission's constraining influence:

> Many things that we did in perfect consistency with FCC rules were later ruled retroactively to be wrong. It was never possible to program your station in an innovative fashion with any assurance that you were conforming to FCC rules. . . .
>
> The seven FCC Commissioners, with one or two exceptions, had had little or no broadcast experience during the era when I was broadcasting. So, it was impossible for a renegade innovator like myself to exist with that bunch of numbskulls. (McLendon, 1981b)

Gordon's low regard for the FCC sprang from the numerous sparring matches between him and the commission during the 1960s. Many of the fights—the KABL case described in an earlier chapter as an example—were relatively minor. But there were two that attained more significant proportions. The first resulted from Gordon's efforts to change the format of the McLendons' Chicago radio station. The second resulted from his and B. R.'s effort to purchase radio station WCAM in Camden, New Jersey.

FORMAT BATTLE AT WYNR/WNUS, CHICAGO

Gordon had wanted a radio station in Chicago for some time because of the city's major-market status (Keyes, 1989). So, when a chance to acquire WGES came along, Gordon jumped at the opportunity. He and B. R. applied to the FCC for transfer of the WGES station license to the McLendon Corporation on October 13, 1961, and the application was approved on June 13, 1962 (*The McLendon Corporation*, 1963a). The station's purchase price was approximately $2 million (*City of Camden*, 1969b, p. 433).

About 80 percent of the WGES program schedule at the time the station was purchased was targeted toward its predominantly black audience ("New WGES," 1962, p. 48). The remainder of the station's program schedule—some thirty-two hours to be exact (*The McLendon Corporation*, 1963a)—consisted of foreign language programming targeted to Polish, German, Italian, Hungarian, Swedish, Slovak and Spanish listeners (*Congressional Record*, 1962, p. 18808). WGES aired four daily programs and six Sunday programs drawn from this particular ethnic mixture ("New WGES," 1962).

An August 23, 1961, McLendon Corporation press release indicated the company's intention to purchase WGES and announced that no programming changes were anticipated at the station. Gordon was quoted in the release as saying that "we never change a station's programming as long as it is established that such programming is the best way to utilize that facility to serve the public needs and tastes" (*Congressional Record*, 1962, p. 18809). A similar statement was made in the license transfer application that the McLendon Corporation had filed with the FCC on October 13, 1961 (*Congressional Record*, 1962, p. 18808). It should be noted that in neither document—the August press release or the October license transfer application—was there a direct statement suggesting that the McLendons would retain the existing WGES program format.

The McLendon Corporation assumed control of WGES on August 8, 1962. On or about August 28, two major decisions were made affecting the station's format. First came the elimination of all foreign language programs (*The McLendon Corporation*, 1963a). Next came the increase of black programming to fill 100 percent of the station's schedule. One more important change was the adoption of WYNR (pronounced "winner") as the station's new call letters ("New WGES," 1962). The new WYNR format became effective on September 1, 1962 ("WYNR Probe," 1963).

Little did Gordon realize what effect his format decision would have on his new station's future. *Broadcasting* magazine described the decision as producing "an explosion" ("New WGES," 1962). Plans for the format change had been known several weeks before their actual implementation. It was during this period that two U.S. congressmen, Roman Pucinski (D-Ill.) and Dan Rostenkowski (D-Ill.) protested Gordon's decision to the FCC. Pucinski protested in writing and Rostenkowski met personally with FCC Commissioner Robert E. Lee ("New WGES," 1962). Both congressmen represented constituents in the Chicago area who were affected in one way or another by the loss of foreign language programming, but Rep. Pucinski had a more personal grievance. His mother produced one of the Polish programs that Gordon had cancelled ("Informal," 1963, p. 52). William C. Klein, producer of one of the German programs that had been cancelled, was said to have filed a formal complaint with the FCC regarding Gordon's format change ("New WGES," 1962).

The FCC responded to these protests by sending a letter to the McLendon Corporation on August 21, 1962, asking that the commission be advised as to whether information about WYNR's discontinuance of foreign language programming was correct. If so, the commission wanted to know "on what basis the decision was made" (*Congressional Record*, 1962, pp. 18808–18809). The FCC received its response from the McLendon Corporation in a letter dated August 28, 1962 (*Congressional Record*, 1962, p. 18809).

Soon thereafter, Gordon called a news conference to publicly explain the reasons for WYNR's format change as contained in the August 28 letter. He said that Chicago's 1.25 million blacks were being underserved by the city's full-time radio stations. Ethnic groups, on the other hand, were being well served. Seven Chicago stations provided a combined fifty hours of Polish programming every week, and four stations provided more than twenty-four hours of Italian programming. Since Gordon wanted WYNR to have a consistent sound—something that would be impossible with the incompatible mix of black and ethnic programming—he elected to go full tilt toward a format specializing in black music and news ("New WGES," 1962). WYNR would be the first all-black radio station in Chicago (Brock, 1971).

Don Keyes was more to the point on Gordon's plans and motivations. "Here was a case . . . of Gordon investing two million dollars," said Keyes. "He ain't gonna get it back playing Lithuanian music. He was there to make a profit. And the void we decided to fill at that time was in the black community" (Keyes, 1989).

The idea for many of the programming concepts that would be employed at WYNR came not from Gordon or Don Keyes but from Ms. Etta Oden Barnett, a respected member of the Chicago black community (Keyes, 1989). Ms. Barnett, in fact, had been appointed WYNR's community relations director and had conducted extensive surveys and interviews within the black community and among Chicago's black leaders to determine what programming would be most attractive to black listeners ("WYNR Probe," 1963). Ms. Barnett had decided that what the Chicago black community wanted and needed would be precisely the kind of programming that WYNR would be capable of delivering twenty-four hours a day.

No more than week after Gordon's news conference on the WYNR matter, he delivered at the World's Fair of Music and Sound the speech cited earlier. His remarks in that speech no doubt had been inspired by events surrounding the WYNR controversy. The speech provided a timely forum for Gordon to protest the kind of program policies that made confrontation with the FCC inevitable, especially given the efforts of Rep. Pucinski to force such a confrontation.

The FCC had forwarded a copy of the McLendon Corporation response to its August 21 inquiry to Rep. Pucinski. After reviewing the response, Pucinski wrote the FCC a lengthy letter of his own on August 31, saying that he felt "more convinced than ever that the Commission should reopen this entire case and compel the McLendon interests to show cause why the license obtained for radio station WGES (now WYNR) should not be revoked" (*Congressional Record*, 1962, p. 18809).

Rep. Pucinski charged that the McLendon Corporation had intentions of dropping foreign language programming before the purchase of WGES and that it had misrepresented this fact to the FCC, to the foreign language program producers and to the licensee from whom the McLendons were buying WGES. "It is quite apparent to me . . . that the McLendon interests did not want to disclose their plans for abandoning the foreign language programs until the ink was dry on the assignment," claimed Pucinski (*Congressional Record*, 1962, p. 18809). The congressman also called attention to the fact that the announcement that foreign language programming would be discontinued came after the August 8, 1962, date when the transfer of the WGES license to the McLendon Corporation was consummated. Had the decision on foreign language programs been publicized prior to that date, claimed Pucinski, then parties interested in retaining the programs could have opposed the license transfer.

Rep. Pucinski's letter criticized two other points made by the McLendon Corporation. He insisted that the evidence showing that black community leaders in Chicago favored an all-black program format was inconclusive. According to his reading of the McLendon Corporation's community leader surveys, Chicago's black leaders approved of a station airing a combination of black programming and foreign language programming, just as WGES had done for years. In addition, even though ethnic programming was available on other Chicago radio stations, as the McLendon Corporation had indicated, many of these stations were located in Chicago suburbs and broadcast a signal too weak to reach all of Chicago's ethnic communities (*Congressional Record*, 1962, pp. 18809–18810).

At no point in Rep. Pucinski's letter did he mention that his mother was one of the producers whose ethnic programs had been eliminated from WYNR's schedule. That fact also was omitted when Rep. Pucinski included his remarks on the WYNR matter along with a copy of his August 31 letter to the FCC in the *Congressional Record* (1962, pp. 18808–18810).

The FCC responded to complaints by Rep. Pucinski and other interested parties by ordering on January 24, 1963 an "inquiry and investigatory proceeding" into representations made by the McLendon Corporation "in connection with its acquisition and operation of Station WGES-WYNR" (*The McLendon Corporation*, 1963a, p. 928). Among the items the FCC wished to examine were the McLendons' programming intentions prior to filing an application for transfer of the WGES-WYNR license. The commission wanted to know if the McLendons told the truth about plans for changing the station's format. Also, how thorough was the McLendons' ascertainment of community needs, and did the new station owners properly consult with foreign program producers about format changes? Finally, the FCC wanted to know what influence the McLendons' community ascertainment results had on their decision to change the WGES-WYNR format (*The McLendon Corporation*, 1963a, pp. 928–929).

The scope of the FCC's inquiry was expanded on March 8, 1963, to include an examination of WYNR's station promotion practices. Complaints had reached the commission regarding damage to public and private property resulting from a WYNR treasure hunt. Other persons had complained of harrassing phone calls and a disturbance in a Chicago public school as a result of other WYNR promotional contests (*The McLendon Corporation*, 1963b, p. 59).

Public hearings on the WYNR matter were conducted in Chicago during a period stretching from April 9 to April 24, 1963. One additional hearing was conducted on May 10, 1963 in Washington, D.C. (*The McLendon Corporation*, 1964, p. 819). *Broadcasting* magazine referred to this particular series of hearings as "one of the most unusual" in the FCC's history ("Informal," 1963, p. 52). The unusual nature of the proceeding rested in the fact that it was simply an informal hearing to allow the commission to determine whether a more formal hearing should be held at a later date ("Informal," 1963, p. 52). Ordinarily, the FCC would have ordered a sanction such as license revocation prior to conducting a hearing, but in the WYNR matter, an FCC hearing examiner conducted the hearing first and then transmitted a certified record of the hearing to the full FCC for any further action ("Pucinski," 1963).

Hearing proceedings began on April 9, under the supervision of the FCC's chief hearing examiner, James D. Cunningham. The McLendon Corporations' counsel was Gordon's longtime friend Marcus Cohn. B. R. McLendon was the first to testify. He said that his and Gordon's interest in buying WGES had begun in 1959 when they first learned that ownership of the station—and a foothold in the lucrative Chicago market—might be possible. Another first-day witness, Ms. Elizabeth Hinzman, part owner of WGES until it was acquired by the McLendon Corporation, testified that a station policy always had been to replace any discontinued foreign language program with a black program, and that this policy eventually would have resulted in 100 percent black programming ("Informal," 1963, pp. 52–54).

Testimony during the hearing's second week came from, among others, Rep. Pucinski, who insisted that his protests of McLendon Corporation policies were not motivated by any personal interests; an official of the Polish-American Congress, who testified that WYNR's cancellation of Polish programs had caused hardship in Chicago's Polish community; and witnesses who told how WYNR promotions had disrupted two Chicago public schools. In support of the McLendon Corporation were witnesses representing the Urban League, United Negro College Fund and the Cook County

Bar Association who praised WYNR's public service efforts ("Pucinski," 1963).

Near the end of the Chicago phase of the FCC's hearing, Gordon was called to testify. He indicated once more that a decision to drop foreign language programs from WYNR's schedule had been made only after studies had indicated it would be a wise move. And the results of these studies were not available until after the McLendon Corporation had finalized its purchase of WGES. Gordon also made an important point about the brokerage arrangements that producers of WGES foreign language programs had with the station, which he had been unaware of until after the station's purchase ("WYNR Probe," 1963). Essentially, the program producers had been acting as time brokers by purchasing air time from WGES and then turning around and reselling the time to advertisers at profitable rates. Since the McLendon Corporation had never allowed such a brokerage policy at any of its other stations, there seemed solid justification for disallowing the practice at WGES by breaking all brokerage contracts with foreign language program producers ("McLendon Defends WYNR," 1963, p. 76).

While the FCC considered the WYNR case in deliberations that now had stretched into 1964, Gordon made a surprise move at the station that would change considerably the complexion of the commission's proceedings. On September 3, 1964, WYNR's programming was transformed into an all-news format, similar to the format with which Gordon was having so much success at XTRA in Tijuana. The station's call letters would also be changed, to WNUS. Gordon said that he had conducted three separate community surveys of Chicago in 1964 and that numerous community leaders had expressed not only an interest in more news, but also great support for an all-news radio station ("McLendon All News," 1964). WNUS was destined to become the "first successful all-news operation based in the United States" (Fornatale and Mills, 1980, pp. 102–103).

Later, when an interviewer asked Gordon why he even had considered a format change at WYNR, Gordon replied that the FCC's criticism of his promotion methods had limited what could be done to attract listeners to the station ("The Top-40," n.d., p. 26). Don Keyes said there were other reasons as well. The entire effort with WYNR's all-black format had not been a good move, in Keyes's opinion. Although WYNR had been successful to some extent with its programming early on, the success did not last. The big blow came when Lenny Chess, owner of Chess Records, purchased a full-time, one-kilowatt radio station in a Chicago suburb, programmed it with a rhythm and blues format and literally yanked away most of WYNR's black audience (Keyes, 1989).

Two months after Gordon changed WYNR's format and call letters, the FCC issued a decision in its McLendon Corporation probe (*The McLendon Corporation*, 1964, pp. 817–820). The decision effectively terminated the lengthy proceedings, although an FCC staff proposal recommended that proceedings continue and that the commission consider license revocation ("FCC Calls Off," 1964).

In its final report on the matter, the FCC stated that there was no evidence to suggest that the McLendon Corporation had attempted to deceive the commission with representations made when applying for license transfer of the original WGES. The commission report also stated that the corporation had been remiss in failing "to assess the community's interest in the foreign language programs before they were cancelled" (*The McLendon Corporation*, 1964, pp. 818–820). However, the report noted that steps were taken to assess the need for programming designed to serve Chicago's black community. Indeed, the FCC report even gave muted praise to the programming, saying that it had "served specific needs and interests not otherwise satisfied by stations in the area" (*The McLendon Corporation*, 1964, p. 820).

The FCC was less complimentary of WYNR's promotional efforts. The commission concluded in its report that contests broadcast by the station "resulted in damage to public and private property; caused harassment, annoyance and interference with the right of privacy of various telephone subscribers; and caused disturbances in several Chicago public high schools and disruption to classes, school work and procedures" (*The McLendon Corporation*, 1964, p. 820). The commission said the licensee deserved to be censured for this but that it would "go no farther at this time only because the record reflects that in each instance, top management of the station, on being notified of the harmful results, took immediate remedial action" (*The McLendon Corporation*, 1964, p. 820). The FCC did emphasize, however, "that carrying of contests and promotions which adversely affect the public cannot be condoned" (*The McLendon Corporation*, 1964, p. 820). These exact words would be repeated in a tersely worded public notice on contests and promotions issued by the FCC in February 1966 (*Contests and Promotions*, 1966).

The FCC terminated its proceedings in this particular case on November 12, 1964 (*The McLendon Corporation*, 1964, p. 820), well after the date when Gordon had announced plans to change the WYNR all-black format to the WNUS all-news format. Nonetheless, the FCC made no mention of this transition, even as it praised WYNR's black programming effort. It is quite likely that no party complained about the format change; thus the commission would have nothing on which to base extending its McLendon Corporation proceedings beyond their original scope.

Within two years of its format change, WNUS was turning a profit. But the station was having to compete with other Chicago radio stations that also had switched to an all-news format and were in many respects doing a superior job of news coverage to what WNUS could manage (Fornatale and Mills, 1980, pp. 102–103). WNUS, which was, after all, primarily a rip-

and-read operation, found competition especially tough once WGN turned to all-news. WGN, owned by the *Chicago Tribune*, had long been a dominant station in the market, and with its newspaper resources there was little that any other radio station could do to compete with it.

WGN was not the only problem that WNUS faced. A radio station airing an all-news format requires a listening audience with generally upscale demographic characteristics. In Chicago, such an audience resides primarily to the north of the city. The WNUS transmitter was located to the south of the city, and the station's limited power hardly could carry its signal to the preferred north-side destination. Even Gordon himself had trouble picking up WNUS on the radio in his Lakeshore Drive apartment. "So, we're in trouble in Chicago from day one. It just didn't work," recalled Don Keyes (1989).

By 1968, Gordon had replaced the WNUS all-news format with a beautiful music format (Routt, McGrath, and Weiss, 1978, p. 169). That switch did not prove particularly successful either. So, Gordon decided eventually to extricate himself from the Chicago market by selling WNUS to the Harlem Globetrotter organization. Regarding Gordon's entire WGES/WYNR/WNUS venture, Don Keyes, commented: "I think that's one of the times he exercised poor judgment in making a purchase" (Keyes, 1989).

CAMDEN'S WCAM AND LICENSE TRAFFICKING ALLEGATIONS

Attorney Marcus Cohn described Gordon's ordeal with the FCC during the WGES/WYNR proceedings as an exasperating experience (Cohn, 1989). A similarly exasperating experience with the FCC occurred during proceedings on the KABL matter, examined in an earlier chapter. The KABL hearing followed in close order the WGES/WYNR hearing. Neither of these two bouts with the federal bureaucracy would try Gordon's patience as much as his third and final confrontation with the FCC. At issue this time around was his and B. R.'s efforts to purchase Camden, New Jersey radio station WCAM.

The WCAM episode began not with that station but with another station, WIFI-FM, in nearby Philadelphia. Word that WIFI-FM was for sale was brought to Gordon and B. R.'s attention in 1967 by broadcast station broker Joseph Sitrick (*City of Camden*, 1969b, p. 439). The McLendons had been interested for quite some time in acquiring radio stations in the top U.S. markets, and so they immediately began exploring the possibility of purchasing WIFI-FM. On August 3, 1967, a formal application was filed with the FCC for transfer of the station's license to the McLendon Corporation (*City of Camden*, 1969b, p. 435).

However, before the FCC could act on the transfer application, the WIFI-FM owner decided to terminate the transaction. In the meantime, Joseph

Sitrick had become aware of WCAM's availability for purchase (*City of Camden*, 1969b, p. 439). The station's location in Camden just across the Delaware River from Philadelphia, still would allow Gordon direct access to the bigger market that was included in the WCAM coverage area (*City of Camden*, 1969a, p. 414). For this reason the McLendon Corporation commenced purchase negotiations with WCAM's owner, the city of Camden. Negotiations were soon concluded and with the FCC's anticipated license transfer approval, the McLendon Corporation appeared the likely new owner of WCAM.

The FCC was not willing to cooperate in this venture, though, once application for transfer of the WCAM license was formally filed with the agency. Obviously memories lingered of the KABL case, where Gordon was accused of programming his Oakland station to serve San Francisco listeners. Because the FCC assumed a similar intent by the McLendon Corporation to locate a radio station in Camden, New Jersey, while planning primarily to serve Philadelphia listeners, the commission informed the McLendons on July 24, 1968, that transfer of WCAM's license would not be approved without a hearing (*City of Camden*, 1968, p. 351).

Gordon and B. R. could have dropped the matter there by giving up their efforts to purchase WCAM, but neither Gordon nor B. R. was about to let the FCC have its way without a fight. The McLendons indicated to the FCC their willingness to submit once more to hearing proceedings (*City of Camden*, 1968, p. 351).

The hearing would focus on two formal issues. The first was "whether the proposed program plans of the McLendon Corporation [were] realistically designed to meet the needs of Camden, N.J., or Philadelphia, Pa." The second was "whether the McLendon Corp., directly, or indirectly through its predecessors, affiliated corporations, or subsidiary corporations, has engaged in trafficking in broadcast authorizations" (*City of Camden*, 1968, p. 351).

The second issue was the more serious one, and quite likely came as somewhat a shock to Gordon and B. R. at this particular juncture in their broadcast careers. "Trafficking" according to the FCC, "occurs when a licensee . . . acquires and/or operates a station for the primary purpose of selling or otherwise disposing of it for profit rather than for the primary purpose of serving the public interest" (*Harriman Broadcasting Co. (WXXL)*, 1967, p. 733). In other words, a broadcast license trafficker is one who seeks a station license "for sale rather than service" (*Folkways Broadcasting Co. v. F.C.C.*, 1967, p. 302).

The FCC had issued a rule on March 23, 1962 (*Voluntary Assignments and Transfers of Control*, 1962, p. 1514) that concluded a proceeding begun on December 7, 1960 and established criteria to be considered regarding evidence of broadcast license trafficking. In justifying its new rules, the FCC commented that the "principles of licensee responsibility make it clear that the accelerated trend in the sale of broadcast properties which has been occurring since 1955, presents serious questions for the Commission's determination" (*Voluntary Assignments*, 1962, p. 1504). Statistics showed that in the two years prior to commencement of FCC license trafficking proceedings (1960 and 1961) the percentage of license transfer applications for broadcast stations whose licenses had been held for less than three years ranged from 53 percent to 45 percent, respectively (*Voluntary Assignments*, 1962, p. 1516).

In its Report and Order released on March 19, 1962 (*Voluntary Assignments*, 1962, p. 1515), the FCC said that it was

> seriously disturbed over the very high ratio of transfer and assignment applications involving short-term ownership of stations in numerous communities. It believes that it has a special obligation to insure that such short-term assignment or transfer applications do not constitute trafficking in licenses. An applicant who seeks to dispose of his license within the first few years encompassed by his initial license period obviously warrants special scrutiny. (*Voluntary Assignments*, 1962, p. 1504)

The Report and Order said that the FCC intended "to embark upon a program of intensified scrutiny of proposed transfers or assignments which occur within a short period," and chose three years as the benchmark period "within which proposed transfers or assignments will be regarded as raising substantial questions of trafficking or undue disruption" (*Voluntary Assignments*, 1962, p. 1505). Unless special circumstances warranted otherwise, the FCC stipulated that it would

> designate an application involving a station held less than three years for hearing, to fully explore and test, through the Commission's hearing procedures, the material and substantial questions presented as to the extent of the licensee's compliance with its responsibilities, and the effect of the transfer or assignment upon the public interest. (*Voluntary Assignments*, 1962, p. 1505)

Formal hearings in the WCAM case convened on October 30, 1968, and continued through the following day. After a brief recess, hearings continued on November 4, 5 and 8. David I. Kraushaar was the hearing examiner who presided at the proceeding (*City of Camden*, 1969b, pp. 427–428). As it happened, Kraushaar was a lucky choice for the McLendons. His conduct of the WCAM hearings and his later assessment of the evidence rendered during the hearings showed him to be one person at the FCC whom Gordon might consider a friend.

The hearing examiner's report, issued on January 2, 1969 (*City of Camden*, 1969b, p. 427) showed that, at least on the subject of broadcast license trafficking, Kraushaar was every bit in agreement with Gordon's longtime criticism of the FCC's retroactive application of its rules. The report began by documenting the McLendon Corporation's record of buying and selling radio and television stations from 1947 through 1968. Of the eleven radio stations purchased and then subsequently sold by the McLendons during that period, only five were held for less than three years. These stations—with length of McLendon ownership in parentheses—included WTAM (less than one year), WYSL (one year and eight months), KLBS and WRIT (both one year and nine months) and KNET (two years and seven months). The six other McLendon Stations, which were held for more than three years, included WAKY (three years and six months), KEEL-AM/FM (four years and five months), KELP (five years and seven months), KZAP-FM (eight years and ten months), KTSA (nine years and four months) and KILT (ten years and eleven months) (*City of Camden*, 1969b, p. 429).

The WCAM hearing report noted that the FCC never had questioned the license transfer or assignment transactions involving any of the above stations, nor had there ever been a question as to the reason for any of the transactions. Moreover, read the report,

> The evidence in the present record shows that, although the McLendons may have sought to acquire certain broadcast facilities for reasons having to do with their desire to try out their concepts of programming in the various communities, or to provide a particular service to the listenerships they were expected to serve, as businessmen of more than ordinary acumen the McLendons also had in mind that the facilities they were seeking to acquire would prove profitable to them. When, subsequently, they sought authorizations to transfer these stations to others, whatever other motivations they may have had, originally, the McLendons have made no bones of their underlying desire to upgrade their holdings to include stations in the top broadcast markets of the country. As to this, indeed, they perceived no difference between their efforts and those of other multiple station licensees who have done the same thing over the years. (*City of Camden*, 1969b, p. 430)

The report stated that WCAM would air a program format similar to the KABL format, and that local news carried on the station would cover not only Camden but also Philadelphia. And while Philadelphia was considered within the WCAM coverage area, Gordon and B. R., said the report, were "unequivocably committed to operate and identify the station as a Camden, N.J., station" (*City of Camden*, 1969b, p. 441). And although WCAM could generate plenty of advertising revenue just by virtue of the approximately 800,000 potential listeners in the station's southern New Jersey coverage area, the McLendons were well aware that Philadelphia could add considerable numbers to WCAM's listenership base, as well as to its potential advertiser pool. In fact, WCAM's sales manager had told B. R. that the station already derived 85 to 90 percent of its advertising income from Philadelphia clients (*City of Camden*, 1969b, p. 441).

The decision to program WCAM with the KABL format came about in two ways. First, the McLendons had retained a local resident to conduct a formal survey of the programming needs of Camden. More important, though, was Gordon's monitoring of local radio stations to ascertain what format likely would be the most popular among Camden listeners (*City of Camden*, 1969b, pp. 441–443).

Much of hearing examiner Kraushaar's concluding comments were composed of criticism lodged against his own agency for its treatment of broadcasters such as the McLendons and for the manner in which it applied questionable policy. The following lengthy passage from the examiner's conclusions stands alone as a remonstrance to the FCC and a vindication of the McLendons with respect to the trafficking issue of their hearing:

> The record in this proceeding summarizes the broadcasting career of the McLendons covering a span of nearly 22 years. It shows, indeed, that Mr. Gordon McLendon has devoted a working lifetime to the broadcast interests he has owned with his father. It shows, further, that although the McLendons have been very successful financially, their concern and interest extended beyond a mundane pursuit of profit, into the realm of ideas and programming of the broadcast facilities they have owned. If entrepreneurs like them are to be condemned to perdition as traffickers for publicly and candidly admitting their ambition to serve the larger and better markets, one may legitimately ask whether it is not also the purpose of government to end, once and for all, the free enterprise system under whose aegis the broadcasting industry was cradled and grew. Or, perhaps, one may merely conjecture whether such people as the McLendons are to be pursued and harassed in order to discourage would-be newcomers from entering the better markets of the country, so as to leave these markets as the exclusive preserves of those multiple broadcast station owners who happened, fortuitously, to get there first. Obviously no such baleful purposes are involved herein. The Commission only desired to look into what appeared, on the surface, to be an all-too-rapid turnover of broadcast properties by the McLendons, in order to ascertain their intentions with respect to the public interest. . . .
>
> Regardless of purpose which, in any event, is beyond the pale of this initial decision to analyze (it being a difficult enough operation to try to "unscramble the eggs"), the problem of proof in this proceeding, calling for the reconstruction of transactions occurring years ago, all with prior Commission consent, has been rather appalling. And the effort to relate whatever facts have been established to the legal concept of trafficking, which in itself received no extended exploration or in-depth study by the Commission until the year 1962, involves some mental gymnastics when, in 1968, one tries to evaluate the McLendons' conduct in the light of behavior patterns prevalent in the broadcast industry during the late 1940's and the 1950's, as against standards that were first clearly enunciated in 1962. In all events, the McLendons have cooperated during the present hearing, even to the point of trying to exhume what, for want of better description, is now ancient history, from their own and government archives. . . .
>
> If the matter of trafficking is largely subjective, as the commission says it is,

> one is free to look beyond the cold record to glean what one can of the McLendons' subjective intent. Therefore, in reaching the result which the examiner believes ought to be reached in this case (i.e., exonerating the McLendons of the offense of trafficking in broadcast licenses), he desires to stress his observations of the McLendons' demeanor while testifying and wishes to state again that he found them to be completely open and above-board throughout. The reasons they have advanced during the hearing, as distinguished from what they told the Commission in filed applications, for the various transactions, are credible and were never impeached. Their desire and ambition to upgrade their holdings by seeking to go to the better markets, always in effect sanctioned by the Commission in the past, indeed, was not sinful, if only because a pattern clearly emerged that evinces their concomitant intent to advance their concepts of programming and to operate each facility in the public interest. (*City of Camden*, 1969b, pp. 446–448)

Examiner Kraushaar spent only a brief space on the programming issue. He noted that the FCC previously had published policy statements declaring the "obligation of broadcast licensees and applicants to seek out and be responsive to community needs and interests," but he emphasized that the commission had left the "methods and means" for meeting those needs and interests "to the discretion and judgment (and good faith) of the licensees" (*City of Camden*, 1969b, p. 448). Accordingly, Kraushaar determined that the McLendons had made a sufficient effort to determine the Camden, New Jersey market's programming needs. Moreover, Kraushaar was satisfied that the McLendons would perform as promised in meeting these needs.

Hearing examiner Kraushaar therefore concluded that the public interest would be served by granting the license of radio station WCAM to the McLendon Corporation (*City of Camden*, 1969b, p. 449). Kraushaar's report and decision on the WCAM matter were issued formally on January 2, 1969 (*City of Camden*, 1969b, p. 427).

The seven FCC commissioners disagreed with both the hearing examiner's decision and his rationale, and they stayed his decision. An additional date was set, on March 10, 1969, for any further oral arguments that parties in the WCAM matter wished to submit before the commission issued its final decision. As it happened, that decision rested entirely upon the programming issue, to which hearing examiner Kraushaar had paid scant attention, while it virtually ignored the license trafficking issue, to which Kraushaar had paid greatest attention (*City of Camden*, 1969a, p. 413).

The FCC stated in the conclusions of its final report on the WCAM matter that

> the steps taken by the McLendons to ascertain Camden's needs and interests were inadequate; their proposed programming cannot be regarded as responsive to properly determined needs; and their representation that WCAM will

> operate principally as a Camden facility is, therefore, in view of other facts reflected by the record, unproductive of assurance that the proposal is realistically for Camden. (*City of Camden*, 1969a, p. 418)

The FCC proceeded in its report to spell out in explicit detail how broadcast licensees were to conduct exhaustive surveys among community leaders in order to ascertain what programming needs there were in the community. Then programming was to be fashioned that would address all or most of these needs (*City of Camden*, 1969a, pp. 418–424). The McLendons had fallen far short of such efforts, said the FCC's report:

> While the McLendons submit that the particular programming selected is a matter of licensee judgment and that because of their long experience in broadcasting they are well qualified to make programming determinations, nonetheless adequate information regarding the community's needs is required for a valid judgment. From what we have seen of the McLendons' effort to ascertain the Camden area's needs, we are not persuaded that a sufficiently careful analysis of those needs has been made so that a solid basis exists for the exercise of licensee judgment. In short, we do not believe that the McLendons' showings are in accord with our longstanding policy that a licensee seek out and be responsive to a community's needs and interests. (*City of Camden*, 1969a, p. 424)

The FCC concluded that the McLendons' "interest in WCAM was apparently generated by a desire primarily to gain a foothold in Philadelphia, not to serve Camden," and as such, "there is no clear or persuasive assurance that the station as proposed to be operated by the McLendons will be realistically programmed as a Camden station. Rather, the likelihood is that the proposed operation will be essentially for the metropolitan area instead of the assigned community" (*City of Camden*, 1969a, p. 425).

Given these findings and conclusions, the FCC decided that granting the McLendon Corporation a license to operate WCAM "would not serve the public interest," and thereupon denied the McLendons' license application (*City of Camden*, 1969a, p. 425). The commission's decision was adopted on June 11, 1969 (*City of Camden*, 1969a, p. 412).

By all accounts, the FCC appeared to be using the WCAM matter to hold Gordon and B. R. accountable for what many commission personnel may have regarded as past indiscretions. "The regulatory climate has changed around here since you came into the broadcast business; so, we are going to hold your feet to the fire on this one," the FCC seemed to be saying.

The full commission would not press forward on the trafficking issue, probably because the agency's own hearing examiner had seen the issue's irrelevance and had defended the business practices of the McLendons so eloquently. Programming, though, was another issue. By holding the

McLendons strictly to the letter of the FCC's community ascertainment regulations, the commission not only could justify denying them the WCAM license, but also perhaps could exact some measure of satisfaction for the agency's failed efforts in the earlier KABL matter. Ironically, since the FCC's implementation of the ascertainment rules in 1960 (*Report and Statement of Policy Res*, 1960), to which it held the McLendons so strictly accountable in 1969, the McLendon Corporation had applied for license grants for six radio stations and one television station, and undertaken ascertainment measures for each station that were no more rigorous than the one undertaken for WCAM and had been granted a license to operate the stations without the FCC voicing any concern whatsoever ("McLendon Defends Claim," 1968, p. 41).

BOWING OUT A WINNER

The WCAM confrontation would be Gordon's and B. R.'s last with the FCC. There would be no more McLendon broadcast station acquisitions. All McLendon Stations still in the fold at the conclusion of the WCAM matter—(KLIF AM/FM, KABL AM/FM, WYSL AM/FM, WNUS AM/FM, KOST-FM, WWWW-FM and KCND-TV)—would be sold by the mid-1970s, with the one exception of KLIF-FM, whose call letters Gordon would change to KNUS-FM.

KNUS-FM had been spun off from KLIF when the latter station was sold in 1971. Gordon and B. R., in fact, had offered to sell KNUS to Fairchild Broadcasting at the same time the company purchased KLIF, but had decided to keep the station when Fairchild offered a buying price that was far lower than expected (Bart McLendon, 1990). So the McLendons were saddled with a radio station that they apparently did not want. They nonetheless made the best of it. Ironically, one of the conditions agreed to when KLIF was sold was that the McLendons would not operate another AM radio station within fifty miles of Dallas for at least ten years (Patoski, 1980, p. 170). Fairchild Broadcasting in only a short time would wish that the agreement had stipulated FM radio as well.

Gordon had changed the KLIF-FM call letters to KNUS in anticipation of someday changing the station's format to all-news. The format was far from all-news, however, during the years prior to its split from KLIF. KNUS, in fact, was a progressive rock station that for its day probably bordered on the heavy metal sound. Bart McLendon had been placed in charge of KNUS as its general manager. Ken Dowe had persuaded Gordon to adopt the progressive rock format as an alternative to the KLIF format. In the process of installing the new KNUS format, Gordon also had won approval to upgrade the station's transmitting power to 100,000 watts (Dowe, 1989).

Bart McLendon's operation of KNUS as what was considered an underground rock station in the early 1970s won the station a sizable following of diehard fans. But Gordon, according to Bart, cared little for the KNUS brand of music, understood little about the station's attraction and "had little, if anything at all, to do with the management of KNUS" (Bart McLendon, 1990).

When KLIF was sold, Gordon became more attentive to the KNUS format. He wanted to change it from progressive rock, but had no immediate idea about what new format to install. Ken Dowe was given the task of devising some new direction for the station with only one proviso from Gordon: "Don't make the format exactly like KLIF. I don't think that would be too nice" (Dowe, 1989).

The format Ken Dowe created was a combination of Top 40 and what later would be called "album-oriented rock." The transition to the new format was not an easy one. Progressive rock devotees bombarded KNUS with letters and phone calls protesting the format change decision. Even Bart McLendon had misgivings about the station's new direction. However, he agreed to see it through and continued as the KNUS manager.

The new KNUS format proved a resounding success. Within a year the station's advertising revenue had jumped from less than $200,000 to over $1 million annually. Better still, KNUS became the top-rated station in Dallas within fifteen months of the arrival of its new format and its split from KLIF (Dowe, 1989). What's more, said Bart McLendon, KNUS became the first Dallas radio station to beat KLIF in the ratings since 1953 (Bart McLendon, 1990).

That would be Gordon's last hurrah in broadcasting. In 1979, he and his father sold KNUS-FM to New York-based SJR Communications for $3.75 million (Pederson, 1979). FCC approval of the transaction brought a formal end to Gordon's broadcast career and to more than thirty years of his and B. R.'s partnership in the operation of a McLendon Station group that had stretched from coast to coast, border to border and beyond.

Gordon's struggles with the FCC were receding into the past by the time he decided finally to depart from radio. These struggles nonetheless had precipitated that departure. But fatigue and a desire to move on to other ventures were the two factors that seemed uppermost among Gordon's reasons for agreeing to sell the last McLendon Station. Edd Routt remarked that Gordon also had tired of hearing people tell him that ideas that had worked so well for radio during the 1950s were no longer workable in the 1970s (Routt, 1989).

Gordon said as much himself during an interview in the late 1970s, while at the same time offering a hint at where he next would turn his creative talents. Speaking of radio broadcasting in artistic terms—as he had seen radio from the very beginning—Gordon remarked that he was kind of tired of painting on that canvas. How many inventive things can you think of to do between records? Motion pictures, to me, represent a broader canvas, they have the element, they have the visual. I'm just kind of tired of painting on a smaller canvas. I've done most of the things you can do in radio. ("The Top 40," n.d., p. 27)

10 *Politics, Moviemaking and Other Interests*

Gordon was engaged in a number of other activities throughout his career besides inventing formats and running broadcast stations. Many of these activities kept him in the public eye, and many were either directly or indirectly related to Gordon's primary interest in broadcasting. His most memorable non-broadcast activities revolved around politics and motion pictures. There were others, certainly, but nothing outside of broadcasting seemed to hold as much fascination for Gordon as these two.

CAMPAIGNING FOR PUBLIC OFFICE

It probably surprised very few of Gordon's confidants when in the mid-1960s he decided to run for public office. Had he been successful, Gordon's career in broadcasting would have come to an abrupt end. But given his lifelong interest in politics, Gordon's effort to see what political life was all about from the public policymaker's perspective was perhaps inevitable.

Why Gordon chose to run for public office when he did is uncertain. His days as the Old Scotchman sports announcer for the Liberty network and the many editorials he had delivered over the McLendons' Texas Triangle radio stations certainly had made Gordon a well-known public figure in Texas. But Gordon's objective for his very first run for public office in 1964 was the U.S. Senate seat that had been occupied by Senator Ralph Yarborough since 1957 (*Congressional Directory*, 1965, p. 159). That Gordon would begin a political career as a novice set to wage battle against a popular and well-seasoned incumbent seemed ill-advised, but Gordon was convinced that he could overcome the heavy odds against his success.

Much has been said already about the political nature of many of Gordon's editorials. Nonetheless, the political positions that Gordon had taken on so many subjects appeared to be only those of an interested citizen. Gordon had given few clues as a part of his editorializing or otherwise prior to 1964 that he had set his sights on public office. An inkling of what McLendon associates thought of Gordon's political potential certainly had been implied. A 1959 *Broadcasting* magazine article, for instance, noted that Gordon held potential as either a senatorial or Texas gubernatorial candidate ("The Story," 1959, p. 44B). And it might be surmised that the idea of running for public office had come up at some time during conversations that Gordon had had with his father-in-law and former Louisiana Governor James Noe.

Whatever the genesis of the idea, the first clue that Gordon might actively enter politics came in a September article in the 1963 Denton, Texas *Record-Chronicle* that quoted Gordon as saying that 1964 would be a good year to challenge Senator Yarborough ("McLendon Cited," 1963). However, Gordon's true intentions were not confirmed until he officially filed as a candidate in the May 2 Democratic primary, only thirty minutes before the midnight, February 3 filing deadline ("Conservative Banner," 1964).

The May 2 Democratic primary was the political turf on which the conservative and liberal wings of the Texas Democratic Party battled to see who later would go through the motions of running against token Republican opponents in the general election (McClellan, 1970, pp. 15–16). The only Democrat to announce his candidacy for Yarborough's seat prior to Gordon's announcement was Dallas public relations executive John Van Cronkhite (Morehead, 1963). The failure of any seasoned conservative Democrat to jump into the U.S. Senate race as 1964 began was attributed to the rumor that President Lyndon Johnson preferred that Ralph Yarborough be reelected and had advised the Texas conservative Democrats not to jeopardize the senator's chances (McClellan, 1970, pp. 70–72, 83–87).

Gordon paid no heed to Johnson's preference, if indeed there was a preference, and plunged headlong into his campaign. Gordon's campaign manager, George Sandlin, had been entrusted with guiding his candidate through a three-month primary campaign whose color and controversy would be described as similar in style and substance to the gubernatorial campaign of W. Lee "Pappy" O'Daniel. O'Daniel had accompanied his fiery oratory with the folksy music of a western band as he rode the campaign trail all the way to Austin and the governor's mansion (Patoski, 1980, p. 170).

Gordon outlined a campaign platform that included precise positions on such issues as labor law, taxation, the national debt, Medicare, foreign aid, states rights, education, farm programs and the federal bureaucracy. The number one issue, though, was civil rights (McLendon, 1964c, pp. 1–7). That issue would be debated throughout the campaign, and it would evoke considerable mudslinging from both the McLendon and the Yarborough camps. But even civil rights took a backseat to what later emerged as *the* campaign issue: personal integrity.

Two matters interrupted the McLendon campaign during its early going that had nothing to do with issues. The first was John Van Cronkhite's decision to withdraw from the senate race in mid-February, leaving Gordon as the lone challenger to Ralph Yarborough (Banks, 1964a). The second matter was a bizarre incident that, had it gone as planned, would have left Yarborough with no Democratic opponent. A deranged woman intending to assassinate Gordon shot instead at a man she mistook for the candidate. No one was injured in the incident, which occurred at Love Field in Dallas, but after subduing the would-be assassin, police said that the woman claimed to have knowledge of Gordon's association with the mafia and that he had intentions of harming her ("Woman Faces," 1964). The woman, Ms. Mary Elizabeth Stone, later was committed to a state mental hospital ("Judge Rules," 1964).

The campaign that had begun with a literal bang eventually would carry Gordon to ninety-three different Texas cities (McLendon, n.d., "A Political Innocent Abroad," p. 11). Reporters at every campaign stop asked questions about Gordon's conservative views. At one point he responded that although he indeed embraced a conservative political philosophy, his was "a good bit short" of the brand of conservatism then being displayed by presidential hopeful Barry Goldwater. Gordon also said that he would even "qualify as liberal" in civil rights (Duncan, 1964).

As much a champion of civil rights as Gordon claimed to be—and the claim appeared justified in view of editorial remarks that he had made on the subject (McLendon, 1963d)—he refused to lend wholehearted support to the then pending Civil Rights Bill, primarily because of the "broad and sweeping powers" of enforcement that the bill would allow the federal government (Banks, 1964b). Senator Yarborough, on the other hand, supported the Civil Rights Bill in its entirety; for that, said Gordon, the senator would have to answer to the citizens of Texas ("McLendon Raps Foe's," 1964).

Gordon stuck to the civil rights theme through early April. By then some glitz had been added to the campaign when two of Gordon's longtime Hollywood friends, John Wayne and Texas native Chill Wills, joined the candidate on the campaign trail. Actor Robert Cummings would join Gordon later to pilot the candidate's plane during the last days of the campaign (Morehead, 1964).

Gordon relied heavily on television to blanket the entire state during the last few weeks prior to the May 2 primary election. He had used his Texas Triangle radio stations since his campaign had begun to thoroughly saturate the Dallas, Houston and San Antonio markets with campaign spot announcements. Eighteen one-minute McLendon spots had aired on each of the stations daily, beginning on February 10, 1964 (*Hon. Ralph W. Yarborough*, 1964).

The absence of any Ralph Yarborough campaign announcements to counter the McLendon spots probably gave the impression that Gordon was using his radio stations to gain an unfair advantage over his opponent. But that was not the case. Gordon had made every effort to be fair with Senator Yarborough regarding allocation of McLendon Station airtime. A memo from Gordon addressed to key station personnel and written at the outset of his senatorial campaign had warned them to treat Yarborough fairly in the manner in which the campaign was reported (McLendon, 1964a). And Gordon had written Senator Yarborough at least seven times throughout the duration of the campaign notifying the senator that, as required by federal equal time law, he was due free campaign announcement time equal to that used by the McLendon campaign on all of the McLendon Stations in Texas.

Not until mid-April, however, did Senator Yarborough decide to avail himself of Gordon's offer (*Hon. Ralph W. Yarborough*, 1964, pp. 163–165). By then the senator had accumulated considerable equal time commitments from his opponent—fifty-seven hours' worth to be exact ("McLendon Has," 1964, p. 72). When Gordon balked at giving Yarborough the entire time due, especially so near the primary election day, Senator Yarborough asked the FCC to force Gordon to provide what had been promised. The FCC agreed that McLendon Station airtime was owed Yarborough, but, since a lump sum of airtime at such a late point in the campaign was at issue, the commission asked that representatives of each candidate determine a more equitable time arrangement (*Hon. Ralph W. Yarborough*, 1964, pp. 163–165). What the two camps finally worked out might not have been numerically equal, but it seemed so to Gordon. "In fact," said Gordon, "during about the last week of the campaign, the stations were giving [Yarborough] 54 one-minute spot announcements a day, three an hour to my one" ("Ralph Got About," 1964).

THE INTEGRITY ISSUE

Ralph Yarborough's efforts to secure McLendon Station airtime might have been less urgent had there not been the need to address a controversial and potentially scandalous issue that arose on April 12. Until then, the senator had appeared comfortably ahead of Gordon in public opinion polling (McClellan, 1970, p. 95). But, the April 12 issue of the *Dallas Morning News* carried a page-one article alleging that convicted swindler Billie Sol Estes had given Yarborough $50,000 in cash in 1960. The report, branded by Senator Yarborough as "an infamous lie" (Banks, 1964c), coincidentally shared the newspaper's front page with an endorsement of Gordon McLendon for the U.S. Senate ("The News," 1964).

Senator Yarborough did not deny a close friendship with Estes, and the fact that Estes had contributed money to the senator's campaigns in the past was a matter of public record. However, there was no record to be found of the $50,000 gift (Banks, 1964c). Since federal law at the time forbade "an elected federal official from taking more than $5,000 in one calendar year from any individual" (Banks, 1964e), Yarborough's alleged receipt of the $50,000 gift from so notorious a donor placed the issue of personal integrity front-and-center during the waning days of the Democratic primary campaign.

The senator immediately called for an FBI investigation of the allegation—an act that Gordon characterized as "the oldest political trick in the world." Noting the short time before the May 2 election, McLendon said that his opponent was "attempting to cloak himself with innocence by asking the FBI into a case he knows would take weeks or months for them to render a decision on" (Duckworth, 1964). Gordon also said that he had not intended to make the so-called "Estes-Yarborough scandal" an issue in the senatorial campaign until Yarborough complained to the FCC about Gordon's radio stations carrying news reports on the matter. That, said Gordon, forced him to defend his station's integrity. His first move came during a statewide television program on April 25, when he produced two witnesses who had signed sworn affidavits that they had seen "Estes hand an envelope to Yarborough and [had] heard Estes say, 'Here is the $50,000 you wanted.' " After the appearance of the two witnesses Gordon declared, "Now, we come face to face with the issue and there is no way to put it delicately. Who is lying?" (Harris, 1964).

Ralph Yarborough answered Gordon during an April 28 statewide television address of his own. With the senator were two witnesses who displayed their own sworn affidavits claiming that they had been present when Yarborough was supposed to have accepted the $50,000 from Billie Sol Estes, and that they had observed no such transaction ("Two Deny," 1964). Yarborough was aided further by Assistant U.S. Attorney General Jack Miller, who told the senator during a May 1 phone call that one of Gordon's witnesses had recanted his story during FBI questioning. The senator quickly released this election-eve disclosure to the press with a demand that Gordon "withdraw from the race because of having based it on perjury and character assassination" (Banks, 1964d).

Gordon's witness who recanted his story would testify later that he had done so under threat of death (Banks, 1964e). That rather startling twist, however, was not disclosed in time to help Gordon counter the effects of Ralph Yarborough's May 1 announcement. News of the announcement, in fact, did not reach Gordon until 4:15 P.M. in the afternoon of May 1, as he was preparing for a televised question-and-answer program in Beaumont. "I hesitated a moment, terribly angry that the Justice Department should have given information to my opponent without giving it to me," Gordon remarked. He then released a press statement saying that "this eleventh hour intervention in our state electoral process by the Federal government is unheard of" (McLendon, n.d., "A Political Innocent Abroad," p. 13).

The May 2 election day of the 1964 Democratic primary finally brought Gordon's senatorial campaign to an end. Ralph Yarborough won his party's renomination to the U.S. Senate with 57.3 percent of the vote. He received 905,011 votes to Gordon's 673,573 (McClellan, 1970, p. 101). Gordon had outspent his opponent by nearly three to one—$311,190 to $123,880 ("Gifts," 1964). His losing effort was nonetheless the "closest race any political newcomer in Texas history ever [had run] against an established incumbent" (McLendon, n.d., "A Political Innocent Abroad," p. 1).

The election was over, but the questions surrounding the Billie Sol Estes gift persisted. After making its May 1 pronouncement about the McLendon witness recantation, the U.S. Justice Department delayed releasing a final report on the subject until late August. The report's conclusion was a terse statement that the "department's investigation found the [Estes gift] allegation to be without any foundation in fact and unsupported by credible testimony" ("Probe Backs," 1964). However, the Texas Department of Public Safety conducted its own investigation of death threats against the recanting witness and found that sworn statements and polygraph tests supported not only the death threat claim but also the original claim that Billie Sol Estes indeed had given Senator Ralph Yarborough the $50,000 (Banks, 1971, pp. 74–76).

END OF THE POLITICAL ROAD

Gordon's effort to win election to public office did not end entirely with his defeat in the 1964 U.S. Senate race. He entered the Texas governor's race in 1968, but due to what he decided were irreconcilable differences with President Lyndon Johnson, Gordon decided to withdraw from the gubernatorial campaign after only fifty days (Gardner, 1968). That short-lived run brought Gordon's political career to a sudden and, unlike his 1964 endeavor, uneventful end.

Why Gordon entered the 1964 U.S. Senate race in the first place always has been somewhat a mystery. Gordon himself never gave a clearly defined reason. Most persons with whom he spoke before announcing his candidacy had advised against it, according to what Gordon said after the election ("The Conservatives' Dilemma," 1967, p. 8). Even Gordon's closest associates could not cite a specific reason why he entered the race, although Don Keyes's thoughts on the subject probably were nearest the target. He concluded that Gordon's run for office was motivated by "ego, plain and simple" (Keyes, 1989).

THEATERS AND MOVIEMAKING

Gordon's ability to perform so well on the political stump was no doubt fostered by his broadcast experience. But he was helped by show business experience of another kind as well. Gordon had been in the motion picture business, first as theater owner along with B. R. and then as producer of motion picture promotion campaigns, and finally as full-fledged motion picture producer, for many years prior to the launch of his short-lived political career. In fact, if the McLendons had a family business to speak of, it was the motion picture business and not broadcasting.

As recounted earlier, the McLendons' motion picture business began when B. R., practicing law in Idabel, Oklahoma, purchased a movie theater from one of his financially strapped clients. That was in 1932, when the country was in the depths of the depression (" 'Mr. Mac,' " 1969). B. R. was to show the entrepreneurial genius that later passed to Gordon by expanding his one-theater holding into a chain of theaters that spread from Oklahoma to Louisiana and Texas. Nineteen of these indoor theaters would be sold during the 1960s so that B. R. and Gordon could concentrate their motion picture exhibition business in Texas (" 'Mr. Mac,' " 1969).

Before Gordon joined B. R. in the Tri-State Theatres company, the senior McLendon had built his first Dallas theater ("Gordon Combines," 1969), the Casa Linda, constructed in 1945 (Porter, 1973). The Casa Linda eventually was joined in Dallas by the Preston Royal, Park Forest and Capri indoor theaters, and the Gemini Twin and Apollo Twin outdoor theaters (" 'Mr. Mac,' " 1969).

Gordon and B. R. later would be joined by Gordon's son Bart as the family's number of drive-in Tri-State Theatres located in Dallas, Houston, Fort Worth, Galveston, El Paso and other Texas cities rose to seventy by 1984 ("The Forbes," 1984). This remained for a number of years the state's largest chain of outdoor movie theaters (Schulz, 1986, p. A–8).

The McLendons were particularly successful with their drive-in theaters, due in part to Gordon's correct forecast that people would flock to such theaters as the urban centers of Texas began their sprawl in the early 1960s. A good climate and an ever-expanding number of motorists also helped make Texas the "drive-in capital of the world" (Thompson, 1983, pp. 47–48).

Actually, it was the property on which the drive-in theaters sat and not the theaters themselves that held B. R.'s attention. A major portion of the money from the sale of the McLendons' radio stations had gone toward purchase of land for drive-in theaters. "The drive-in theaters were always land-placed; they were never anything more than that," said Bart McLendon.

> They were just something to put on the land to help make a little money until it's time to either develop them for their highest and best use—put office

> buildings on them or shopping centers or whatever—or it was time to turn around and sell them. And it's not that he [B. R.] had any great affinity for the drive-in movie business. He really didn't. It was just a way to make some money. (Bart McLendon, 1990)

The McLendons may have had their eyes on property value, but in 1964 their intentions were to pioneer a new concept in motion picture theaters—the multiscreen drive-in (Shultz, 1986, p. A–1). The Gemini drive-in theater would be the first to have twin screens that would accommodate some 2,000 automobiles, and it would be the biggest theater of its kind in Texas. The theater would cost nearly a million dollars to build ("McLendon Corp. to Expand," 1964).

B. R. and Gordon's intentions eventually were to build 200 such drive-in theaters across the country (" 'Mr. Mac,' " 1969). That number never would be reached, but the McLendons' interest in pushing the multiscreen theater idea to its limits led them to construct a four-screen drive-in theater, the Century IV in Grand Prairie-Arlington near Dallas, and the Capri 7 indoor theater in downtown Dallas, both of which, as of the mid-1970s, were said to have been the biggest multiscreen outdoor and indoor theaters ever built (Raffetto, 1973). Gordon eclipsed the McLendons' own record for world's biggest theater when in 1982 he built the six-screen "I-45" drive-in theater in Houston. The theater could accommodate more than 3,000 automobiles (Thompson, 1983, p. 46).

MOTION PICTURE PROMOTION CAMPAIGNS

Success with the exhibition side of the motion picture business, coupled with Gordon's burgeoning success in the broadcast business, especially with radio station promotion, quite naturally led him to try his hand at motion picture promotion. Once again, Gordon's Midas touch was at work. Former KLIF disc jockey Ron Chapman said that Gordon's creative instincts made motion picture promotion both artistic and exciting. By itself, said Chapman, a McLendon motion picture promotion was more than just a mere radio commercial. "It oftentimes took on the appearance of a main event" ("Tribute," 1986). Gordon's innate sense of the dramatic, said one-time Liberty Broadcasting System music director Tom Merriman, allowed him to create movie promotions that by themselves made people want to see the movie (Merriman, 1990).

Gordon's first movie promotion aired on KLIF in 1954, according to Bill Meeks's recollection (Meeks, 1990). The talent that Gordon showed for that and subsequent promotions caught the eye of major motion picture companies. By the late 1950s, they had enlisted his expertise in producing promotion campaigns for major Hollywood releases. The promotions were distributed to radio stations nationwide. By 1960, the McLendon Corporation had become the largest company in the United States engaged in producing such promotional campaigns (McLendon, 1960a). By 1961, Gordon was handling between fifteen and twenty motion picture promotion campaigns per year, at a cost to his customers of $5,000 per film ("Zany," 1961, p. 131). And for a period of time from 1963 to 1966, Gordon was under an exclusive contract with United Artists studios to produce promotion campaigns for all of the company's new releases ("Gordon Combines," 1969). Several motion picture studios even tried to persuade Gordon to move to Hollywood and produce promotional campaigns full-time, but he refused to leave Dallas (Porter, 1990).

Gordon himself wrote and voiced several of the hundreds of motion picture promotional spots produced by the McLendon Corporation between 1955 and 1970 (The McLendon Organization, n.d.; "Inventory," n.d.). Mitch Lewis also wrote a number of the spots, but Les Vaughn recalled that "Don Keyes wrote about 90 percent of the promos" (Vaughn, 1989). Vaughn, who provided the audio engineering for all of the motion picture promotional spots, described the process involved in their creation:

> We'd screen the movie and record the sound track while we were watching it. And Gordon or Mitch or Don would sit there and take their notes. . . . They would tell me what excerpts they wanted pulled out of the sound track. I'd have to go back down through the sound track again and take out what they wanted. And they'd write the commercial, and I had to pick the sound effects, music, etc. . . . and blend it all together to come up with either a twenty-five-second commercial or a fifty-five-second commercial. (Vaughn, 1989)

The creative philosophy behind Gordon's motion picture promotional campaigns was simple. He followed the principle of "painting a word picture in the listener's mind. No canvas is as large as the imagination," Gordon would say (Porter, 1972, p. 1E). It was the same principle he had applied so successfully to his baseball game recreations years earlier (McLendon, 1969a). Gordon eventually gave a name to the principle, calling it "imagery transfer" (McLendon, 1960d, p. 4). Though imagery transfer was meant to appeal to the imagination, the ultimate objective of its use was far more practical. "Our main thought with any announcement is to get people *talking*," said Gordon. "Conversation begets controversy. Controversy begets interest. Interest begets action—at the box office" (McLendon, 1960d, p. 5).

Gordon was not content with creating just one promotional spot for each motion picture. He felt listeners would become easily bored after hearing the same announcement several times. To relieve the tedium and to increase the interest, Gordon produced several different spots for every movie. The number of spots per motion picture sometimes would run as high as fifteen (Porter, 1986).

Some of Gordon's more memorable motion picture promotional campaigns were for such films as *The Guns of Navarone*, *The Bridges at Toko-Ri*, *Samson and Delilah*, *The High and the Mighty*, *From Russia With Love*, *Goldfinger*, *Barefoot in the Park*, *The Country Girl* and *Where Eagles Dare* (McLendon, 1979a). Perhaps even more memorable were the promotional campaigns Gordon created for rereleased movies that had not fared too well at the box office during their initial release, or that simply had been out of circulation for several years. After McLendon campaigns for rereleases of such films as *Citizen Kane* and *From Here to Eternity*, these movies often not only did better at the box office than when originally released, but also outdistanced first-release movies playing at competing theaters (McLendon Corporation, 1959, p. 3).

MOTION PICTURE PRODUCTION

Gordon's showman instinct provided a natural inclination for his decision to push the family movie exhibition business into the movie production business. Moreover, Gordon was attracted to the glitter element of the movie industry. Rubbing shoulders with movie stars and important directors and producers appealed to him (Keyes, 1989). There also is the suspicion that Gordon, having screened so many motion pictures as a part of the movie promotion business, became convinced that he could create movies as good as and perhaps even better than many of those that he had seen.

Gordon and B. R. created the McLendon Radio Pictures Corporation as the production arm of their motion picture enterprise (McLendon, 1960a). Mitch Lewis was named the company's advertising and publicity head, and James H. Foster was named company vice president (McLendon Corporation, 1959, p. 3). For the company's studio and production headquarters, Gordon purchased a 500-acre tract of land on the shores of Lake Dallas near Denton, Texas, about a thirty-minute drive from downtown Dallas. Gordon paid $500,000 for the land and spent $250,000 more to build a sound stage and lodge to house cast and crew during filming (McLendon Corporation, 1959, p. 1). This new production center would be called Cielo Studio.

By midsummer 1960, Gordon could boast that Cielo Studio possessed "a combined studio-location advantage" that even Hollywood did not have, that Cielo Studio was the only one "where there is a combined studio-location-living quarters arrangement," and that Cielo Studio was the only nonstock studio in America "where one closely-held company assumes all the risks" (McLendon, 1960c, pp. 1–2). Gordon also noted that "no studio in the country produced more pictures outside Hollywood last year than were produced by the Cielo Studios" (McLendon, 1960c, p. 1).

Gordon was referring to the three motion pictures that the McLendon Radio Pictures Corporation had produced in 1959, certainly an impressive accomplishment for a company so new to the business (McLendon, 1960c, p. 1). Gordon had decided early in the year to produce the three films, but to wait a while before producing anymore. "We have all seen so many companies rush into the motion picture business, over-expand and fall by the wayside, that we do not want to make the same mistake," Gordon told his business associates in January 1959 (McLendon, 1959a, p. 2). He had been somewhat reluctant even to produce the third film, preferring instead to see whether his company was "on the right track" after production of the first two films (McLendon, 1959a, p. 2).

Gordon's first motion picture was *The Killer Shrews*, a science-fiction story shot entirely at Cielo for $125,000 (McDougal, 1984, p. 18). The movie starred two of the lesser-known performers of their time, James Best and Ingrid Goude. Both actors had performed only in bit roles to this point, although Best carried better acting credentials than his costar. Ingrid Goude had achieved her greatest fame as Miss Sweden of 1957 and later as runner-up for Miss Universe. Ken Curtis was also featured in the movie, and served as its producer (McLendon, 1959d, pp. 1–2). Curtis, later to gain fame as the character Festus on the "Gunsmoke" television series (McDougal, 1984, p. 18), probably was one of the most recognizable faces in *The Killer Shrews*, since he had appeared in a number of movies directed by his father-in-law, John Ford.

Gordon also took a cameo role in *The Killer Shrews*, to, in his words, "give it a little more name value because I am well-known in many states as a broadcaster" (McLendon, 1959d, p. 1). Gordon portrayed a mad scientist in the movie who was "unceremoniously chewed to death in his brief but crucial cameo appearance" (McDougal, 1984, p. 1). One critic noted years later that Gordon's role in *The Killer Shrews* "remains one of the lesser, if more curious, credentials on the resume of a true Texas character" (McDougal, 1984, p. 1).

Gordon's second movie, *The Giant Gila Monster*, also featured two unknown performers. Don Sullivan played the male lead, and Miss France of 1957 Lisa Simone played the female lead. Ms. Simone had never previously acted in a movie, but Gordon felt that her presence might increase his movie's marketability in France. Veteran character actors Fred Graham and Shug Fisher filled out the remaining major roles in *The Giant Gila Monster*. Ken Curtis also produced *The Giant Gila Monster*, and Ray Kellogg directed both *The Giant Gila Monster* as well as *The Killer Shrews* (McLendon, 1959d, p. 2).

While their collective experience may have been limited, most of the persons selected for lead roles in Gordon's first two movies did have some attachment to the film business. That was not so for the minor character roles. For these Gordon rounded up several of his KLIF employees, especially the disc jockeys (Blackwell, 1986, p. 6C).

The Giant Gila Monster was shot back-to-back with *The Killer Shrews* at

Cielo. Gordon felt that shooting the films simultaneously would cut expenses, save time and make use of an already assembled production crew (McLendon, 1959a, pp. 1–2). As it happened, both movies were completed in little more than two months, beginning in January and ending prior to mid-March 1959 (McLendon, 1959e). This might not have been a record, but it had to have been close. His experience as motion picture mogul evidently was not at all what Gordon had anticipated, judging from a letter he wrote to an acquaintance prior to beginning production on *The Killer Shrews.* "I am going very quietly crazy getting ready to shoot our two epic productions starting here in January," Gordon lamented. "These are turning out to be horror pictures in every sense of the word, but we are looking for tremendous grosses in Southern Tibet" (McLendon, 1958d).

The Killer Shrews and *The Giant Gila Monster* were scheduled to premiere as a double-feature billing at the Majestic Theater in Dallas and the Palace Theatre in Fort Worth on June 25, 1959 (McLendon, 1959f). Gordon pulled out all the stops in promoting the premiere (Routt, 1989). The movies were advertised in the *Dallas Morning News* on the day preceding their premiere as "Horror Masterpieces!" (Movie Promotion, 1959a). Advertising on the day of the premiere noted that the Majestic Theater would open at 8:15 A.M. for a special morning showing of the movies (Movie Promotion, 1959b).

One month before Gordon premiered his first two movies, he started production at Cielo on his third movie, to be entitled *My Dog Buddy* (McLendon, 1959f). The movie, costing a mere $73,000 to produce, was described as a "quintessential kiddies' melodrama about a boy, a dog, and their enforced separation occasioned by the death of the boy's parents in a car accident . . . a case of boy meets dog, boy loses dog, and, finally boy finds dog—or, rather, dog finds boy" (Hirschhorn, 1989, p. 238). *My Dog Buddy* was written and directed by Ray Kellogg, and starred Travis Lemmond as the young lead and "London" the German Shepherd in the canine role of "Buddy." Ken Curtis was making his third appearance in as many McLendon motion picture productions. He was joined in supporting roles by McLendon employees Ken Knox and James H. Foster. Gordon also cast friends Jane Murchison and Bob Thompson in supporting roles (Hirschhorn, 1989, p. 238).

All three of Gordon's movies eventually were distributed nationally—*The Killer Shrews* and *The Giant Gila Monster* by American International and *My Dog Buddy* by Columbia Motion Pictures Corporation (McLendon, 1969a). One Dallas film critic kindly made note of the two firsts associated with *The Killer Shrews* and *The Giant Gila Monster*—the first feature-length films produced in Dallas and the first movies to premiere as double features (West, 1959). Reviews of all three of Gordon's movies in *Variety*, a publication whose views were meant more for movie exhibitors than for the public (Porter, 1990), were only lukewarm. The movies' technical production was seen as their major strength. *Variety* critics nevertheless suggested that all three McLendon movies probably would draw audiences (*Variety Film Reviews*, 1983).

Critics whose comments were meant specifically for moviegoers, especially those living outside of Dallas, did not greet Gordon's moviemaking efforts with any great critical acclaim. To the contrary, the movies were roundly panned. One critic said of *The Killer Shrews*: "Shrews are the tiniest of rodents, but some crazy scientist has enlarged them to 100 pounds each. Strange how these giant killer shrews resemble Irish setters in blackface" (McDougal, 1984, p. 18). Another critic went so far as to call *The Killer Shrews* one of the worst motion pictures ever made. Gordon, who could not help but be honest in his own appraisal of his three film creations, put tongue in cheek and responded to the critic: "I resent your allegation that *The Killer Shrews* was one of the worst movies of all time. I made two other movies that were worse than that" (Blackwell, 1986, p. 6C).

In later years Gordon recalled "those first little mincing steps" taken to produce his first motion pictures (Porter, 1980, p. 4-M). He said that they had been made "experimentally . . . literally to make mistakes" in order that he and his production staff might learn the rudiments of film production. Over time, these early lessons, said Gordon, would prove beneficial as his motion pictures improved and became more serious (McLendon, 1969a). And while Gordon "never pretended he was creating high art" with his first movies, he did prove that he could produce movies and that they could be made in Dallas (Porter, 1986).

Gordon also proved that moviemaking could be profitable. He eventually quintupled his original investment in his first three motion pictures (McDougal, 1984, p. 18). Each would pop up occasionally on the television late show schedule (Porter, 1980, p. 4-M), and *The Killer Shrews* would gain "a special sort of cult infamy" in the pantheon of forgettable but intriguing motion pictures (McDougal, 1984, p. 18).

With three motion pictures produced in 1959, the McLendon Radio Pictures Corporation was well on its way in the moviemaking business. Gordon envisioned Cielo becoming a full-fledged production center, not only for motion pictures but for television as well. In mid-1960 he spoke of plans to produce major movies at Cielo starring such screen luminaries as John Wayne, Gregory Peck and Jennifer Jones. And plans also were underway to produce a television police series and Western series—perhaps even to transfer production of the popular television series "Have Gun Will Travel" to Cielo (McLendon, 1960c, p. 2). A fourth motion picture, *Tuffy Scott's Dog*, was scheduled to begin shooting at Cielo in July 1960 (McLendon, 1960a), and a long list of movie projects was lined up for 1961.

Practically all of the planned movies were heavily oriented toward the youth market. One of the movies, *Tom Sawyer's Treasure*, would be based upon Mark Twain characters, but the actual story, about a treasure hunt on a deserted island, would be based upon an original screenplay written by Gordon himself (McLendon, 1961, 1969a).

None of the motion pictures planned for production in 1961 were ever produced. Several reasons seemed to foreclose on Gordon's intentions. One had to do with the declining market interest in children's movies. Another had to do with the discouraging financial returns thus far experienced by the McLendon Radio Pictures Corporation (McLendon, 1962d). Added to these were pressures from B. R. to extinguish any further moviemaking ideas for fear of losing money (Bart McLendon, 1990).

So, by December 1962, Mitch Lewis was telling Gordon's associates that McLendon Corporation broadcast interests "have been taking up 100% of our time and it leaves other projects either undone or at loose ends. As a result, it would seem very doubtful that we would be interested in any film projects in the foreseeable future" (Lewis, 1962).

Gordon's attention to broadcast and political matters in the mid-to-late 1960s pushed his ambitions toward motion picture production further and further into the background. There still remained a desire on Gordon's part to return to moviemaking, but time constraints simply would not allow it. Plus, there was the realization, slow to take hold, that Dallas, after all, did "not have the qualified personnel to elevate it to any sort of feature film producing center" (Lewis, 1966). As a result, Mitch Lewis was instructed to begin selling the McLendon Radio Pictures Corporation inventory of cameras and other film production hardware, a task that was nearly complete by early May 1966 (Lewis, 1966).

Gordon's interest in producing motion pictures was not entirely dead, though. By 1969, he was talking of getting back into the business, and *Tom Sawyer's Treasure* was being mentioned once more as a top project (McLendon, 1969a). Gordon was not just talking, either. He had started construction of a Western town at Cielo in May 1969 that would serve as both a movie and television set (Chism, 1969). The set never would be used for any of his own film projects, although other film companies often used it to shoot commercials, and at least one spaghetti Western starring Rhonda Fleming was shot there (McDougal, 1984, p. 21).

Gordon's moviemaking intentions were sidetracked for a while longer, but in the meantime the McLendons' movie exhibition business was running at full throttle. In February 1969, the McLendon Corporation announced plans to construct seventy-five new movie theaters in twenty states ("McLendons Plan," 1969). Bob Hartgrove, a veteran theater operator whom the McLendons had hired to manage their theater chain, made the announcement (McLendon, 1969a). The expansion would cost nearly $100 million and take some five years to complete. The plan called for construction of both indoor theaters in large shopping centers and triple- and quadruple-screen drive-in theaters around the United States ("McLendons Plan,"

1969). In little more than four years, the McLendons jumped from a pre-1969 ownership of five movie theaters to ownership of ninety theaters. By 1973, practically every major city in Texas was the site of a McLendon theater (Raffetto, 1973).

The McLendons appeared to be moving ahead at an amazing pace in their theater business when suddenly, in October 1973, B. R. announced that the entire McLendon chain of theaters was being sold (Porter, 1973). The decision to sell their theaters, coming as it did during the same period when the McLendons also were selling many of their radio stations, seemed to have been well-timed financially. A firm headed by B. J. Hardy and based in Tyler, Texas was paying in excess of $21 million for all the McLendon theater properties. The transaction was said to be the biggest of its kind in Texas history. Hardy was to assume ownership one month after B. R.'s October announcement (Raffetto, 1973). Theater business insiders were speculating, however, that the McLendons' exit from the business was not permanent and that they would be back in one form or another at some future date (Porter, 1973).

How right the insiders were. The deal fell through, and the McLendons retained their theaters. In 1976, though, the entire chain was leased for ten years to FLW, a theater management company located in Detroit (Porter, 1987; 1986). FLW's lease agreement required that it pay the McLendon Corporation a monthly rental fee and a percentage of the gross from box-office receipts (Kerns, 1981).

When the FLW lease expired in 1986, the McLendon Corporation, then headed by Gordon's son Bart, took back its original control of a rapidly diminishing number of McLendon theaters. The competition from cable television, home video and indoor theaters especially had led to the closing of drive-in theaters across the country during the late 1970s and early 1980s (Frank, 1986). Ironically, it was the appearance of these new media with their voracious appetite for movies that would cause Gordon's return to moviemaking.

Gordon seemed never to be too far from the moviemaking business. In the late 1970s, along with business associate Sy Weintraub, he began thinking seriously of buying huge chunks of stock in Columbia Pictures, one of Hollywood's biggest film production companies. The two businessmen did not have their eye on owning Columbia so much as on buying what they considered undervalued stock in a company that was ripe for eventual takeover. Together, Gordon and Sy Weintraub became the largest owners of Columbia stock, each owning 125,000 shares in the company, before the Coca-Cola Company bought Columbia. Gordon's and Sy Weintraub's takeover hunch had proved correct. Stock that they had purchased at eighteen dollars per share was sold to Coca-Cola for seventy-four dollars per share (McDougal, 1984, p. 20).

That encounter with the film industry at the business level reignited Gordon's interest in moviemaking at the creative level. This would be the third time in the last three decades that Gordon would try to shape his dreams of making movies into a reality. This time, though, Gordon approached matters with a decidedly different perspective. Asked about his reentry into moviemaking, Gordon said that he now realized that he would "never have the time in my lifetime to devote to being a line producer or a director" (Kerns, 1981). These were the creative roles that Gordon so relished. Applying his creative touch to moviemaking "was one of the things in life I really, really wanted to do, and I realize now that there won't be enough years left for me to do it. . . . I used to kid myself that it could still happen," said Gordon, "but I'm getting a little too old to kid myself anymore" (Kerns, 1981).

Gordon's creative ambitions may have been thwarted, but he still regarded the role of executive producer as a viable alternative. In this capacity he would be able to invest his own considerable wealth into motion picture production. There was an indirect creative touch here in that Gordon could choose which movie to produce based upon his assessment of the movie's script (Porter, 1980, p. 4-M).

Moviemaking in the 1980s held another appeal for Gordon as well. The new video technologies had expanded the exhibition potential and thus the profit potential for movies. "If you've got cable television fighting subscription television for movies, fighting the movie theaters for movies and fighting the television networks for movies, it will be a wonderful thing for the motion picture industry," Gordon maintained (" 'Old Scotsman' Reentering," 1980). And he added, "He's got to make a pretty bad motion picture not to have a market for it. . . . If he makes a good picture . . . holy mackerel" (" 'Old Scotsman' Reentering," 1980).

Gordon leaped back into the moviemaking business as executive producer of a "high adventure" film entitled *Escape to Victory*. The movie's $15 million budget was far removed from the $100,000 budgets of Gordon's first films. And the cast members carried credentials and name recognition that also were in an entirely different league. Michael Caine, Sylvester Stallone and Max von Sydow filled the lead roles. Brazilian soccer star Pele also played an important role in the movie, whose story line about a group of American prisoners of war forced to play a soccer match with their German captors was fashioned around his athletic talents (Porter, 1980, pp. 1–M, 4-M).

This impressive cast had been assembled by Gordon as one of his executive producer duties. A bigger coup than pulling these actors together, however, was Gordon's success in nabbing John Huston to direct *Escape to Victory*. Apart from reading the film's script, suggesting changes and hiring Huston, Caine, Stallone, von Sydow and Pele, Gordon's only other major chore was to finance the movie. After that was accomplished there was little left for him to do but stay out of the way. After all, said Gordon, "when you see John Huston sitting there in a director's chair, he looks positively awesome and you certainly don't feel safe offering him suggestions" (Kerns, 1981). Gordon actually spent most of the time when *Escape to Victory* was in production working in Dallas (Porter, 1980, p. 1-M), although he did manage to visit the film location in Budapest, Hungary occasionally.

Gordon's decision to produce *Escape to Victory* had its profit motive, to be sure. "I wouldn't get involved with any film that I didn't feel had real financial potential, no matter how artistic," Gordon said (Kerns, 1981). And he felt that the international flavor of the movie's cast would make *Escape to Victory* more popular in the world market and thus stretch its financial potential even more.

But Gordon had another motive, too. This particular movie would be fun to make. He emphatically did not want to get involved in serious "message" movies, but instead preferred movies that would entertain their audience (Kerns, 1981).

Escape to Victory finally was released in 1982 with its title shortened to *Victory*. The movie did not attract the crowds anticipated and virtually flopped at the box office. Gordon was disappointed, but he wisely had arranged to recoup his own investment in the movie (McDougal, 1984, p. 18).

By 1984, Gordon and several of his associates were pooling their resources for an $80 million production fund that would underwrite several movies in the coming years. Some of the projects Gordon had set his sights on producing were a film version of his philosophical mentor Ayn Rand's novel, *Atlas Shrugged;* a film version of James Ramsey Ullman's novel, *The Sands of Karakorum;* the remake of a 1937 movie based on James Hilton's best seller, *Knight Without Armor;* and the film version of one of the stories in F. Scott Fitzgerald's *Babylon Revisited* short story collection (McDougal, 1984, pp. 1, 18). All of these titles suggested much more adult themes than the kind of films Gordon had wanted to produce in his earlier years as a moviemaker. Remaining from those days, however, was Gordon's desire to produce his beloved *Tom Sawyer's Treasure*. "Once more after some years I think it's time to test the waters of pure children's movies," Gordon said during a 1984 interview (McDougal, 1984, p. 18).

Tom Sawyer's Treasure also was Gordon's link to an earlier and more carefree time in the moviemaking business. As it happened, not only was *Tom Sawyer's Treasure* never produced, but none of the other projects that Gordon had lined up ever moved from the planning stage. Gordon's health precluded his ever advancing beyond one major movie release during his on-again, off-again moviemaking career.

OTHER PROFESSIONAL AND PUBLIC PURSUITS

Gordon's professional interests were not entirely directed toward radio, cinema and politics. Much of his time away from business was taken up by personal civic endeavors and KLIF public affairs activities. Texas state chairperson of the March of Dimes, honorary national commander of the VFW Poppy Drive, Dallas Theatre Center and Dallas Symphony Orchestra board member, member-at-large of the Dallas Area Council of the Boy Scouts of America and board of stewards member of the Dallas Highland Park Methodist Church were just a few of the voluntary roles that Gordon assumed through the years ("Gordon McLendon for United States Senator," 1964). Gordon said that of all his volunteer service, he enjoyed working with youth most of all. That work was even more gratifying when it contributed toward their education, he added (McLendon, 1969a).

Gordon's volunteer work took an international turn in the early 1960s when he was enlisted as a Peace Corps communications advisor by Peace Corps director Sargent Shriver (McLendon, 1969a). Shriver referred to Gordon as one of the Peace Corps pioneers, and paid particular tribute to his work in helping establish an educational television system in Colombia, South America (Shriver, 1964).

Gordon's interest in working with young people, especially those seeking to better themselves, led to a project that he had considered doing for some time, called the "Magnificent Seven." The project's aim was to develop the broadcast management skills of young persons who were interested in broadcasting as a career. Gordon, along with several persons from his staff, developed a seminar curriculum for the Magnificent Seven project that included instruction in everything from engineering to programming to sales (Dowe, 1989).

Once the curriculum was in place, Gordon solicited seminar applications through newspaper and trade magazine advertisements (Brock, 1971). Applicants were screened, and eventually seven were chosen as seminar participants (Dowe, 1989). The Magnificent Seven were brought to Dallas in 1971 for a one-month, all-expense-paid, intensive indoctrination into the world of broadcasting. Gordon housed his students and conducted his seminar at Cielo (Brock, 1971).

While there certainly was an altruistic motive in creating the Magnificent Seven seminar, Gordon had a selfish purpose as well. He hoped that at least someone in the group eventually would emerge with the kind of talent that could be useful as a McLendon Station employee. And that indeed was the result for the top seminar graduate, who went on to manage the McLendon's Detroit radio station (Dowe, 1989).

The success of Gordon's first Magnificent Seven seminar led eventually to a second one. For this one, however, Gordon selected only minority participants. And instead of just seven, nine persons—seven blacks, a Puerto Rican and a Mexican-American—were brought to Cielo and put through the same crash course in broadcasting as their predecessors (Brock, 1971).

Gordon said that he hoped to conduct another Magnificent Seven seminar at some point (Brock, 1971), but the likelihood of that happening became more and more remote as his sights shifted away from radio. Once that shift began, the range of interests that now would occupy Gordon's time and attention and to which he would apply his considerable talent appeared nearly limitless. "His mind was so fertile that trying to keep it in one direction was impossible," said Bart McLendon. So . . . after he mastered the radio business, he went in several different directions, one of which was the financial arena, and became quite an expert in precious metals, international currencies, strategic metals, to an extent stocks and bonds and options" (Bart McLendon, 1990).

Just how far-ranging the McLendon financial empire happened to be is somewhat confusing, but there is no doubt of the diversity of interests it included.

In what appears to have been the first public attention given to Gordon's and B. R.'s post-Liberty Broadcasting System financial dealings, *Business Week* magazine reported in 1961 that Gordon was the president of seventeen corporations ("Zany," 1961, p. 124). The number of corporations overseen by Gordon and B. R. had increased to twenty-five by 1968, according to another source (Ford, 1968), but *Newsweek* magazine reported in the same year that Gordon owned thirty companies ("The Gall," 1968).

Did Gordon and B. R. really own and operate this many corporations and/or companies? Not really, said Bart McLendon. "Before they realized . . . the proper way to structure a business," said Bart, "they probably were thinking that they had to have one corporation for each radio station; you know, a corporation for each little part of the jigsaw puzzle. But then they put it all within two partnerships, being the McLendon Company and Tri-State Theatres" (Bart McLendon, 1990).

The diversification of interests found in the McLendon financial portfolio represented two investment phases. Banking, chemical and oil investments (McLendon, 1969a) and to some extent real estate investments were made alongside radio and television station investments during phase one. By the early 1970s, though, Gordon's and B. R.'s fears of unsteady U.S. economic conditions led to a shift in their investment strategy (McDougal, 1984, p. 20). They divested themselves of their broadcast interests and replaced them with investments in strategic and precious metals, real estate and art objects (McLendon, 1980a, p. 1).

For Gordon, about whom it was once said with regard to his oil investments that "his attitude toward oil epitomizes his business philosophy: He wants wildcats, not development drilling" ("Zany," 1961, p. 131), the new investment strategy was rooted in providing greater investment security (McDougal, 1984, p. 20). Gordon's ascent to *Forbes* magazine's list of the wealthiest persons in the United States during the 1980s, with a wealth estimated in excess of $200 million, suggests that the strategy worked ("The Forbes," 1983; 1984; 1985). But, there was more than security involved. Gordon, when asked by *Forbes* in 1985 for his key to financial success, replied with tongue in cheek: "Never invest in anything that eats or needs painting" ("The Forbes," 1985). The reply actually carried more meaning than it seemed, for it implied a personal philosophy of investing that had accompanied Gordon's "phase two" investment strategy. And that philosophy was to "have fun" (McDougal, 1984, p. 18). After all, said Gordon, "How many jollies do you get from a passbook account?" (McDougal, 1984, p. 21).

Gordon had some jollies and made headlines at the same time in 1981 when he paid more than $155,000 for a fifth-century B.C. Greek coin. The price for the silver piece was the highest ever paid for such a coin at a U.S. public auction (Knutson, 1981). Gordon's very expensive coin was added to his collection, considered to be the world's largest, of ancient seals and cylinders dating back to at least 4,000 B.C. (McDougal, 1984, p. 20).

Gordon invested in gold in the 1970s at a time when its cost was far below the $300 an ounce to which the price eventually would climb (Shultz, 1986, p. A-1). In fact, a considerable amount of the proceeds from the sale of KLIF was said to have been used to purchase gold when the price for the precious metal was twenty-six dollars an ounce (Hitt, 1986a, p. A-8). Moreover, at least some of the more than $150 million from the sale of all but one of the remaining McLendon radio stations between 1972 and 1977 ("The Forbes," 1983) was said to have gone toward purchase of gold when the metal's price hovered around forty dollars an ounce (Hitt, 1979).

The huge profit that Gordon eventually stood to make by converting his gold into cash was but a reminder of how he managed always to be ahead of his time (Kerns, 1981). Being ahead of his time was not always so profitable, though. Just as Gordon had discovered earlier that failure sometimes resulted from moving too quickly ahead with innovative radio formats, so was failure possible when moving ahead too quickly with particular financial arrangements and investments.

One of Gordon's financial missteps, in Bart McLendon's opinion, was his decision to abandon radio when he did. Although the McLendons correctly predicted the decline of AM radio, and managed to sell KLIF for more than ten times what the station would be worth in a decade, Bart said that Gordon somehow "never did really see the coming of FM radio" and never "really saw how truly powerful FM was going to be" (Bart McLendon, 1990). Gordon and B. R. had scored such success early on with their AM radio stations that Gordon evidently misjudged FM radio's eventual rise to dominance among the two services, and thus underestimated the value of FM stations. And even though the McLendons owned powerful Class C FM stations in major markets such as Dallas, Detroit, Buffalo and Chicago, they sold them at a fraction of what their selling price would have been just a few years later. KNUS-FM in Dallas, for example, sold "for three million and change," as Bart McLendon put it, and ten years later the entry price for a comparable Class C FM station was "something in the neighborhood of $20 million" (Bart McLendon, 1990).

Another financial misjudgment on Gordon's part occurred in the late 1960s, when he attempted to launch a project called "Car-Teach". The idea behind Car-Teach, as well as the project's name, originated with Mitch Lewis (Vaughn, 1989). Car-Teach was designed to utilize the driving time of people living in highly mobile urban areas by providing them with academic and self-help courses recorded on audiocassette tapes. Gordon had determined that commuters in many cities spent anywhere from one to two hours per weekday driving back and forth to work. Why not offer these people a way to utilize that time in some constructive way (McLendon, 1969a)?

Car-Teach was formally incorporated in March 1967 (CAR-TEACH, Inc., n.d.), and was placed in the newly created educational division of the McLendon Corporation (McLendon, 1969a). Joining Gordon in his Car-Teach venture was good friend and fellow investor Roy Lofton. Lofton introduced two other investors with high name recognition—entertainer Arthur Godfrey and former White House press secretary Pierre Salinger—to the project (Routt, 1989). These people formed the financial and promotional nucleus of a unique venture that, according to Gordon, no other business yet had entered (McLendon, 1969a).

One of the reasons that Car-Teach was operating in virgin territory was the relative newness of the technology being utilized. Audiocassettes and cassette record/playback units only recently had entered the consumer marketplace (McLendon, 1969a). In fact, since the success of Car-Teach relied entirely on the availability of cassette playback units, Glenn Callison was dispatched to Japan to search for a manufacturer that could supply units for Car-Teach distribution. Callison managed to negotiate an agreement with a company to manufacture playback units only, which without a record mechanism made them relatively inexpensive (Callison, 1989).

Eleven Car-Teach courses eventually appeared between 1967 and 1968. Each course was available on individual audiocassettes, accompanied by a verbatim transcript of each tape in book format. The courses, whose taped versions presumably were voiced by their authors, covered a somewhat eclectic array of subjects that included, among others, Morton Yarmon's *How to Buy Stocks and Bonds*, Del Rayburn's *How to Write Fiction That Sells*, Elmer Wheeler's *Successful Salesmanship*, William C. Monroe's *The Study of Philosophy*, Charles R. Boyles's *How to Get Into Court and Win Without a Lawyer*, and Horace Zachary's *Sex in Marriage*. Two titles, *Style in Letter Writing* and *Style in the Use of English*, were authored by Gordon himself. One of the most peculiar titles was Arther Leif's *Piano Playing Skills I* (CAR-TEACH, n.d.). Obviously, this title did little good for the commuter.

Car-Teach seemed to be on the success track. Gordon even commented in 1969, one-and-a-half years after introducing Car-Teach, that the venture had reached a break-even point financially, and that people who had taken the Car-Teach courses were quite pleased (McLendon, 1969a).

Gordon's enthusiasm for the potential of Car-Teach may have been genuine, but reality showed the venture to be in a precarious financial condition. Whatever the cause—and that remains obscure—the business arrangement between Gordon, Roy Lofton, Arthur Godfrey and Pierre Salinger collapsed, leaving Gordon with a hefty bill for bailing out what remained of Car-Teach, Inc. (Routt, 1989).

Bart McLendon noted that the failure of Car-Teach quite likely ranked as one of Gordon's greatest professional disappointments (Bart McLendon, 1990). Had Gordon been able to hold on for a while longer, or had he waited a few years to exploit the Car-Teach idea, he would have found conditions for success much more favorable. By the 1980s, automobiles were being manufactured equipped with cassette players, and a plethora of self-help books, many of which were available on audiocassettes, were crowding bookstore shelves.

There were numerous other business decisions, most not as well known nor as public as the above, that required the keen business skills of the Gordon/B. R. McLendon partnership. And certainly, decisions that both made were more often right than wrong. When asked to evaluate the business acumen and skills of his father and grandfather, Bart McLendon said;

> Granddad had the great business mind. Although he wasn't the only one. Dad had a pretty fair business head on his shoulders too. You don't amass that kind of wealth by simply being a good programmer. You just don't do it. . . . He made some very sound, very good business decisions. But Granddad was the business partner. And he ran the company, *Granddad ran the company*. Let there be no question about that. Dad was second in command at all times. (Bart McLendon, 1990)

High on B. R.'s investment agenda was real estate. Estimating land value and making deals to buy property were skills that were fully within B. R.'s realm of expertise. Gordon "knew absolutely nothing about the real estate business and cared a lot less," said Bart McLendon (1990). And while Gordon was buying gold and other precious metals with one portion of the proceeds of the McLendon Station sales, B. R. was buying land with the other portion (Bart McLendon, 1990).

The land and the gold, of course, would appreciate tremendously in value over the coming years, but not unlike other Texans, B. R. always had a greater attraction to land ownership than to any other kind of investment. In fact, the value of all the land accumulated by B. R. accounted for roughly 40 percent of the McLendon holdings, said Gordon during a 1984 interview. "It's the biggest single investment we have," he added (McDougal, 1984, p. 18). What's more, approximately 1,000 acres of the McLendon land was reportedly prime metropolitan real estate.

Perhaps not surprisingly, much of that prime acreage had been occupied at one time by a drive-in movie theater ("The Forbes," 1984). As noted earlier, B. R. always had set property value as the most important criterion in deciding where to build a McLendon outdoor theater.

One example of B. R.'s ability to pick the right spot for his drive-in theaters is the piece of land on which he placed the Gemini Twin Theater in Dallas. The twenty-eight acres of land on which the now closed theater sits (Bart McLendon, 1990) occupies a space near the corner of two major Dallas traffic arteries—LBJ Freeway/I–635 to the north and North Central Expressway to the west. Don Keyes recalled B. R. telling him years ago that the land on which the Gemini Theater sat one day would be worth more money than anything the McLendons owned (Keyes, 1989). Time would prove him right. Bart McLendon said that during the pre-1985 "heyday of Texas real estate," the property was appraised at $70 million. Since then the value "has been affected by the Texas economy just like all properties have," Bart said during a 1990 interview. But, he added, "In my opinion it is still the most valuable piece of property left in the city of Dallas" (Bart McLendon, 1990).

During the late 1970s, with McLendon real estate matters left in the able hands of B. R., for the time-being, Gordon turned his attention fully toward domestic and foreign economic problems and the investment potential for rare coins and precious metals (Odom, 1990). He became quite adept at predicting economic trends as his expertise on the subject grew. Bart McLendon recalled that Gordon had an uncanny ability to predict fluctuations in U.S. and foreign currency values. Maybe Gordon was only guessing, Bart said, but if so, they were "darned accurate" guesses (Bart McLendon, 1990).

Gordon spent much time also during the late 1970s and 1980s attending and speaking at investment and financial conferences around the world (Odom, 1990). In September 1980 he once more entered broadcasting on the performance side as a financial commentator (McLendon, 1980a, p. 1). Gordon's commentaries were aired four times daily on Dallas television station KNBN ("Gordon McLendon," 1980). Gordon also had planned to produce another series on financial matters for national syndication. The series, entitled "The Money Picture," would have combined Gordon's financial commentaries with interviews with leading financial experts from around the world ("The Money Picture," n.d.).

Gordon made a major contribution to financial education with the 1980 publication of his book *Get Really Rich in the Coming Super Metals Boom*. The book was given high marks by one reviewer, who called it a very readable guide for novice and seasoned buyer alike who might be looking to invest in those necessary but nonetheless rare metals referred to as "strategic metals" (Biffle, 1981).

Gordon told another reviewer that he and B. R. had discovered the investment potential for strategic metals when studying the "gold-and-silver situation" in the mid-1970s. Once he had conquered the labyrinthine procedures for purchasing strategic metals, Gordon said, he was determined to pass on that information in somewhat simplified form to others (Eyrich, 1981). A *Forbes* magazine article about Gordon's book noted that "radio's supershowman is metals' supersalesman," and that Gordon's investment ideas put him "right in step with Wall Street—maybe a step ahead" (Bagamery, 1981, pp. 98–102).

Sales of Gordon's book did remarkably well, making both the B. Dalton and Waldenbooks best-seller lists for trade publications (Biffle, 1981). Gordon planned a sequel to *Get Really Rich in the Coming Super Metals Boom* that would enhance even more the investment skills of its readers (McLendon, 1980b, p. 119). The book, though, never would be written.

11 *Reflections*

Writer Joe Nick Patoski had grown up listening to the Top 40 programming of a McLendon Station, so he was well acquainted with the public persona of Gordon McLendon when he interviewed him in 1979 for an article later to appear in *Texas Monthly* magazine (Patoski, 1980, p. 101). Patoski's objective was to do a retrospective piece on Gordon's career in broadcasting, a career from which Gordon only recently had retired. Several weeks of interviewing concluded with Patoski accompanying Gordon on a flight from Dallas to New York City, where Gordon was to appear on the "Tomorrow" television program, hosted by former McLendon Station disc jockey Tom Snyder. Regarding observations made during that flight, Patoski wrote:

> Though his broadcasting empire, once the focus for his tremendous energy, no longer existed, McLendon remained very much a driven man, living out of suitcases as he shuttled between residences in Geneva, Stockholm, Liechtenstein, Los Angeles, Palm Springs, and Dallas. . . . During the two-and-a-half-hour plane ride, he spoke passionately of finance, of balancing the national budget, and of the men he has most admired: the lone eagles, the gamblers, and the risk takers. (Patoski, 1980, p. 171)

The passion with which Gordon drove home his points did not escape the attention of another writer who earlier had interviewed Gordon for an article that appeared in *Newsweek* magazine. Noted the writer: "McLendon can hardly sit still for 30 seconds before furrowing his black brows in silent concentration or delivering sermonettes on his latest brainstorm" ("The Gall," 1968).

But Joe Nick Patoski had caught sight of something else during the Dallas-to-New York flight that created an altogether different impression of Gordon. "Life in the fast lane had certainly extracted its price," Patoski thought as he watched Gordon "slowly make his way down the aisle of [the] eastbound jet. His [58-year-old] face was drawn and his hair combed forward in a futile grasp at lost youth. . . ." For a man whose energy level had seemed nearly boundless in earlier times, Gordon now appeared burdened by the simple act of walking (Patoski, 1980, p. 171).

One can rightfully argue that fatigue will finally overtake even the most robust person who follows the kind of work and travel routine that Gordon maintained. But Patoski saw something in Gordon that was an ominous sign. The health of this once-vigorous man was beginning to decline. The decline was not rapid at first, and it certainly did not immediately diminish Gordon's spirit or drive. Nonetheless, time was running out for the Old Scotchman.

Chapter after chapter of Gordon's life began closing as he moved through the 1980s. One of the most monumental events was the death of his father in October 1982. B. R. suffered a heart attack and died while en route to a business meeting. He was eighty-two years old ("Movie Theater Owner," 1982). The partnership that Gordon and B. R. had forged so successfully nearly forty years before was now at an end. One need only be aware of the "father-son worship relationship" that existed between these two to understand the emotional pain that Gordon must have suffered (Odom, 1990).

Now by himself, Gordon decided to move the McLendon Corporation offices to Cielo in May 1983 (McLendon, 1983). He adjusted to running the affairs of his company well enough, but it was at this time that Billie Odom said Gordon began to appear physically frail (Odom, 1990).

In September 1984, Gordon traveled to Los Angeles to appear at the NAB/NRBA Programming Convention in honor of broadcast consultant Kent Burkhart. The trip was not meant as a farewell gesture to his colleagues of so many years, but as it happened, Gordon's Los Angeles public appearance would be his last before a gathering of broadcasters ("Radio Pioneer," 1986, p. 3).

A few months later, in early 1985, Gordon was off on one of his farflung journeys once more. This time the destination was Australia. When Gordon returned to Dallas, he was hoarse. The same condition had persisted for several months, but it was bad enough this time to seek medical attention (Bart McLendon, 1990).

What doctors discovered was esophageal cancer (Hitt, 1986a, p. A-8). Such news normally is devastating to anyone first hearing it, and one might expect that it would have devastated Gordon. But not so, at least not outwardly. "He did well," Bart McLendon recalled. "I don't think any of the rest of us did very well, but he did very well. He took it very matter-of-factly. He was a fighter" (Bart McLendon, 1990).

Adding one more burden to Gordon's shoulders was the death of his mother, Jeannette Eyster McLendon, in July 1985. Mrs. McLendon died of a heart attack in a Dallas hospital at the age of eighty-six ("McClendon [sic] Services Set," 1985).

Attention turned now to battling the cancer. For this Gordon relied on the chemotherapy treatments of Houston cancer specialists. There were signs of the cancer's remission at times, but the drugs Gordon took weakened him and left him confused and disoriented for a few days following his treatment. It was during one of these times in early December 1985 that Gordon shot himself with a .38-calibre handgun that Bart McLendon said his father had purchased for protection. A housekeeper found Gordon lying on the floor of the main room at Cielo. He had lost considerable blood and a bullet had broken his jaw, but a helicopter managed to transport Gordon to a local hospital for treatment.

Mystery surrounded the shooting. Bart McLendon contended that it was an accident caused by Gordon's inept handling of his firearm while trying to clean it (Brady, 1985, p. 28-A). The contention had a firm foundation, considering Gordon's well-known limitations when it came to handling mechanical things. Ken Dowe even said that Gordon could hardly dial a phone without assistance (Dowe, 1989).

The Denton County sheriff's office, whose responsibility it was to investigate the shooting incident, withheld immediate judgment as to what had happened. The only statement issued by the sheriff's office on the matter said: "The motive for the shooting has not yet been established, and investigators have not ruled out the likelihood of suicide" ("Broadcasting Pioneer," 1985). Nothing further seems to have been said officially about Gordon's shooting.

Gordon was listed in critical condition when admitted to the hospital ("Broadcasting Pioneer," 1985). He spent nearly a month recovering from his injury before doctors were ready to allow Gordon to return to Cielo. There his gunshot wound healed, but the cancer that had settled in his throat and caused a paralysis of his vocal cords was having its way (Schultz, 1986, p. A-1). There was little humor in Gordon's plight, but there was much irony. For someone whose livelihood for so long had depended on his voice, the agony of losing that voice to such a relentless disease was "a pain worse than death" (Brady, 1985, p. 1-A).

Gordon clearly was losing his battle with cancer by the spring of 1986. Doctors felt that death was imminent in April. But Bart was certain his father would "hang tough" a while longer (Hitt, 1986a, p. A-8). And he was right. Gordon held on for five more months. But at 9:15 P.M., on September 14, 1986, Gordon died at his beloved Cielo. He was sixty-five years old (Schultz, 1986, pp. A-1, A-8). The only immediate family members surviving Gordon were his four children—Jan, Bart, Kristen and Anna Gray—and his sister, Marie Wheeler (Drape, 1986, p. 10A).

Gordon's death was announced across the land. Both *Variety* and *Broadcasting* magazine carried lengthy obituaries that recounted Gordon's exploits in radio ("Obituaries," 1986; "Deaths," 1986). The *Dallas Morning News*, in whose pages many articles about Gordon had appeared over the years, managed to misspell his last name in its headline to his obituary (Drape, 1986, p. 1A). The "McClendon" spelling actually had been a common error over the years in articles related to the McLendons, but such a mistake in what might have been the hometown newspaper's final article on the Old Scotchman was the kind of thing that likely would have brought a big grin to Gordon's face.

Sports Illustrated carried a memorial piece that recalled Gordon's "friendly Texas twang and spicy use of simile" from his Liberty Broadcasting days. " 'Fast as the lead dog in a coon hunt' is vintage McLendon, as are 'mad as a rooster that overslept' and 'uncertain as a dish of Tuesday's hash' and 'dangerous as a radio announcer without a script,' " noted the magazine ("Gordon McLendon," 1986). Also recalled was Gordon's reply when someone asked whether "he had any moral qualms about fictionalizing real ball games." Gordon shot back: "This kind of question infuriates me. . . . I was happy as hell to be able to entertain our listeners. What harm is there in making 100,000 people happy on a hot summer afternoon?" ("Gordon McLendon," 1986).

There were many tributes paid Gordon in the broadcast trade press, but perhaps none was so able to cut to the essence of the man and his contributions to radio as this tersely worded commentary that appeared in *The Pulse of Broadcasting:*

> The stubborn innovator of Top 40 radio lost the big battle this week—a long-time bout with cancer. Gordon McLendon is dead in Dallas. Living beyond him, however, is a heritage in the broadcast business known as Top 40 radio, and in an industry that tends to forget where they borrowed ideas, McLendon's name has become a legend. ("Radio Pioneer," 1986, p. 3)

A memorial service for Gordon instead of a funeral was scheduled at Cielo on Saturday, September 20 (Shultz, 1986, p. A-1). Gordon had requested that no funeral be held. In fact, more than a decade earlier, he had outlined in a memo precisely the procedure he wanted followed upon his death. His body was to be cremated, and his ashes were to be scattered in the Kiamichi Mountains. There was to be no funeral or memorial service. And all loved ones were to resume their regular activities within twenty-four hours of Gordon's death. To these instructions Gordon added the postscript that he wished to be cremated "in the least expensive coffin available" (McLendon, 1973b).

This memo revealed much about Gordon's values. The request that his ashes be scattered in the Kiamichi Mountains of southeastern Oklahoma, near his boyhood home of Idabel, said something of Gordon's glance backward to a less complicated and maybe even happier time and place.

Bart McLendon honored all of his father's wishes, including a later change of mind on Gordon's part to have a memorial service (Bart McLendon, 1990). But Gordon had decided that such a service would be appropriate only if his friends gathered to celebrate his life instead of mourn his death (Porter, 1986). The occasion would be a happy one, Gordon instructed, in what Bart said was his father's last memo.

There was much happiness but still tears to be shed as the 300 or so people gathered in the courtyard of Cielo's main building for Gordon's Saturday memorial service (Hitt, 1986c). The whole service lasted for about an hour. Everyone was seated in a lawn chair beneath the hot Texas sun; it was a gorgeous day. Don Keyes remembered "the whole thing was a remarkable service" (Keyes, 1989). In attendance were Gordon's close working associates, such as Keyes, Sy Weintraub, Marcus Cohn and many others. Robert Page, former custodian at the McLendon Building, was there, as was multimillionaire Bunker Hunt. Bart McLendon told all the men present to remove their coats and loosen their ties. And everyone was to have a good time.

Three speakers were chosen to deliver eulogies. They stood on a flower-bedecked podium to reminisce about Gordon. Wes Wise told of his days at Liberty Broadcasting and how, when he was drafted, Gordon had urged radio listeners to send Wise a postcard. Sack after sack of mail arrived at Wise's Fort Benning address as a result.

Marcus Cohn told of Gordon's practical jokes. He especially recalled the time Gordon managed to contact him by postcard during a vacation in Italy. The card had been torn so that most of the message was missing. The only part of the message that Gordon so carefully had left intact were the words "crisis," "disaster," "emergency" and "immediately" (Hitt, 1986c).

Don Keyes began his eulogy by saying: "Let there be no tears at Cielo today. Cielo means heaven, and that's where Gordon is." His entire eulogy lasted only about twenty-five seconds, but, Keyes said, "It took me days to write it. . . . There was the constant urge to get maudlin. With my writing ability and knowing [Gordon] and his romanticism, I had to fight it. I knew he wouldn't like it, and I knew I probably couldn't read it without breaking down" (Keyes, 1989).

PROFESSIONAL DIMENSIONS

Tributes to the character, personality and creative genius of Gordon McLendon flowed freely both during and after his memorial service. Allowing himself time to reflect on his friend's unique qualities, Marcus Cohn later described Gordon as "the most creative person I have ever known. To him, the usual and ordinary were boring; they were almost repulsive" (Cohn,

1986). Don Keyes added to Cohn's description, saying that Gordon "was at once charming and demanding, picky and generous . . . but above all, exhilarating to be with, absolutely exhilarating" (Keyes, 1989).

But the best description of Gordon's professional demeanor may have been drawn by fellow broadcast executive Robert Eastman while Gordon still was in his prime. Introducing Gordon before a speech he was to deliver in 1966, Eastman called him "a human time-stretcher. . . . Get to know him, if anyone can—charming, exasperating, unpredictable, frustrating, daring, restless, unsatisfiable, critical, self-critical, tough, charitable, demanding—a human chameleon of contrasts whom it is an experience to know, a fascination to watch, and impossible to describe" (Eastman, 1966, p. 3).

Gordon probably would have smiled approvingly at all of the many words said about him, certainly the kind ones and maybe even the ones that bordered on the unflattering. But he might have felt most comfortable with the characterization of him that appeared in a 1968 *Newsweek* magazine article. Describing Gordon as a "nervous, lanky man (5 feet 11 inches, 145 pounds)," the article said: "Even in Texas, the 46-year-old millionaire hardly blends with the crowd" ("The Gall," 1968). Indeed, while there was so much about Gordon that was common and ordinary, there was so very much more that was uncommon and extraordinary.

Gordon considered himself a maverick in every sense of the word. In fact it was said that when greeting new acquaintances at Cielo, Gordon handed them a sheet of paper containing the dictionary definition of the word "maverick" and then asked that the definition be read aloud as he nodded approvingly ("The Gall," 1968). Gordon was fond of doing things his own way. Ideas were constantly streaming through his mind—ideas for things yet untried or ideas for new ways of doing what had been done already. "He was always thinking and always right on the cusp of something new that was going on. . . . He was there to explore it. He had an incredible penchant for inquiring about things that other people didn't think about," observed Ken Dowe (1989).

Gordon had an "uncanny ability to see a trend developing . . . to spot a trend before it happened," recalled Tom Merriman (1990). Moreover, said former Liberty Broadcasting System sportscaster Lindsey Nelson, "Gordon lived the life he lived because he was not bound by restrictions that the average person lives by. Gordon would try anything" (Nelson, 1988). So often was he trying something new, said Dave McKinsey, that "you could never tell what was going to happen next" (McKinsey, 1990). Gordon carried "reams of paper in his coat covered with notes, data and ideas that have come to him during the day," Don Keyes once wrote a friend (Keyes, 1958). And he left behind a string of unfinished projects; as soon as one project would begin, ideas for a new one would pop up, which often caused the previous project to be pushed aside (Harp, 1989).

The note taking was only one example of Gordon's compulsive nature.

Another was his tenacity. "Gordon would set out to do something, and if he made up his mind to do it, you'd better get out of his way because he's going to do it," recalled political advisor George Sandlin. "He was a goer. He was a doer. And he wasn't afraid of anybody or anything" (Sandlin, 1990). Gordon had the mind, the drive and the wherewithal to try just about anything, and to succeed at most things. He expected people who worked for him to have the same drive, determination and mindset, and to be available when needed. Sometimes that meant being available twenty-four hours a day. Even when Gordon traveled he often called members of his staff in the middle of the night with instructions to do this or that. Time differences between Dallas and wherever he might be meant nothing to Gordon (Odom, 1990).

Gordon's hectic, nonstop work schedule has already been noted. "When Dad was in his heyday, no three men could stay with him from a work standpoint," said Bart McLendon. "He'd work them all in the ground. Through his twenties, thirties and a large part of his forties, he was absolutely driven" (Bart McLendon, 1990).

Gordon's pace gave him an apparently ubiquitous presence that could terrorize his employees. One of Gordon's favorite terror tactics was to set his alarm clock for some early hour such as 3 A.M., wake up and begin listening to one of his radio stations. Whenever he heard one of his disc jockeys—(who probably thought no one would be listening at that time of the morning)—make a mistake, Gordon immediately phoned him with instructions to be more careful. After a while, Gordon had his disc jockeys convinced that he never slept.

Gordon was naturally impulsive. He was not one to abide by a schedule, nor did he follow a routine. His impulsive habits sometimes overwhelmed McLendon Station employees. Bart McLendon told of his father going to Houston one time and phoning the KILT program director with instructions to meet with him in his hotel room. That meeting lasted for seventy-two uninterrupted hours while the two talked about radio programming ideas (Blackwell, 1986, p. 6C).

Edd Routt provided another example of Gordon's impulsiveness that happened when Routt served as Gordon's administrative assistant:

> [Gordon] called me from Love Field, which was then the airport for the Dallas area, and wanted me to meet him out there and bring some files and folders. We were going to kick some things around. I got out there, and we got to talking, and he said, "Look, I'm going to go on to Mexico City, and I've got thus and so to do. Why don't you just go with me?" I said, "Oh, Gordon, I've really got a lot to do. I've got this, this and this working." "Well," he said, "you'll only be gone 24 hours."
>
> So he called his secretary and had her go by my house and get some clothes for an overnight trip. And we went to Mexico City, and from there we went

> to New York City, and from there we went to Detroit, and from there we went to Chicago. . . . I got home three weeks later. (Routt, 1989)

Asked how Gordon was able to maintain the pace he did and to accomplish as much as he did, Don Keyes said that Gordon had "tremendous stamina, tremendous capacity mentally to handle it all. . . . He was a workaholic. He just reveled in it" (Keyes, 1989). Edd Routt added that Gordon

> was good at delegating. And he could keep 16 fires going by using his aides and assistants. He simply, in that respect, was a very good executive. He made good use of people. He often would get exasperated when somebody couldn't get something done. He'd just move in and take over. . . . He never was off-duty. And when you're that way, you can keep a lot of things going. (Routt, 1989)

Les Vaughn said that Gordon's low tolerance for anything short of perfection affected his treatment of McLendon Corporation personnel. "I don't care how good you were at whatever job you were supposed to be doing," said Vaughn. "If [Gordon] told you to do something and you didn't do it right, your days were numbered. He was just that way" (Vaughn, 1989).

Although Gordon disliked firing people, he nonetheless was said to have fired entire radio station staffs in order to replace them with staffs from competing stations (Patoski, 1980, p. 168). Bill Stewart, in fact, may have held the record for the number of times that Gordon fired him. The firings generally came by way of a note pushed under Stewart's door saying, "You're not with me anymore. You're fired." This was Gordon's way of avoiding confrontation. "He didn't confront people very well," Ken Dowe said of Gordon. "And that probably was one of the more unattractive character flaws that Gordon had. He could be a bully. I'm not certain that he was all that brave. . . . Gordon just didn't like to confront" (Dowe, 1989).

Gordon often showed great care and affection for his employees. But, said Bart McLendon, his father's disposition toward employees sometimes showed a less than saintly side (Blackwell, 1986, p. 6C). "Gordon made me mad several times," Les Vaughn said. "I'm sure he's made everybody else mad, too. He's made me so mad sometimes I'd want to quit. . . . He mistreated some of the employees, he really did. And it was only those who understood him that he could do these things to" (Vaughn, 1989).

Vaughn's decision, and most likely the decision of others, to stay with Gordon after he had rubbed them the wrong way showed that they indeed did understand him and were willing to tolerate his temperament. They understood Gordon's drive, his high energy level and his work ethic, and were willing to be caught up in the excitement that seemed always to surround him. "I was a pretty tough taskmaster," Gordon freely admitted on one occasion. "But I believe that I both worked as hard as any of my employees and didn't demand anything from them that I wasn't able to do myself" (Patoski, 1980, p. 168).

Much of Gordon's work ethic came from his grandfather. He once related to a group of college students in Arkansas what Jefferson Davis McLendon had shared with him as a youth:

> My Grandad [sic] engrained in me his own philosophy that we do not begin to live in any true and satisfactory sense until we have learned to take each day by itself, to make the most of *that* day as if it were our last and our all, dismissing tomorrow as a mere phantom that may never appear. Each day, he told me, offered me opportunities, and one of life's most precious possessions, time itself. (McLendon, 1969b, p. 3)

Gordon's dogged determination to succeed, and the fact that he accomplished so much of what he set out to do, did not cloud Gordon's views of his limitations. His reference to himself at one point as "an optimist who always carries a raincoat" was a sure indication that Gordon was a pragmatist (Kerns, 1981). There were disappointments along the way. They were to be expected, but they were not to dampen the spirit when encountered. Besides, Gordon contended, disappointments could be beneficial as learning experiences. "There are many defeats more important than victories," he would say (McLendon, n.d., "A Political Innocent Abroad," p. 17). Learn from them, but don't let them consume you. Keep moving forward. As baseball legend Satchel Paige, whom Gordon was fond of quoting, would say, "Don't look back; they may be gaining on you" (Bart McLendon, 1990).

PERSONAL DIMENSIONS

Gordon possessed other personality traits that friends and associates in time came to recognize. Some of these were annoying, some endearing and some were just plain peculiar.

Gordon was not at all a family man. His marriage to Gay of some twenty years ended in the mid-1960s (McLendon, 1967a), and a second marriage to actress Susan Stafford in 1973 ("Miss Stafford," 1973) also ended in divorce ("The Forbes," 1984). Gordon "was not a prototypical father," according to son Bart. "I don't think that Dad really enjoyed doing the things that a parent . . . has to do" (Bart McLendon, 1990). "He was gone a lot," Bart said, but then he hastened to add:

> There was never a moment in my life that I ever questioned the fact that he loved me or that he wouldn't have been there within milli-seconds if I needed him. . . . But as far as being an involved parent, no, he wasn't. I don't think he enjoyed that, and I think that he was probably too busy doing some other things. But, he loved his kids abidingly. (Bart McLendon, 1990)

Besides his children, Gordon was most devoted to his parents, especially his father, B. R. The two men, business partners for practically all of Gordon's professional career, shared a love, admiration and respect for one another that was absolute. Nonetheless, Billie Odom recalled vividly how the two used to argue (Odom, 1990). B. R. most often would emerge victorious from those arguments, usually by the sheer force of his dominating character. Ken Dowe recalled that B. R. "put the fear of God into everybody, including Gordon" (Dowe, 1989). Bart McLendon said that B. R. "was a dictatorial man, and he had very broad powers over Dad. From an emotional standpoint, Dad . . . leaned on [B. R.] a lot" (Bart McLendon, 1990).

Gordon's mother, Jeanette, had a personality just opposite that of B. R. "She was a warm, loving spirit," said Bart McLendon. It was her influence, Bart added, that brought out the "smoother edges" of Gordon's personality (Bart McLendon, 1991).

The depth of Gordon's feelings toward his parents perhaps was best expressed on the dedication page of his book, *Get Really Rich in the Coming Super Metals Boom*. There Gordon wrote:

> Dedicated to my long-suffering, remarkable, famously moral, patient and incredibly loving father, and to my mother, who is not only all of that but carries with her a sweetness of disposition that has its own special importance in the lives of all whom she touches. Without the continually courageous and understanding help of my father, I believe I would have done little, and without my mother, nothing at all. Both of them I love unabashedly. (McLendon, 1980b, p. 4)

Among Gordon's most endearing traits, said Bart McLendon, were his big, infectious smile and laughter. He had a wonderful sense of humor and could laugh at himself, Bart said (1990). Don Keyes also recalled Gordon's "winning smile and a puckish sense of humor" that prevented him from taking anything too seriously. "The world would be going to hell and Gordon always had a smile and a quip," said Keyes (1989). He was "a very quick wit" and "great on practical jokes," Keyes added.

Gordon tried to remember everybody he met, and he kept track of numerous birthdays and anniversaries of friends through a card file maintained by Billie Odom. The cards contained each person's name, address, occupation, spouse's name and other pertinent data. Gordon used the file to make certain his friends and acquaintances always received a card and/or note on special occasions (Odom, 1990).

Gordon shared friendships with persons ranging from the powerful, such as George Bush and the Hunts—H. L., Herbert and Bunker—to the imprisoned Jack Ruby, who had murdered presidential assassin Lee Harvey Oswald. Gordon happened to be the recipient of the last letter Ruby wrote from prison before he died (Bane, 1982, p. 11). These were distant friends, though. Closer to Gordon were Clint Murchison, Bob Thompson, Mitch Lewis, Sy Weintraub and probably Billie Odom. Of this smaller group, Bart McLendon said that Clint Murchison and Gordon were "very close to best friends" (Bart McLendon, 1990). But, said Billie Odom, Gordon really "didn't have any bosom buddy friends" (Odom, 1990).

Gordon's workaholic ways did not allow time for him to nurture close friendships with anyone. He was by nature a loner. "I'm not saying he was an antisocial man," Bart McLendon said of his father, "but he was as close to an antisocial man as you'll ever meet" (Bart McLendon, 1990). He was not at all keen, for instance, on the kind of partying and socializing that many of "the legion of Dallas millionaires" found an obsession. Gordon found them only mildly diversionary (Dowe, 1989). And besides, Gordon had his own agenda of interests, most of which were far outside the social swirl. Marcus Cohn said that Gordon was a loner in some respects because he felt, with plenty of justification, that he was intellectually superior to many of those in his own social circle (Cohn, 1989).

Nothing about Gordon's antisocial nature should be construed as meaning that Gordon was distant or insincere with persons he did consider friends. Once he knew he could trust a person to be honest with him and that that person had no ulterior motives for seeking or claiming Gordon's friendship, then that person was considered a friend (Odom, 1990).

Edd Routt talked about just what Gordon's friendship could mean to a person, and what it meant especially to Routt:

> If he embraced someone, he cared about that person. And the care never diminished unless a big disappointment came along. "I am your friend until you prove to me that you are not worthy of my friendship." And a lot of people proved that to him. But, he was staunchly loyal to his friends. He would support his friends. He would tolerate no negativism about his friends. He was a very caring man with a lot of heart and a lot of intellect to give. I don't know really what my life would have been without him. Very dull for one thing. But he was my motivator. He inspired me. He was my teacher, benefactor in many ways from money to advice. He was not a religious man, but I think he believed in God. But, you wouldn't catch him in church every Sunday. He was a "oner." There wasn't anybody like him before, and there won't be anybody like him again. The people whose lives he touched will never forget him. (Routt, 1989)

Much has been said already about Gordon's professional demeanor. He was a taskmaster and a perfectionist who demanded nearly total dedication from his employees. Gordon "was a man of tremendous honor and integrity," said Ken Dowe. "As long as you were straight . . . and candid with him, he was always at least that with you" (Dowe, 1989). Cross him, and Gordon "could be a devastating enemy. You didn't want him to be your enemy," said Dowe (1989). But even in situations that Gordon found to his disliking, he seldom let his temper get the best of him. Billie Odom, in fact, said that Gordon was generally "laid-back" and that he "made a great effort to control his temper" (Odom, 1990).

Gordon "was soft-spoken" and had basically a "gentle, shy disposition," Billie Odom said. "The shyest, most retiring person I know was Gordon McLendon," she added (Odom, 1990). But, said Bart McLendon, Gordon "was a man fed by ego." His ego was certainly comparable in size to those of his wealthy friends Clint Murchison and Bunker Hunt (Bart McLendon, 1990). Gordon's ego also reflected many of the essential ingredients of the Ayn Rand philosophy that he so admired (Keyes, 1989). The self-centered objectivist philosophy viewed the individual's quest to achieve personal happiness and success as his or her ultimate goal (Rand, 1965, pp. 22–23). Billie Odom, however, did not feel that Gordon was nearly as consumed by his ego as those less aware of his true personality might have thought. She felt that the "appearance of ego was more bravado" and that it really helped conceal a certain vulnerability that Gordon possessed (Odom, 1990).

Gordon was given to occasional spells of moodiness. And for a man who so often was in the public eye, he enjoyed his solitude (Dowe, 1989). Gordon also grew more introspective with the passage of time (Odom, 1990), due perhaps to a romanticism that Edd Routt said always had softened the hard-nosed business exterior that Gordon tried to project (Routt, 1989). The nature of that romanticism, while not easily described, may be found between the covers of one of Gordon's favorite novels. James Ramsey Ullman's *The Sands of Karakorum* depicts the journey of its main character into faraway Tibet and through the corridors of Eastern religious mysticism as he seeks ultimate knowledge and communion with a higher power (Ullman, 1953). "Read the book," said Billie Odom, "and you'll understand Gordon" (Odom, 1990).

Gordon did not seem to possess very liberated views toward the opposite sex. Perhaps his romantic nature caused Gordon to associate the role of women with something more reminiscent of their role in bygone days. Whatever the origin of his attitudes, Billie Odom did not hesitate to label Gordon a "male chauvinist." But, she was quick to add that regardless of his chauvinistic tendencies, Gordon "was such a gentleman. He was such a charmer. He could just charm anybody" (Odom, 1990). Don Keyes agreed: "He had tremendous charm, tremendous leadership ability. He could put you in his pocket with a hug, a smile, a touch. He was a touching person" (Keyes, 1989).

For all of his wealth, Gordon never gave the appearance of being wealthy. He was an informal person given to eccentricities, especially in his attire (Dowe, 1989). Gordon oftentimes had a "rumpled" look about him, as though he had "slept in his clothes," said Billie Odom (1990). "He was not a fancy dresser," Edd Routt recalled (1989). Billie Odom "would have to corral him and make him sit still while she got a tailor in to get him some new suits, 'cause he would wear one just forever" (Routt, 1989). Routt also remembered Gordon as traveling light because "he wore these old nylon shirts—white—that you could wash. . . . He'd wash his underwear and his shirts and hang them up in the bathroom of the hotel" (Routt, 1989). Bart McLendon said that his father "had no sense of fashion. He had no sense of style and didn't care" (Bart McLendon, 1990).

Even when he did manage to fit inside a three-piece suit, Gordon often conducted his office business with feet casually propped up on his desk (Patoski, 1980, p. 101). But the three-piece suit often gave way to a more comfortable blue denim shirt, blue denim pants and brown cowboy boots ("Tribute," 1986). This was precisely the same outfit that Gordon wore at Cielo (Routt, 1989). In fact, the same combination became something of a uniform for Gordon, as Ken Dowe was to discover. Dowe said that his job required extensive travel to the various cities where McLendon Stations were located, and that he usually stayed in penthouse apartments maintained by Gordon in each of the cities. The first time he traveled to Chicago and stayed in Gordon's apartment there, Dowe said, "I got my bag to go put in the closet. And I looked inside the closet and there must have been 24 blue, Big-Mack shirts and 24 blue Penney's bluejeans and 24 pairs of boots" (Dowe, 1989).

Gordon would change his mode of dress somewhat in later years. Writer Dennis McDougal, interviewing Gordon at Cielo in 1984, noted Gordon's "predilection for gray cardigans, drab trousers and no neckties" (McDougal, 1984, p. 18).

If Gordon's priorities did not include dress, neither did they include some other elements of daily life that more or less are taken for granted. "Gordon never carried a billfold," Les Vaughn said, because his wife "wouldn't let him. He never carried any money, because he didn't know how to take care of money. He'd just as soon leave a thousand dollar bill on the table as pay for a 15-cent lunch" (Vaughn, 1989). As a result, Gordon often depended on others to pick up checks in restaurants and to pay for items he purchased. "I bet the guy owes me a thousand or 15 hundred dollars . . . for cigarettes alone, to say nothing of lunches, coffee, whatever," said Vaughn (1989).

Gordon was forgetful, too. He always traveled with inexpensive suitcases due to the number of times he failed to retrieve his luggage at the airport (Harp, 1989). Gordon also managed to lose a rental car, or so the story goes. Edd Routt told of hearing from others at KLIF that people from a Dallas rental car agency came looking for a car that Gordon had rented two months earlier. The car eventually was found in a parking lot (Routt, 1989).

Gordon did own cars, but they were not a passion with him. His cars were never the "big, flashy" ones, Bart McLendon said, although he remembered Gordon breaking down at one point and buying himself a Thunderbird with a car phone (Bart McLendon, 1990). In later years Gordon did allow himself the luxury of a Mercedes, "but nothing flashy, not the little two-door convertible," said Don Keyes (1989).

It was just as well that Gordon cared little about cars, since he was such a poor driver. The less time Gordon spent behind a steering wheel, the safer he, his passengers and other drivers would be. Gordon used to weave all over the highway while his thoughts were focused on ideas and projects (Harp, 1989). "He was not a safe driver. I'm just surprised that he didn't get killed in a car wreck, because his mind was constantly going," said Edd Routt (1989).

Gordon's disinterest in cars might have stemmed in part from his problems operating mechanical things, problems that probably also accounted for why Gordon was forever lugging along a vintage early 1900s manual Royal typewriter during his travels. Gordon needed a typewriter for all of his writing, but he never was able to adjust to a newer electric typewriter (Dowe, 1989).

Reading was one of the few recreations Gordon allowed himself. Another was traveling (Bart McLendon, 1990). In fact, traveling where and when he wanted was one of just a few visible signs of Gordon's great wealth. The other was Cielo. "A lot of guys put on the emblems of rank—corporate aircraft, the Rolex, the whole shot. [Gordon] never did that," said Don Keyes. "He never tried to impress people with his wealth" (Keyes, 1989). But Cielo was different. Cielo was to Gordon what the corporate jet and Rolex were to others. "The ranch was his pride and joy," recalled Keyes.

> He loved to show that around. It was a very personal thing, that ranch. He loved it, and he loved to take people out there. This was the only thing that I ever saw that said, "Look at me. I've arrived. I've done something to allow me to live in this lifestyle, in this lovely place called Cielo." (Keyes, 1989)

Gordon was neither ostentatious nor conceited. He "never viewed himself as a celebrity," and "was always available to people," said Billie Odom (1990). Regardless of who needed to see him, Gordon made certain that that person had a chance to meet with him. And whomever he was with, Gordon always preferred that he be addressed by his first name. He "didn't want anyone to call him 'Mr. McLendon,' " Billie Odom said (1990). *Dallas Times Herald* newspaper columnist Bob Porter remembered Gordon as being "accessible" and "down-to-earth." He "was always friendly and outgoing and very candid," said Porter. And he added that Gordon "seemed to be very open to anyone approaching him and talking to him" (Porter, 1990).

Gordon's reputation and the control he maintained over McLendon Station personnel nonetheless made him somewhat intimidating for employees to approach. Chuck Blore, for instance, said "it was like talking to God when you talked to Gordon" (Blore, 1990). Even so, Blore, like so many others who worked for Gordon, said he came to idolize the man.

Quite likely, Gordon's low-key lifestyle, unassuming personality and disregard for flamboyance were the reasons that his name rarely was mentioned along with other Dallas or Texas luminaries. And that was fine with Gordon. In fact, not until his name began appearing regularly among the *Forbes* magazine list of the nation's wealthiest persons did Gordon's wealth gain him notoriety. Gordon credited that notoriety with his decision to seclude himself at Cielo, where he conducted most of his business during his last years (McDougal, 1980, p. 20).

Gordon may not have flaunted his wealth, but he nonetheless was proud of it. Bart McLendon, in fact, said his father probably would have counted his being named to the *Forbes* list of wealthiest Americans as his proudest achievement. But the money was only a symbol, a "scorecard" to Gordon, said Bart (1990). Gordon himself was quoted by *Forbes* magazine as saying much the same. "Pity the guy who uses money as an end. Because none of us are going to get out of this thing [life] alive," he said ("The Forbes," 1984). Money never had been the motivation for his hard work, Gordon said during a 1972 interview. He simply enjoyed working (Porter, 1972, p. 13E).

THE NATURE OF A MAVERICK

Time and time again, when Gordon's friends and associates were asked to describe him, they responded with what they considered to be a simple truth—that Gordon indeed was a genius. But when Gordon himself was asked what he thought of being labeled a genius, he replied that it was "a lot of hooey. . . . [I]f I were a genius," said Gordon, "I could have done things a hell of a lot easier" (Kerns, 1981). His accomplishments were owed not to genius, Gordon declared, but rather to working hard at doing the things he loved. Success had been dependent upon another factor, too. "A factor called luck. . . . And God knows I've been lucky," said Gordon (Kerns, 1981).

Luck may have played a role, but the creative instinct that Gordon possessed derived undeniably from genius. Ironically, the creativity that had contributed so significantly to the radio industry was not universally appreciated or respected by Gordon's broadcast peers.

> [Gordon] was among the most inventive of station owners, and among the most widely imitated. Respected, but not loved, his feuds were famous, his gaffes legendary, his ego enormous . . . and [he] was thought to be arrogant and obnoxious by many of his competitors, even though he was admired for his success. (Fornatale and Mills, 1980, p. 28)

Gordon early on had earned a reputation as "enfant terrible of radio" ("Zany," 1961, p. 124). Ken Dowe characterized him as "a spirited competitor and extremely dogmatic and dedicated and tireless, and he did not suffer fools gladly" (Dowe, 1989). Gordon "almost had contempt for other broadcasters, because what had they done? They do what the FCC tells them," remarked Marcus Cohn. Gordon simply "refused to conform, to be a part of the crowd" (Cohn, 1989).

Gordon was not bothered by what other broadcasters thought of him. And he admitted to being an iconoclast, as much from necessity as by choice. Being part of the establishment meant falling in line and doing what the others were doing and playing by their rules. But Gordon could not abide by such constraints. "Remember," he said, "what I was doing was attacking an establishment, a journalistic and radio establishment set like a grand piano in concrete. So I *had* to be an iconoclast" (Patoski, 1980, p. 171).

Marcus Cohn said that one of Gordon's great stimulants was battling the establishment, particularly when that meant challenging the FCC. The antagonism that the agency and Gordon had toward one another seemed never to wane. Had the FCC allowed Gordon always to do what he wanted, Cohn said, "part of the spark would have left him" (Cohn, 1989). What's more, said Cohn, whenever FCC policies required broadcasters to do one thing, Gordon was determined to do just the opposite. His contempt for the FCC stretched beyond mere policy matters. Gordon had little respect for the abilities of most FCC employees. He had a special low regard for commission attorneys, whom he felt should have been better than they were. Marcus Cohn said that during the several occasions when Gordon testified before the FCC, he often grew restless and belligerent, because he knew that he could outperform every commission attorney present (Cohn, 1989).

At the local level, harsh feelings toward Gordon were of a different nature. Bart McLendon felt that his father was resented by Dallas broadcasters because of the competition they faced from KLIF. The station's ratings were constantly bashing in the heads of other Dallas radio stations (Bart McLendon, 1990). Even among his detractors, though, Gordon eventually earned—even if begrudgingly—a genuine respect. Proof of that came in 1987, when the National Association of Broadcasters recognized Gordon's contributions to the radio industry by electing him posthumously to its hall of fame ("Trout, McLendon," 1987).

FINAL COMMENTS

The hotel where KLIF's basement studios first were located still stands at 329 E. Colorado in Oak Cliff. By 1990 the hotel had become the Cliff Towers Nursing Home. Nothing about the building would suggest that one of America's greatest radio stations and one of its most popular radio networks both were born there. Nor is there anything about the triangular building standing at the intersections of Jackson, Commerce and Central Expressway in downtown Dallas to suggest that it once housed that great station during its halcyon days. The building stood empty as of 1990, stripped of the giant KLIF marquees that once adorned its apex. In earlier times the marquees lit the way to what thousands of Top 40 fans regarded, reverentially, as almost a shrine.

For so many people who listened to KLIF and/or the Liberty Broadcasting System, or who played a role in creating KLIF and LBS programming, the transformed buildings from which the programs originated stand now as reminders of a more exciting, a more imaginative and a more innocent time in their lives. For Gordon McLendon, there was no doubting it. Those days when KLIF was just getting off the ground and Liberty Broadcasting was already perhaps the most powerful sports voice in America were the best days of his life.

Gordon did not follow sports much after his Liberty Broadcasting days. He did broadcast a few professional tennis matches in later years, but he claimed to have little time or interest for sports beyond that. He confessed to not even attending games of the Dallas Cowboys football team, even though he was a member of the Cowboys board of advisors and his best friend Clint Murchison owned the team. When someone once asked Gordon why he never attended sports events, he jokingly replied that he had once earned a thousand dollars a day when covering football and baseball games on the radio, and that he never had gotten "used to not being paid to go into the stadium" (McLendon, 1969a).

Near the end of his life, though, Gordon tried to rekindle his love affair of so many years ago with baseball and radio. In early 1985 he approached Eddie Chiles, then owner of the Texas Rangers baseball team, about doing radio play-by-play for the ball club. Gordon was not the least bit interested in what or if he would be paid, and he faced the task of reeducating himself about a sport that he had neglected over the years (Bart McLendon, 1990). Nonetheless, here he was, making arrangements to pick up once more from where he had stopped more than thirty years earlier.

Gordon's bout with cancer cut short his announcing comeback. His effort to revive a dormant career in radio was tinged with irony, given Gordon's determination to distance himself from the broadcast business during the late 1970s. But too much of Gordon's life was interwoven into the very fabric of radio for him to ignore the obvious. The passion for radio that had ignited during his youth continued to burn deep in Gordon's soul. And during his final days, that passion rose once more to the surface.

That Gordon failed in his comeback attempt is of little consequence when one considers the lofty position he already held in the annals of radio. Gordon's legacy as a maverick—forever challenging the odds and defying the conventional—would live long after him. Gordon McLendon had touched radio as it had been touched by no one before, and radio would never be the same.

References

NOTE: The abbreviated "McLendon Papers" notation follows source citations for items from the Gordon McLendon Papers, located in the Southwest Collection of Texas Tech University, Lubbock, TX.

Adams, Val. (1950, September 17). "Just Like Topsy": The Saga of the Liberty Broadcasting System. *New York Times*, sec. II, p. 11.

Adams, Val. (1965, December 24). All-Commercial FM Station Proposed to F.C.C. *New York Times*, p. 41.

Ads Are Broadcast For 16 Hours a Day. (1967, January 21). *Editor & Publisher*, pp. 14, 20.

Ad Station Seeks Help of ANCAM. (1966, July 23). *Editor & Publisher*, p. 41.

Advertisement. (1947, November 9). *Dallas Times Herald*, p. 7, sec. 2.

Advertisement. (1950, February 12). *Dallas Morning News*, sec. I, p. 16.

Advertisement. (1954, January 9). *Dallas Times Herald*, p. 5.

Advertisement. (1955a, August 29). *Broadcasting/Telecasting*, p. 39.

Advertisement. (1955b, September 5). *Broadcasting/Telecasting*, back cover.

Advertisement. (1956, July 30). *Broadcasting/Telecasting*, p. 51.

Advertisement. (1957, July 22). *Broadcasting/Telecasting*, p. 38.

Advertisement. (1963, August 28). *Washington Post*, p. C19.

All-Ad FM Intrigues FCC. (1966, July 4). *Broadcasting*, p. 38.

All-News Format Is Winning Friends. (1966, June 27). *Broadcasting*, pp. 100–103.

Bagamery, Ann. (1981, May 11). All that Glitters. *Forbes*, pp. 98–102.

Bane, Michael. (1982, September 5). Gordon McLendon: A Contemporary Texas Fairy Tale. *Westward*, pp. 6–12.

Banks, Jimmy. (1964a, February 19). McLendon Says Ex-Rival Backing Him for Senate. *Dallas Morning News*, n.p.

Banks, Jimmy. (1964b, March 24). McLendon Needles Rival Over Failure to Debate. *Dallas Morning News*, n.p.

Banks, Jimmy. (1964c, April 12). Estes Says He Gave $50,000 In Cash to Sen. Yarborough. *Dallas Morning News*, p. 1.

Banks, Jimmy. (1964d, May 2). Yarborough Demands McLendon Withdraw. *Dallas Morning News*, n.p.

Banks, Jimmy. (1964e, June 7). $50,000 Question Still Unresolved. *Lubbock Avalanche-Journal*, n.p.

Banks, Jimmy. (1971). *Money, Marbles and Chalk: The Wondrous World of Texas Politics.* Austin: Texas Publishing.

Barker, Bill. (1957, May 15). McLendon's "Texas Triangle." *Variety*, pp. 37, 52.

Baseball: Broadcast "Regulations" Charted. (1950, December 11). *Broadcasting/Telecasting*, p. 23.

Baseball: Opposition Mounts Despite New Rules. (1949, November 7). *Broadcasting/Telecasting*, p. 38.

Baseball Ban Prompts WARL To Ask for Anti-Trust Action. (1947, October 6). *Broadcasting/Telecasting*, p. 82.

Baseball Coverage: Ban Threat Subsides. (1950, December 18). *Broadcasting/Telecasting*, pp. 25, 47.

Baseball Outlook: Leagues Hit Radio-TV. (1950, November 6). *Broadcasting/Telecasting*, pp. 23, 36.

Baseball Probe: Justice Suspends Action; Eyes New Major Rules. (1949, October 31). *Broadcasting/Telecasting*, pp. 23, 81.

Baseball Re-Creation Investigation Foreseen. (1950, July 3). *Broadcasting/Telecasting*, p. 4.

Baseball's Gate: Jordan Cites Radio-TV Effect. (1950, November 20). *Broadcasting/Telecasting*, pp. 19, 32–33.

Baseball Suit: McLendon Asks $12 Million. (1952, February 25). *Broadcasting/Telecasting*, p. 27.

Beatty, J. Frank. (1950, November 27). Radio Helps Gate: Liberty, MBS Views. *Broadcasting/Telecasting*, pp. 19, 91.

Beatty, J. Frank. (1951, October 15). Baseball Future Bright: Justice Probes Football. *Broadcasting/Telecasting*, pp. 25, 105.

Biffle, Kent. (1981, May 10). McLendon Puts Golden Touch to Work for Metals. *Dallas Morning News*, n.p.

Biggest Radio-Only Sale. (1967, July 3). *Broadcasting*, p. 36.

Blackwell, M. I. (1986, September 21). And Radio Was Never the Same Again. *Dallas Morning News*, pp. 1C, 5C–6C.

Blore, Chuck. (1990, December 12). Telephone interview.

Boyles, Chuck. (1967, December 4). [Letter to His Excellency, the French Ambassador. Editorial File]. McLendon Papers.

Brady, Jim. (1985, December 7). Radio Pioneer's Goal Was to Get Back on Air. *Dallas Times Herald*, pp. 1-A, 28-A.

Broadcasting Pioneer Listed Critical After Gunshot Wound. (1985, December 7). *Lubbock Avalanche-Journal*, p. 8-A.

Brock, Bob. (1971, May 23). Broadcaster McLendon Conducts Unique Seminar. *Dallas Times Herald*, n.p.

Bureau Wants Lower Fine for KABL. (1966, April 18). *Broadcasting*, pp. 47–48.

Callison, Glenn. (1989, May 5). Personal interview. Richardson, TX.

Carleton, Don E. (1985). *Red Scare!* Austin: Texas Monthly Press.

CAR-TEACH. (n.d.). [Collection of books and tapes]. McLendon Papers.
CAR-TEACH, Inc. (n.d.). [Articles of Incorporation]. McLendon Papers.
Carter, Roy E. (1951). Radio Editorializing Aboard the "New Mayflower." *Journalism Quarterly* 28, pp. 469–473.
Chism, Olin. (1969, June 18). New Movie Town Is Going Up At Gordon McLendon's Cielo. *Dallas Times Herald*, p. 10-B.
City of Camden et al., 14 FCC 2d 351 (1968).
City of Camden et al., 18 FCC 2d 412 (1969a).
City of Camden et al., 18 FCC 2d 427 (1969b).
Classified-Ad Format Flops in L.A. (1967, August 21). *Broadcasting*, p. 34.
Cohn, Marcus. (1986, October 9). Letter to Bart McLendon.
Cohn, Marcus. (1989, December 3). Telephone interview.
Congressional Directory. (1965). Washington, D.C.: Government Printing Office.
Congressional Record. (1935, June 20), p. 9813.
Congressional Record. (1952, May 30). Gordon McLendon letter to U.S. Rep. Patrick Hillings, pp. A3744-A3746.
Congressional Record. (1962, September 6). Pp. 18808-18810.
Conrad, Glenn R., ed. (1988). James Albert Noe. In *A Dictionary of Louisiana Biography*. New Orleans: Louisiana Historical Association.
Conservative Banner Worn By McLendon. (1964, February 4). *Dallas Times Herald*, n.p.
The Conservatives' Dilemma. (1967, March 31). *The Texas Observer*, pp. 8–9.
Contests and Promotions Which Adversely Affect the Public Interest, 2 FCC 2d 464 (1966).
Crater, Rufus. (1948, December 13). Baseball Probe: Anti-Trust Law Said Violated in Air Rights. *Broadcasting/Telecasting*, pp. 21, 80.
Crater, Rufus. (1949, August 15). Baseball Broadcasts: Justice Dept. Showdown Looms. *Broadcasting/Telecasting*, pp. 23, 67.
Cullen, Hugh Roy. (n.d.). [Recorded interview with Ed Kilman]. Houston Public Library Metropolitan Research Center, Houston, TX.
Curtis, Jim. (1987). *Rock Eras: Interpretations of Music and Society, 1954–1984*. Bowling Green, OH: Bowling Green State University Popular Press.
Deaths: Gordon McLendon. (1986, September 22). *Broadcasting*, p. 110.
de la Villesbrunne, Gerard. (1968a, January). French Rebuttal #1. [Editorial]. McLendon Papers.
de la Villesbrunne, Gerard. (1968b, January). French Rebuttal #2. [Editorial]. McLendon Papers.
de la Villesbrunne, Gerard. (1968c, January). French Rebuttal #3. [Editorial]. McLendon Papers.
de la Villesbrunne, Gerard. (1968d, January). French Rebuttal #5. [Editorial]. McLendon Papers.
de la Villesbrunne, Gerard. (1968e, January). French Rebuttal #6. [Editorial]. McLendon Papers.
Dowe, Ken. (1989, November 23). Personal interview. Dallas, TX.
Drape, Joe. (1986, September 15). Broadcast Pioneer McClendon [sic] Dies. *Dallas Morning News*, pp. 1A, 10A.
Dry Run Precedes KFWB's Switch to All News. (1968, March 11). *Broadcasting*, p. 66.

Duckworth, Allen. (1964, April 29). McLendon Says Foe Using Oldest Trick. *Dallas Morning News*, n.p.
Dugger, Ronnie. (1964, April 17). The Old Scotchman's Bankruptcy. *Texas Observer*, pp. 7–9.
Duncan, Dawson. (1964, February 14). McLendon Says Mail Backs Race to Unseat Yarborough. *Dallas Morning News*, n.p.
Earlybirds of Modern Radio. (1962, May 28). *Sponsor*, pp. 35–36, 53–54, 59.
Eastman, Robert. (1966, March). [Introduction to Gordon McLendon for unidentified occasion]. McLendon Papers.
Eberly, Philip K. (1982). *Music in the Air*. New York: Hastings House.
Editorial File. (n.d.). McLendon Papers.
Editorializing By Broadcast Licensees, 13 FCC 1246 (1949).
Elliott, Carolyn. (1978, June 28). Radio Changes After Appearance of Television. *San Antonio Light*, p. 6-E.
End of Liberty. (1952, June 9). *Time*, pp. 92–94.
Eyrich, Claire. (1981, August 2). By Any Other Name, It's Still a Gold Rush. *Fort Worth Star-Telegram*, n.p.
Fanfare: The Curse of Consistency. (1959, November 30). *Broadcasting*, p. 78.
FBI Probes Baseball: On Radio-TV Rights. (1951, May 28). *Broadcasting/Telecasting*, pp. 25, 73.
FCC Calls Off Probe of WNUS Chicago. (1964, September 21). *Broadcasting*, p. 95.
Federal Baseball Club of Baltimore, Inc. v. National League of Professional Baseball Clubs, et al., 259 U.S. 200 (1922).
Floating Swedish Radio Shut. (1962, July 3). *New York Times*, p. 2.
Folkways Broadcasting Co. v. F.C.C., 375 F. 2d 299 (1967).
The Forbes Four Hundred. (1983, Fall). *Forbes*, p. 119.
The Forbes Four Hundred. (1984, October 1). *Forbes*, pp. 133–134.
The Forbes Four Hundred. (1985, October 28). *Forbes*, p. 199.
Ford, Jon. (1968, January 4). McLendon in Race as "Moderate to Conservative." *San Antonio Express*, n.p.
Fornatale, Peter, and Joshua Mills. (1980). *Radio in the Television Age*. Woodstock, NY: Overlook Press.
Fowler, Gene, and Bill Crawford. (1987). *Border Radio*. Austin: Texas Monthly Press.
Frank, Jay. (1986, August 31). The Last Picture Show. *Houston Post*, p. 3J.
Freedgood, Seymour. (1958, February). The Money-Makers of "New Radio." *Fortune*, pp. 122–124, 222–226.
French Will Answer McLendon. (1968, January 19). [McLendon Corporation news release]. McLendon Papers.
From #1 Air Talent to #1 Voiceover Talent . . . Come On Down! (1987, January 19). *The Pulse of Broadcasting*, pp. 8–9, 32–33.
The Gall of Gordon. (1968, February 5). *Newsweek*, p. 84.
Gardner, William. (1968, February 28). McLendon Leaves Governor's Race. *Houston Post*, n.p.
Gifts and Spending Reported by the Candidates For Two Major Offices in the May 2, 1964, Texas Primaries. (1964, May 29). *Texas Observer*, p. 4.
Glick, Edwin L. (1979, Spring). The Life and Death of the Liberty Broadcasting System. *Journal of Broadcasting* 23, pp. 117–135.

A Gordian Knot for the FCC. (1965, December 27). *Broadcasting*, pp. 34–35.
Gordon, Mitchell. (1965, October 11). Pirate Broadcasters. *Barron's*, pp. 5, 15–17.
Gordon Combines Radio, Theater. (1969, August 15). *Dallas Times Herald*, p. 6-B.
Gordon McLendon: The Legend Lives On. (1980, August 25). *Broadcasting*, p. 60.
Gordon McLendon, 1921–1986. (1986, September 29). *Sports Illustrated*, p. 26.
Gordon McLendon for United States Senator. (1964, February 22). [Campaign handbill]. Texas State Library, Austin.
Griffith, Emlyn I. (1950). Comments: Mayflower Rule—Gone But Not Forgotten. *Cornell Law Quarterly* 35, pp. 574–591.
Group Ownership, (1961/62–1973). *Broadcasting Yearbook.*
Hall, Claude, and Barbara Hall. (1977). *This Business of Radio Programming*, New York: Billboard Publications.
Harp, Dennis. (1989, February 10). Personal interview. Lubbock, TX.
Harper, Jim. (1986, Spring). Gordon McLendon: Pioneer Baseball Broadcaster. *Baseball History*, 42–51.
Harriman Broadcasting Co. (WXXL), 9 FCC 2d 731 (1967).
Harris, Lewis. (1964, April 26). McLendon Challenges Senator To Take Lie Detector Test. *Dallas Morning News*, n.p.
Hirschhorn, Clive. (1989). *The Columbia Story*. New York: Crown Publishers.
Hitt, Dick. (1979, May 18). Stroke of a Pen Ends Old Scotchman's Broadcasting Era. *Dallas Times Herald*, n.p.
Hitt, Dick. (1986a, September 15). Lasting Memories of a Singular Man. *Dallas Times Herald*, pp. A-1, A-8.
Hitt, Dick. (1986b, September 18). Memories of a Genius Broadcaster. *Dallas Times Herald*, p. A-21.
Hitt, Dick. (1986c, September 23). A Heartfelt Signing Off for a Friend. *Dallas Times Herald*, p. A-11.
Hon. Ralph W. Yarborough, 2 RR 2d 163 (1964).
Hunnings, N. March. (1965, April). Pirate Broadcasting in European Waters. *International and Comparative Law Quarterly* 14, pp. 410–436.
Husserl, Paul. (1951, November 3). Texas Oil on Troubled Air Waves. *The Nation*, pp. 370–371.
Informal Chicago Hearing Erupts. (1963, April 15). *Broadcasting*, pp. 52–55.
Inventory of the Papers, 1917–1979, of Gordon McLendon. (n.d.). Southwest Collection, Texas Tech University, Lubbock, TX.
Johnson, Lyndon. (1958, May 12). [Letter to Gordon McLendon. Political File]. McLendon Papers.
Johnson, Lyndon. (1960a, February 25). [Letter to Gordon McLendon. Political File]. McLendon Papers.
Johnson, Lyndon. (1960b, April 25). [Letter to Gordon McLendon. Political File]. McLendon Papers.
Johnson, Lyndon. (1960c, October 6). [Letter to Gordon McLendon. Political File]. McLendon Papers.
Judge Rules Woman Must Be Committed. (1964, March 5). *Dallas Morning News*, n.p.
Kebbon, Richard A. (1964, August). "Pirates" of the Airwaves. *Media/scope* 8, pp. 52–56.
Kerns, William D. (1981, July 26). Gordon McLendon: A Story of Riches & Regrets. *Lubbock Avalanche-Journal*, p. E-5.

Keyes, Don. (1958, February 25). [Letter to Jack Elliot. Policy Book]. McLendon Papers.

Keyes, Don. (1961a, March 21). [Memo to All McLendon Disc Jockeys. Policy Book]. McLendon Papers.

Keyes, Don. (1961b, November 30). [Memo to All Managers, All Program Directors. Policy Book]. McLendon Papers.

Keyes, Don. (1961c, December 14). [Memo to All McLendon Station Managers. Policy Book]. McLendon Papers.

Keyes, Don. (1961d, December 15). [Memo to All McLendon Station Managers. Policy Book]. McLendon Papers.

Keyes, Don. (1962, January 10). [Memo to All McLendon Station Managers. Policy Book]. McLendon Papers.

Keyes, Don. (1963, June 25). [Memo to All Managers, All Program Directors. Editorial File]. McLendon Papers.

Keyes, Don. (1989, March 21). Personal interview. Tallahassee, FL.

Kilman, Ed, and Theon Wright. (1954). *Hugh Roy Cullen: A Story of American Opportunity.* New York: Prentice-Hall.

KITE Agrees to Withdraw Protest Against KTSA Sale. (1956, September 10). *Broadcasting/Telecasting,* p. 82.

KITE Protests KTSA Sale. (1956, June 11). *Broadcasting/Telecasting,* p. 76.

KLIF DJs To Return For a Day. (1970, August 27). *Dallas Times Herald,* n.p.

KLIF to Start 24-Hour Schedule. (1950, February 12). *Dallas Morning News,* sec. IV, p. 7.

Knutson, Ted. (1981, September 8). Gordon McLendon Pays $155,000 for Coin. *Dallas Morning News,* n.p.

KTSA San Antonio Acquired By McLendon for $306,000. (1956, March 12). *Broadcasting/Telecasting,* p. 7.

Kushner, James. (1972, Summer). KADS(FM): Want-Ad Radio in Los Angeles. *Journal of Broadcasting* 16, pp. 267–276.

Lawyer Named L.B.S. Receiver. (1952, June 7). *Dallas Morning News,* sec. 1, p. 1.

LBS on the Air: Nation-Wide Service Starts. (1950, October 9). *Broadcasting/Telecasting,* pp. 25, 89.

LBS Expands: 150 Affiliates Under Contract. (1950, February 27). *Broadcasting/Telecasting,* p. 16.

LBS-Majors Case Delayed By Court to Next Jan. 11. (1953, May 18). *Broadcasting/Telecasting,* p. 66.

LBS Official Asserts Chain Still Solvent. (1952, May 14). *Dallas Morning News,* sec. 1, p. 1.

LBS Plans: Expands to 48 States in October. (1950, September 4). *Broadcasting/Telecasting,* pp. 25, 59.

LBS Plans: Network Underway; Rate Policy Set. (1950, March 20). *Broadcasting/Telecasting,* p. 28.

LBS Successors: Several Regionals Planned. (1952, May 26). *Broadcasting/Telecasting,* p. 26.

LBS to Quit Air Pending Court Ruling. (1952, May 16). *Dallas Morning News,* sec. 1, pp. 1–2.

Lewis, Mitch. (1962, December 12). [Letter to Fred Gebhardt. Motion Picture File]. McLendon Papers.

Lewis, Mitch. (1966, May 7). [Letter to Mark Armistead. Motion Picture File]. McLendon Papers.
Lewis, Mitch. (1967, December 4). [Memo to All Managers, All News Directors, Editorial File]. McLendon Papers.
Lewis, Mitch. (1968a, July 29). [Memo to Gordon McLendon. Editorial File]. McLendon Papers.
Lewis, Mitch. (1968b, August 15). [Letter to Walton A. Foster. Editorial File]. McLendon Papers.
Liberty Agrees to Bankruptcy. (1952, May 30). *Dallas Morning News*, sec. 1, p. 1.
The Liberty Broadcasting System, Inc. (1952). *1952 Broadcasting/Telecasting Yearbook*, pp. 56–57.
Liberty Broadcasting System v. National League Baseball Club of Boston, Inc., et al., 7 RR 2164 (1952).
Liberty Expands: Plans Nationwide Coverage. (1950, June 12). *Broadcasting/Telecasting*, p. 18.
Liberty Network Sues Thirteen Ball Clubs for $12,000,000 Over Broadcasting Curbs. (1952, February 22). *New York Times*, p. 25.
Liberty Properties Will Be Sold Here. (1952, July 9). *Dallas Morning News*, sec. 1, p. 8.
Liberty Seeks Last-Minute Court Relief. (1952, April 14). *Broadcasting/Telecasting*, p. 5.
Liberty Suspends: McLendon Hits Baseball "Monopoly." (1952, May 19). *Broadcasting/Telecasting*, pp. 25, 93.
Liberty Web Goes National. (1950, February 25). *The Billboard*, p. 12.
McClellan, Jim R. (1970). *Labor and Senator Yarborough: 1964*. Master's thesis, University of Texas at Arlington.
McClendon [sic] Services Set for Saturday. (1985, July 27). *Dallas Morning News*, n.p.
McDougal, Dennis. (1984, March 18). Tall Tales of the Texas Tycoon. *Los Angeles Times Calendar*, pp. 1, 18–21.
MacFarland, David. (1973). *The Development of the Top 40 Radio Format*. Ph.D. diss., University of Wisconsin, Madison.
Macias, Vicki. (1981, September 25). There's a Story Behind Those Radio, TV Call Letters. *Houston Post*, p. 4B.
McInnis, Doug. (1979, May 17). McLendon's Sale of KNUS Ends Colorful Radio Career. *Dallas Times Herald*, pp. 1, 5.
McKinsey, Dave. (1990, September 14). Personal interview. Boston, MA.
McLendon, Bart. (1990, May 22). Personal interview. Dallas, TX.
McLendon, Bart. (1991, June 19). Telephone interview.
McLendon, Gordon. (1952, May 15). [Speech by Gordon McLendon over the Liberty Broadcasting System]. McLendon Papers.
McLendon, Gordon. (1954, July 27). [Letter to Joe Roddy. Policy Book]. McLendon Papers.
McLendon, Gordon. (1955, December 9). [Reminder Sheet distributed at announcers meeting. Policy Book]. McLendon Papers.
McLendon, Gordon. (1956, March 19). News: The Ace Up Radio's Sleeve. *Broadcasting/Telecasting*, pp. 80–81.
McLendon, Gordon. (1957a, January 5). Do Rating Hypos Help Stations? *Sponsor* (reprint), n.p.

McLendon, Gordon. (1957b, January 9). [Untitled Speech to Dallas Jaycees]. McLendon Papers.
McLendon, Gordon. (1957c, August 13). [The Battle of Giants: Radio vs. Newspapers. Speech to Georgia Association of Broadcasters]. McLendon Papers.
McLendon, Gordon. (1958a, March 9). [Revolution in Radio. Speech to Pop Disc Jockeys Convention. Kansas City, MO]. McLendon Papers.
McLendon, Gordon. (1958b, June 20). [Letter to Lyndon Johnson. Political File]. McLendon Papers.
McLendon, Gordon. (1958c, September 10). [Endurance Flight Publicity By Dallas News and Dallas Times Herald. Editorial]. McLendon Papers.
McLendon, Gordon. (1958d, December 19). [Letter to Sy Bartlett. Motion Picture File]. McLendon Papers.
McLendon, Gordon. (1958e, December 30). [Letter to R. L. Thornton. Promotion File]. McLendon Papers.
McLendon, Gordon. (1959a, January 9). [Statement prepared for Meeting with Hollywood Film Corporation. Motion Picture File]. McLendon Papers.
McLendon, Gordon. (1959b, February 2). [Memo to Dave Muhlstein. Editorial File]. McLendon Papers.
McLendon, Gordon. (1959c, February 5). [KLIF 50,000 Watts Editorial]. McLendon Papers.
McLendon, Gordon. (1959d, February 12). [Letter to Jerome Balsam. Motion Picture File]. McLendon Papers.
McLendon, Gordon. (1959e, March 18). [Letter to Douglas Laurence. Motion Picture File]. McLendon Papers.
McLendon, Gordon. (1959f, May 26). [Letter to Sy Weintraub. Motion Picture File]. McLendon Papers.
McLendon, Gordon. (1959g, November 24). [Definition of a KLIF Disc Jockey. Memo to All Managers and Program Directors. Policy Book]. McLendon Papers.
McLendon, Gordon. (1960a, April 21). [Letter to Marcus Cohn. Motion Picture File]. McLendon Papers.
McLendon, Gordon. (1960b, May 25). [The Changing Face of Radio. Speech to San Francisco Advertising Club]. McLendon Papers.
McLendon, Gordon. (1960c, June). [Untitled Speech to Denton Chamber of Commerce. Denton, TX]. McLendon Papers.
McLendon, Gordon. (1960d, September 13). [The Day the Theatre-Owners Stopped Dreaming. Speech to Theatre Owners of America. Los Angeles, CA]. McLendon Papers.
McLendon, Gordon. (1961). [Film Project Outline for 1961. Motion Picture File]. McLendon Papers.
McLendon, Gordon. (1962a, January 31). [Radio Moscow Newscasts. Editorial]. McLendon Papers.
McLendon, Gordon. (1962b, March 7). [Letter to Otto Passman. Policy Book]. McLendon Papers.
McLendon, Gordon. (1962c, April 6). [The American Corporate Form and Its Effect Upon Democracy. Speech delivered at Princeton University. Princeton, NJ]. McLendon Papers.

McLendon, Gordon. (1962d, July 4). [Letter to Sy Weintraub. Motion Picture File]. McLendon Papers.
McLendon, Gordon. (1962e, July). [Capital Punishment. Editorial]. McLendon Papers.
McLendon, Gordon. (1962f, September 6). [Radio: The Years to Come. Speech to World's Fair of Music and Sound. Chicago, IL]. McLendon Papers.
McLendon, Gordon. (1962g, November 26). [Memo to All Managers, All Program Directors, All Managing Editors. Editorial File]. McLendon Papers.
McLendon, Gordon. (1963a, April). [Capital Punishment. Editorial]. McLendon Papers.
McLendon, Gordon. (1963b, June). [Baseball Announcers. Editorial]. McLendon Papers.
McLendon, Gordon. (1963c, June 9). [Fink, Texas. Editorial]. McLendon Papers.
McLendon, Gordon. (1963d, August 27). [The Great March. Editorial]. McLendon Papers.
McLendon, Gordon. (1964a, February 7). [Untitled memo. Political File]. McLendon Papers.
McLendon, Gordon. (1964b, March 2). [First Political Rally Speech]. McLendon Papers.
McLendon, Gordon. (1964c, April 14). [Major Political Speech By Gordon McLendon, Statewide Television Presentation]. McLendon Papers.
McLendon, Gordon. (1965, November 30). [Free Market Place for Radio. Speech to Dallas Ad League]. McLendon Papers.
McLendon, Gordon. (1966a, March 30). [The Coming Faces of Radio. Speech to Chicago Federated Advertising Club]. McLendon Papers.
McLendon, Gordon. (1966b, July 12). [Letter to Frank Lester. Policy Book]. McLendon Papers.
McLendon, Gordon. (1967a, February 21). [I Only Know What My Children Tell Me. Speech to Triple A's]. McLendon Papers.
McLendon, Gordon. (1967b, April 11). [Letter to Ben Waple. Policy Book]. McLendon Papers.
McLendon, Gordon. (1967c, November 28). [Charles de Gaulle. Editorial]. McLendon Papers.
McLendon, Gordon. (1967d, December 3). [Charles de Gaulle. Editorial]. McLendon Papers.
McLendon, Gordon. (1967e, December 6). [Charles de Gaulle. Editorial]. McLendon Papers.
McLendon, Gordon. (1967f, December 17). [Charles de Gaulle. Editorial]. McLendon Papers.
McLendon, Gordon. (1967g, December 17). [French Poll. Editorial]. McLendon Papers.
McLendon, Gordon. (1968a, January 14). [General de Gaulle. Editorial]. McLendon Papers.
McLendon, Gordon. (1968b, January 16). [General de Gaulle's Government. Editorial Response]. McLendon Papers.
McLendon, Gordon. (1968c, January 29 & 30). [General Charles de Gaulle—Reply to French Rebuttal. Series of seven editorials aired in rotation]. McLendon Papers.

McLendon, Gordon. (1968d, February 27). [. . . A matter of honor. Statewide Television Address]. McLendon Papers.
McLendon, Gordon. (1968e, March 23, 24, 25). [All the Way With LBJ. Series of six editorials aired in rotation]. McLendon Papers.
McLendon, Gordon. (1968f, April 7). [LBJ. Editorial]. McLendon Papers.
McLendon, Gordon. (1969a, March 13). Recorded interview with Dr. Clifton Ganus, Jr. Harding University. Searcy, AR.
McLendon, Gordon. (1969b, March 14). [All of the Wonderful Days That Will Be. Speech delivered at Harding College. Searcy, AR]. McLendon Papers.
McLendon, Gordon. (1969c, March). [Abortion Laws in Texas (Clark Bill). Editorial]. McLendon Papers.
McLendon, Gordon. (1969d, April 29). [The Time Before This. Speech to Alpha Epsilon Rho. Detroit, MI]. McLendon Papers.
McLendon, Gordon. (1970a, June). [Abortion Reform. Editorial]. McLendon Papers.
McLendon, Gordon. (1970b, August). [Abortion Reform. Editorial]. McLendon Papers.
McLendon, Gordon. (1972, October 27). [Jack Robinson Tribute. Editorial]. McLendon Papers.
McLendon, Gordon. (1973a, March). [Abortion Decision Right. Editorial]. McLendon Papers.
McLendon, Gordon. (1973b, September 28). [Memo to Whom This May Concern. General File]. McLendon Papers.
McLendon, Gordon. (1977a, June). [Civil Wrongs, Editorial]. McLendon Papers.
McLendon, Gordon. (1977b, August). [United Church of Christ vs. Anita Bryant Movement. Editorial]. McLendon Papers.
McLendon, Gordon. (1978). Recorded interview with Tom Snyder. "Tomorrow Show," NBC television network. Provided by Dennis Harp, Texas Tech University.
McLendon, Gordon. (1979a, January 1). [Biography. General File]. McLendon Papers.
McLendon, Gordon. (1979b, February 16). [Susan Meade for City Council, Place 9. Editorial]. McLendon Papers.
McLendon, Gordon. (1980a, October 9). [Curriculum Vitae. General File]. McLendon Papers.
McLendon, Gordon. (1980b). *Get Really Rich in the Coming Super Metals Boom.* New York: Pocket Books.
McLendon, Gordon. (1981a, February 26). Recorded interview with Dr. James Harper, et al. Texas Tech University. Lubbock, TX.
McLendon, Gordon. (1981b, February 26). Recorded interview with Dr. David Murrah. Texas Tech University. Lubbock, TX.
McLendon, Gordon. (1981c). Recorded press conference. Texas Tech University. Lubbock, TX.
McLendon, Gordon. (1983, May 15). [Letter of Notification on Cielo Office Move. General File]. McLendon Papers.
McLendon, Gordon. (n.d.). [Letter to Joe Roddy. Policy Book]. McLendon Papers.
McLendon, Gordon. (n.d.). [On Continuing Change and the Little Things. Memo. Policy Book]. McLendon Papers.
McLendon, Gordon. (n.d.). [A Political Innocent Abroad]. McLendon Papers.

McLendon All News at Chicago Station. (1964, August 24). *Broadcasting*, p. 68.
McLendon Cited as Senate Hopeful. (1963, September 27). *Dallas Morning News*, n.p.
McLendon Corporation. (1955, April 14). [News Promotional Announcement. Policy Book]. McLendon Papers.
McLendon Corporation. (1959, March 1). [Untitled press release. Motion Picture File]. McLendon Papers.
McLendon Corporation. (1962, January 28). [Untitled press release. Policy Book]. McLendon Papers.
The McLendon Corporation, 24 RR 927 (1963a).
The McLendon Corporation, 25 RR 55 (1963b).
The McLendon Corporation, 3 RR 2d 817 (1964).
McLendon Corporation. (1968a, January 19). [French Will Answer McLendon. Press Release. Editorial File]. McLendon Papers.
McLendon Corporation. (1968b, January 29). [McLendon Refuses French Film. Press Release. Editorial File]. McLendon Papers.
McLendon Corporation. (1978, August 10). [Memo to All McLendon Editorial Subscribers. Editorial File]. McLendon Papers.
McLendon Corp. to Expand Radio, Theater Businesses. (1964, August 27). *Dallas Morning News*, n.p.
McLendon Defends Claim to WCAM. (1968, December 30). *Broadcasting*, pp. 40–41.
McLendon Defends WYNR Programming. (1963, August 19). *Broadcasting*, pp. 76–77.
McLendon Faces Maximum Fine. (1966, May 16). *Broadcasting*, p. 48.
McLendon Gets Green Light for No-News FM. (1968, March 11). *Broadcasting*, pp. 66–67.
McLendon Has a Big Equal Time Problem. (1964, April 27). *Broadcasting*, pp. 72–73.
McLendon Jabs Get French Reply. (1968, January 23). *Dallas Morning News*, n.p.
McLendon May Be Aim of Card's Countersuit. (1952, February 23). *Dallas Morning News*, sec. 1, p. 5.
McLendon, Noe Organize NOEMAC Station Group. (1955, September 5). *Broadcasting/Telecasting*, p. 7.
The McLendon Organization. (n.d.). Glenn Callison personal papers. Richardson, TX.
McLendon Pacific Corporation, 6 RR 2d 131 (1965).
McLendon Pacific Corporation, 5 FCC 2d 855 (1966a).
McLendon Pacific Corporation, 5 FCC 2d 862 (1966b).
The McLendon Pacific Corporation, et al., 4 FCC 2d 722 (1966).
McLendon Raps Foe's Rights Stand. (1964, March 23). *Dallas Times Herald*, n.p.
McLendon Rites Set for Friday. (1954, July 9). *Dallas Morning News*, n.p.
McLendon Sells Two Stations. (1967, June 28). *Dallas Times Herald*, n.p.
McLendon's New Gimmick: All Ads, No Programs at All. (1965, December 20). *Broadcasting*, pp. 28–29.
McLendons Plan Chain of Theaters. (1969, February 5). *Dallas Times Herald*, n.p.
McLendon Station Would Air Only Classified Ads. (1965, December 27). *Advertising Age*, p. 8.

Major League Baseball Replies To Network's $12,000,000 Suit. (1952, November 18). *New York Times*, p. 38.

Majors Seeking Compromise. (1955, January 11). *Dallas Morning News*, sec. 1, pp. 14-15.

Manning Dorothy. (1990, July 10). Personal interview. Plano, Tx.

In the Matter of Primer on Ascertainment of Community Problems by Broadcast Applicants, Part I. Sections IV-A and IV-B of FCC Forms, 27 FCC 2d 650 (1971).

Maule, Tex. (1955a, January 26). Referee Ponders $200,000 Settlement Issue for LBS. *Dallas Morning News*, sec. 1, p. 11.

Maule, Tex. (1955b, January 27). Liberty Trustee to Take $200,000. *Dallas Morning News*, sec. 1, p. 18.

The Mayflower Broadcasting Corp., 8 FCC 333 (1941).

Media Pioneer Dies at Baylor. (1982, October 13). *Victoria Advocate*, n.p.

Meeks, Bill. (1990, July 9). Personal interview. Richardson, TX.

Meeks, Bill. (1991, June 19). Telephone interview.

Merriman, Tom. (1990, May 23). Personal interview. Dallas, TX.

Miller, Robert. (1987, December 10). Friends Plan Gathering to Remember Mitch Lewis. *Dallas Morning News*, p. 3D.

Miss Stafford to Wed Gordon McLendon. (1973, February 5). *Dallas Morning News*, n.p.

The Money Picture. (n.d.). [Promotion brochure]. McLendon Papers.

Morehead, Richard M. (1963, December 10). Observers Attempt to Pick Opponent for Yarborough. *Dallas Morning News*, n.p.

Morehead, Richard M. (1964, April 7). McLendon Jabs at Rival About Rights Bill. *Dallas Morning News*, n.p.

Morris, Willie. (1967). *North Toward Home.* Boston: Houghton Mifflin.

Movie Promotion Advertisements. (1959a, June 24). *Dallas Morning News*, sec. 3, p. 6.

Movie Promotion Advertisements. (1959b, June 25). *Dallas Morning News*, sec. 3, p. 9.

Movie Theater Owner, Lawyer Barton Robert McLendon Dies at 82. (1982, October 12). *Dallas Morning News*, p. 10C.

Moyers, Bill. (1963, September 3). [Letter to Gordon McLendon. Editorial File]. McLendon Papers.

"Mr. Mac." Chairman of Board: Entered His Theater Business by Accident. (1969, August 15). *Dallas Times Herald*, n.p.

Nelson, Lindsey. (1985). *Hello Everybody, I'm Lindsey Nelson.* New York: Beech Tree Books.

Nelson, Lindsey. (1988, October 7). Telephone interview.

Nelson, Lindsey, and Al Hirshberg. (1966). *Backstage at the Mets.* New York: Viking Press.

Neville, John W. (1947). Baseball and the Antitrust Laws. *Fordham Law Review* 16, pp. 208–230.

Newport, Frank. (1981, December). Poor Reception: Whatever Happened to KILT? *Houston City Magazine*, pp. 41–43.

New WGES Format Draws Hot Words. (1962, September 3). *Broadcasting*, p. 48.

News and Nothing But the News on X-TRA. (1961, June 19). *Broadcasting*, pp. 108–109.

The News Endorses. (1964, April 12). *Dallas Morning News*, p. 1.

1950 Broadcasting Yearbook, pp. 55–57, 64.

1948 Broadcasting Yearbook, p. 240.

Obituaries—Gordon McLendon. (1986, September 17). *Variety*, p. 118.

Odom, Billie. (1990, February 28). Personal interview. Dallas, TX.

The Old Scotchman. (1950, September 4). *Time*, p. 61.

"Old Scotsman" Reentering Broadcasting. (1980, June 19). *Lubbock Avalanche-Journal*, p. D-7.

Operation Matthew. (1961). [Various memos. Policy Book]. McLendon Papers.

Osbon, John. (1950, February 27). Baseball Coverage: Regionals Map Plans. *Broadcasting/Telecasting*, pp. 15–16.

Owens, Gary. (1990, December 5). Telephone interview.

Papers View Want Ads as Private Domain. (1966, January 10). *Broadcasting*, p. 34.

Passman, Arnold. (1971). *The Deejays*. New York: Macmillan.

Patoski, Joe Nick. (1980, February). Rock 'n' Roll's Wizard of Oz. *Texas Monthly*, pp. 101–104, 167–171.

Pederson, Rena. (1979, January 9). End of the McLendon Network. *Dallas Morning News*, n.p.

Picture Caption. (1954, May 3). *Broadcasting/Telecasting*, p. 74.

Pioneer Broadcaster Recalls Career. (1984, March 3). *Lubbock Avalanche-Journal*, p. 10-B.

Porter, Bob. (1972, December 14). Gordon McLendon. *Dallas Times Herald*, pp. 1E, 13E.

Porter, Bob. (1973, October 2). McLendon Era May End. *Dallas Times Herald*, n.p.

Porter, Bob. (1980, August 31). Dallas Producer Gets a Kick Out of Film. *Dallas Times Herald*, pp. 1-M, 4-M.

Porter, Bob. (1986, September 21). McLendon Was Master of Film Hoopla. *Dallas Times Herald*, p. C-3.

Porter, Bob. (1987, June 10). Flagship Theater Celebrates Reopening. *Dallas Times Herald*, p. F-8.

Porter, Bob. (1990, May 22). Personal interview. Dallas, TX.

Presley, James. (1983). *A Saga of Wealth: An Anecdotal History of the Texas Oilmen*. Austin: Texas Monthly Press.

Probe Backs Yarborough. (1964, September 1). *Dallas Morning News*, n.p.

Pucinski in Spotlight at Hearing. (1963, April 22). *Broadcasting*, p. 84.

Pulse Makes Quarter-Hour Studies. (1962, November 19). *Broadcasting*, pp. 97–98.

Radio—The Industry in Perspective. (1988, March 14). *The Pulse of Broadcasting*, pp. 8–10, 27.

Radio Days II: More of What It Was Really Like. (1987, April 13). *The Pulse of Broadcasting*, pp. 1, 22–25.

Radio in Transition: Music-and-News Are Only Building Blocks. (1957, September 7). *Sponsor*, pp. 38–41.

Radio Jingles' Beginnings As a Venture. (1987, June 22). *The Pulse of Broadcasting*, pp. 8–9, 32.

Radio Needs to Editorialize. (1955, September 19). *Broadcasting/Telecasting*, pp. 140–151.

Radio Pioneer Gordon McLendon Dead at Age 65. (1986, September 29). *The Pulse of Broadcasting*, pp. 3, 6.

Radio Plea Denied by Federal Court. (1952, April 15). *New York Times*, p. 32.
Radio Program Schedule. (1950a, February 13). *Dallas Morning News*, sec. III, p. 3.
Radio Program Schedule. (1950b, July 11). *Dallas Morning News*, sec. I, p. 19.
Radio Program Schedule. (1951, July 11). *Dallas Morning News*, sec. II. p. 5.
Radio Program Schedule. (1953, June 1). *Dallas Morning News*, sec. I, p. 10.
Radio Program Schedule. (1954, June 14). *Dallas Morning News*, sec. I, p. 11.
Radio Program Schedule. (1955, June 1). *Dallas Morning News*, sec. I, p. 25.
Radio's Merry Maverick. (1961, May). *Coronet*, pp. 128–132.
Radio Station KLEE Becomes Liberty's KLBS. (1952, May). *Houston Magazine*, n.p.
Radio Vessel Got Equipment in U.S. (1961, April 3). *New York Times*, p. 8.
Raffetto, Francis. (1973, October 2). McLendon Circuit Is Reported Sold. *Dallas Morning News*, n.p.
Ralph Got About Equal Time. (1964, May 15). *Houston Post*, n.p.
Rand, Ayn. (1965). *The Virtue of Selfishness: A New Concept of Egoism.* New York: New American Library.
Re-Creations: McLendon to Broadcast Ball Games. (1953, April 12). *Dallas Morning News*, sec. 2, p. 3.
Reed, Bill. (1971, May 27). McLendon Selling KLIF. *Dallas Times Herald*, n.p.
Report and Statement of Policy Res: Commission en banc Programming Inquiry, 44 FCC 2303 (1960).
Return on Soft Drink Empty: $50,000. (1956, December 17). *Broadcasting/Telecasting*, p. 50.
Rogers, John William. (1965). *The Lusty Texans of Dallas.* Dallas: Cokesbury Book Store.
Routt, Edd. (1968, October 24). [Memo to All Managers, All Program Directors. Editorial File]. McLendon Papers.
Routt, Edd. (1972). *The Business of Radio Broadcasting.* Blue Ridge Summit, PA: TAB Books.
Routt, Edd. (1974). *Dimensions of Broadcast Editorializing.* Blue Ridge Summit, PA: TAB Books.
Routt, Edd. (1989, May 4). Personal interview. Malakoff, TX.
Routt, Edd, James B. McGrath and Fredric Weiss, (1978). *The Radio Format Conundrum.* New York: Hastings House.
Rydbeck, Olof. (1963). Broadcasting in Sweden. *Gazette* 9, pp. 243–248.
Safran, Don. (1975, May 13). McLendon Knocks Role in Movie. *Dallas Times Herald*, n.p.
Salzman, Ed. (1961, May 13). The All-News Radio Station. *Saturday Review*, pp. 65–66.
Sandlin, George. (1990, March 1). Personal interview. Austin, TX.
Sayre, Alan. (1980, June 2). Audio Alone Not Fun Anymore, So McLendon to Get into Video. *Houston Post*, p. 5B.
Seek and You May Find. (1955, June 20). *Broadcasting/Telecasting*, p. 97.
The Shape of Things. (1951, October 6). *The Nation*, p. 270.
Shriver, Sargent. (1964, November 4). [Letter to Gordon McLendon. Public Service File]. McLendon Papers.
Shultz, Gary. (1986, September 15). Radio Pioneer Gordon McLendon Dies. *Dallas Times Herald*, pp. A-1, A-8.
Sigma Delta Chi Awards for Distinguished Service in Journalism. (1954). [1954 Ra-

dio Division Entry of Radio Station KLIF, Dallas, Texas. Policy Book]. McLendon Papers.

Sitrick, Joseph. (1990, January 23). Telephone interview.

Smith, Curt. (1987). *Voices of the Game.* South Bend, IN: Diamond Communications.

Sports Package: LBS May Sign Oil Firm. (1952, January 28). *Broadcasting/Telecasting*, p. 32.

Station KLIF Takes Air from Cliff Towers Hotel. (1947, November 9). *Dallas Times Herald*, p. 7-2.

Station KLIF to Take Air Here Sunday Afternoon. (1947, November 9). *Dallas Morning News*, n.p.

Sterling, Christopher. (1984). *Electronic Media: A Guide to Trends in Broadcasting and Newer Technologies, 1920–1983.* New York: Praeger.

Sterling, Christopher, and John M. Kittross. (1978). *Stay Tuned: A Concise History of American Broadcasting.* Belmont, CA: Wadsworth.

The Story of the McLendon Corp. (1959, February 16). *Broadcasting*, pp. 44B–44H.

Strickland, J. A. (1959, October 31). [Letter to Gordon McLendon. Policy Book]. McLendon Papers.

Sweden: *Bon Soir, Bon Jour.* (1962, August 17). *Time*, pp. 72–74.

Sweden: Piracy by Radio (1961, April 14). *Time*, pp. 35–36.

Sweden in Radio Test. (1961, May 5). *New York Times*, p. 59.

Tatum, Henry. (1984, May 13). Growing Up With Big KLIF. *Dallas Morning News*, n.p.

Texan Owns Liechtenstein Operator of Nicaragua Ship Smuggling Radio to Sweden. (1961, April 10). *Advertising Age*, p. 8.

Thompson, Toby. (1983, July–August). The Twilight of the Drive-In. *American Film*, pp. 44–49.

Thornton, R. L. (1959, January 6). [Letter to Gordon McLendon, Promotion File]. McLendon Papers.

Tolbert, Frank X. (1947, November 10). Parrot Does Announcing. *Dallas Morning News*, sec. 1, p. 4.

Tolbert, Frank X. (1952, March). Man Behind a Network. *Nation's Business*, pp. 56–60.

The Top-40 Story: Gordon McLendon. (n.d.). *Radio & Records* (Special Supplement), pp. 18–27.

Tribute to Gordon McLendon. (1981). Recorded for Texas Tech University Department of Mass Communication Hall of Fame Induction Ceremony.

Tribute to Gordon McLendon [Radio program]. (1986). KVIL, Dallas, TX.

Trinity Files for New Am, Decides to Drop Dallas Uhf. (1956, January 9). *Broadcasting/Telecasting*, p. 66.

Trout, McLendon, Storz to Hall of Fame. (1987, March 2). *Broadcasting*, p. 68.

Two Deny Senator Took Estes Money. (1964, April 29). *Dallas Times Herald*, n.p.

Ullman, James Ramsey. (1953). *The Sands of Karakorum.* Philadelphia: Lippincott.

U.S. Congress. House. Subcommittee on Study of Monopoly Power of the Committee on the Judiciary (1951). *Study of Monopoly Power.* Serial No. 1, part 6. Organized Baseball. (Hearings). 82nd Cong., 1st sess. Washington, D.C.: Government Printing Office.

U.S. Congress. Senate. Subcommittee of the Committee on Interstate and Foreign

Commerce. (1953). *Broadcasting and Televising Baseball Games.* (Hearings). 83rd Cong., 1st sess. Washington, D.C.: Government Printing Office.

Variety Film Reviews, 1907–1980. (1983). [Review dates: 1 July 1959, 15 July 1959 and 18 May 1960]. New York: Garland Publishing.

Vaughn, Les. (1989, May 4). Personal interview. Quinlan, TX.

Voluntary Assignments and Transfers of Control, 23 RR 1503 (1962).

Watch Liberty Grow. (1951, August 20). *Time,* p. 63.

Weiss, Michael. (1982, September 26). Changing Times Led to KLIF's Decline, Fall. *Dallas Morning News,* pp. 1A, 15A.

West, Wanda. (1959, June 26). Dallas-Made Films In World Premiere. *Dallas Times Herald,* p. B-7.

Wiskari, Werner. (1961, April 2). Radio Ship Off Sweden Evades Ban on Broadcast Commercials. *New York Times,* pp. 1, 21.

Woman Faces Gun Count; McLendon Intended Victim. (1964, February 20). *Dallas Times Herald,* n.p.

WYNR Probe Recesses. (1963, April 29). *Broadcasting,* p. 60.

Zany Stunts Put Radio Chain in Clover. (1961, September 9). *Business Week,* pp. 124–131.

Index

About the Author

RONALD GARAY is Associate Professor at the Manship School of Journalism, Louisiana State University. He is the author of *Congressional Television* (1984) and *Cable Television* (1988).

Recent Titles in
Contributions to the Study of Mass Media and Communications

The Course of Tolerance: Freedom of the Press in Nineteenth-Century America
Donna Lee Dickerson

The American Trojan Horse: U.S. Television Confronts Canadian Economic and Cultural Nationalism
Barry Berlin

Science as Symbol: Media Images in a Technological Age
Lee Wilkins and Philip Patterson, editors

The Rhetoric of Terrorism and Counterterrorism
Richard W. Leeman

Media Messages in American Presidential Elections
Diana Owen

The Joint Press Conference: The History, Impact, and Prospects of American Presidential Debates
David J. Lanoue and Peter R. Schrott

The Media in the 1984 and 1988 Presidential Campaigns
Guido H. Stempel III and John W. Windhauser, editors

The Democracy Gap: The Politics of Information and Communication Technologies in the United States and Europe
Jill Hills, with S. Papathanassopoulos

Journalism for the 21st Century: Online Information, Electronic Databases, and the News
Tom Koch

Public Television: Panacea, Pork Barrel, or Public Trust?
Marilyn Lashley

The Cold War Guerrilla: Jonas Savimbi, The U.S. Media, and the Angolan War
Elaine Windrich

Political Controversy: A Study in Eighteenth-Century Propaganda
Robert D. Spector